Guardian Angel Academy
YEAR 1: RENEGADE

TAMARA HART HEINER

Year 1: Renegade Guardian Angel Academy

Tamara Hart Heiner

paperback edition
copyright 2021 Tamara Hart Heiner
cover art by Fantasy Designs

Also by Tamara Hart Heiner:
Perilous (WiDo Publishing 2010)
Altercation (WiDo Publishing 2012)
Deliverer (Tamark Books 2014)
Priceless (WiDo Publishing 2016)
Vendetta (Tamark Books 2018)

Goddess of Fate:
Inevitable (Tamark Books 2013)
Entranced (Tamark Books 2017)
Coercion (Tamark Books 2019)
Destined (Tamark Books 2019)

Kellam High:
Lay Me Down (Tamark Books 2016)
Reaching Kylee (Tamark Books 2016)

The Extraordinarily Ordinary Life of Cassandra Jones:
Walker Wildcats Year 1: Age 10 (Tamark Books 2015)
Walker Wildcats Year 2: Age 11 (Tamark Books 2016)
Southwest Cougars Year 1: Age 12 (Tamark Books 2017)
Southwest Cougars Year 2: Age 13 (Tamark Books 2018)
Southwest Cougars Year 3: Age 14 (Tamark Books 2019)
Springdale Bulldogs Year 1: Age 15 (Tamark Books 2020)

Tornado Warning (Dancing Lemur Press 2014)

Eureka in Love Series
Shades of Raven (Tamark Books 2020)
After the Fall (Tamark Books 2018)

Print Edition, License Notes:
This book is licensed for your personal enjoyment only. This book may not be resold or given away to other people. If you would like to share this book with another person, please purchase an additional copy for each recipient. If you're reading this book and did not purchase it, or it was not purchased for your use only, then please purchase your own copy. Thank you for respecting the hard work of this author.

This is a work of fiction. Names, characters, businesses, places, events and incidents are either the products of the author's imagination or used in a fictitious manner. Any resemblance to actual persons, living or dead, or actual events is purely coincidental.

In the beginning, there were two realms: Shamayim, where the superior, celestial beings dwelled in Light and glory, and Sheol, where the Forsaken, or dejected beings, were sentenced to languish in Darkness and misery.

CHAPTER ONE

"It's safe to open your eyes now."

My stomach dropped in churning anxiety as the thick, dark embrace of the archangel's wings opened and spread away from me. Light slashed through my eyelids, and I flinched, but I did not open my eyes. I had trouble breathing, and my pulse shuddered in my throat, terrified and uneasy.

It's not heaven, I reminded myself. *You don't need to be afraid.*

No, of course it wasn't heaven. I would have been incinerated the moment I stepped foot onto that celestial plane. This was something else, a cross between the mortal world and celestial ground. A place for those waiting for heaven's approval to enter.

But I was not waiting for heaven. Heaven would never approve of me. I still couldn't believe I was here, and I still wasn't sure why.

Choice is a double-edged sword. One might choose freedom only to find the choice leads to misery and captivity.

Or one might choose to sacrifice what they had in hopes of something more.

Such was my case.

Archangel Barachiel's wings fluttered near my face, the softness of the air stroking my flaming cheeks.

"Jezbathasat," he said, his voice soft like falling rain yet holding a strain of command, "open your eyes."

The word whispered around me, my name, the lexicology that forever branded me a daughter of hell. I swallowed hard and pried my lids open. The white Light of purity and holiness did not assault me or burn me to cinders as I feared it would, and my shoulders relaxed slightly.

"Welcome to the Guardian Angel Academy at Yishuv," he said.

I looked at him as his golden wings folded and withdrew into his body, leaving him looking as common as the wingless men of the damned I'd witnessed in the depths of Sheol.

Which was my home. Not heaven.

"We are not in heaven," he said, and I flinched. Were the rumors true? Could angels read the thoughts of lesser beings?

"I know that," I snapped. "And you should learn respect for privacy." But my words lacked any venom. I'd made the choice to come here, and in truth, I was terrified. While his motives remained questionable, the archangel had shown kindness to me. I didn't want to leave the protective embrace of his wings.

Archangel Barachiel walked in front of me without a backward glance, expecting me to follow. His dark brown hair was cut short, and his face held no lines. He did not look any older than a thirty-year-old mortal. He wore a dark suit and concealed his wings, giving no indication of his status. But I knew he was a master at GAA at Yishuv.

Guardian Angel Academy.

I could hardly think the words to myself. I was the newest enrolled student at GAA, but there was no hiding what I really was. In a few brief moments, every student at the academy would know.

And they would hate me.

"Where are we?" I asked. "Are we still in Gehenna?"

Gehenna was an in-between land, a spiritual realm where the newly dead souls gathered to acclimate to their new status before moving onto a more permanent destination. It was a neutral plane, and I'd been deposited there from Sheol so Barachiel could retrieve me. He had too much Light to descend to Sheol.

But this place felt too solid to be Gehenna.

"This is Arcadia. It's a hidden realm within earth itself, a land of peace and harmony that can only be reached by those who know the way. All three campuses are here, though Yishuv is the biggest. You will only see the other two if you show talents that lead to their specialties."

Peace. Harmony. Words foreign to my being. Goosebumps popped up over my whole body, and I shuddered, feeling the invasion of righteousness to my soul.

"Where is the campus?" I asked, drudging the words up from somewhere.

"In front of us. We will arrive when you are ready."

I nodded. I would not be able to return to Sheol until I knew the location well enough to travel between the two. I would stay put until then just to make sure I didn't get lost. Hell would freeze over before I'd ask an angel for help.

An angel. Hatred for the celestial beings, the ones who placed themselves at a higher standard and thought they were superior to my kind, bubbled up in my chest. How would I tolerate going to school with them, learning their ways, sharing a room with one of them?

I glanced at Barachiel, wondering if he heard my thoughts. He said nothing.

Perhaps because he knew they would hate me as much as I hated them, but it would be one of me against hundreds of them.

"Do not be afraid."

So he was listening. I knew it. "They will not accept me. They will know what I am."

He stopped and looked back at me, his eyes trailing over the black chains crisscrossing my exposed flesh, wrapping around my arms and claiming me. Hasatan had relinquished me to the academy so I could become "informed enough to make my choice," but he had not relinquished the chains that bound me to Sheol. They branded my skin, burying themselves into my body like a sentient tattoo. I tugged on my dark hair, pulling it over my shoulder, but I couldn't conceal the chains.

"Learning acceptance and forgiveness is part of the curriculum at GAA. You will make a fine candidate for practicing what we preach."

"Just what I hoped," I said sarcastically, but he only smiled.

He continued walking, and I rolled my eyes before trailing after. The archangels and master instructors had already graduated from GAA. Supposedly they had mastered their baser emotions, and it would take much more than the attitude of a Forsaken to rile him up.

We walked for an eternity through rolling green hills and fields of purple grain and deep valleys with winding rivers. Would he let me wander forever? Peace and harmony weren't so bad. I could live out the rest of my damned forever here.

"Jezbathasat," he said, interrupting my reflections, "it's time."

I stopped walking and steeled myself for my first glimpse of Guardian Angel Academy — and GAA's first glimpse of me. "Just Jez," I said softly. "Tell them my name is Jez."

He nodded, and I sucked in a breath.

The horizon wavered, trembled, and then the snow-capped mountains in the distance became obscured by tall, spiracle buildings. I caught my breath in spite of my determination to remain aloof. I'd never seen structures like this in the land of fire and brimstone. One twisted up so high, the final spiral disappeared into the clouds. Others appeared as medieval castles, squatting possessively over the perfect grass.

"This is a school," I said in awe.

"This is your school," he said. "As long as you wish it to be."

I saw students now, wandering the grounds dressed in dark slacks and skirts. Black and white wings jutted out from their button-up shirts, folded tight against their bodies or spread wide like an eagle's as they milled about, school books in hands.

I had not seen adolescent angels before. All of the mortals who died in their adolescence went to Gehenna and were offered the location of their choice to finish out their learning. If they chose to descend to the dark world, they lost their youthful appearance and continued to age through the coming millennia, but they didn't die.

Because only angels of Light were allowed to be young.

The injustice burned through my veins, but I swallowed it back, wishing to mask my feelings from Barachiel. The time for retribution was not yet at hand.

But it would come. And I would bring it.

A chime sounded, ringing out over the courtyard, and the students turned toward it. One by one, most of the black-winged angels stepped into the shortest building on the grounds, a long, rectangular edifice that looked out of place among the sweeping, rounded structures. The white wings dispersed as well, heading into various buildings.

"Come. That is your cue."

"I—I'm not sure I can." Fear gripped me, and my feet remained rooted to the spot. I looked down at my black clothing, my nonstandard halter and torn skirt. My outward appearance reflected my inner self: unsure, nonconforming, and tattered.

Barachiel did not move. "It is your choice. But you will not regret this, Jezbathasat."

His words rang with truth and promise. Was it a manipulation, or could I believe him?

But I didn't really have a choice. Hasatan had warned me of the consequences of failure. And his words I could trust.

"I will go," I said, and I moved my feet forward, closing the distance between myself and the building of my own accord.

Barachiel led me through a side door and to a seat tucked

at the back of the massive hall. I sat with Barachiel as a wingless female with almond-shaped eyes and jet black hair in a white business suit stepped onto the stage.

"Welcome, angelings," she said, her face wreathed in a dazzling light as she smiled. I squinted against it, fearing I'd go blind. "I'm Archangel Selaphiel. I coordinate new student orientation. I'm also the master for Human Relations, a class you will all be required to take in your second year.

"I know there is so much new information for you, but let me start by saying, I'm sorry you find yourselves here."

For one brief moment, I thought she spoke directly to me. And then I remembered every new student was here because they'd recently died. I wasn't the only one in a new place.

"I know it's a shock," she went on. "I'm here to help you adjust, and we will also have classes geared toward teaching you what you need to know to move forward in this life. We've tailored the school to be a familiar environment for you, with customs and technologies like what you had on earth."

I leaned toward Barachiel and whispered, "Do the other students know about me?"

He shook his head. "You are just one more new student starting your first year at the academy."

A few students glanced back at us at the low murmur of his voice, and I sank lower in my seat, grateful for the darkness around us. Darkness. Good for hiding.

Not so much all the Light that surrounded the campus and kept trying to penetrate my shield.

I wrapped my hands around my arms, wishing for something to cover myself. As if not having wings wasn't bad enough . . .

"Now let me tell you about the goals of the school," the woman continued. "The mission of Guardian Angel Academy is to provide you with the knowledge and experience you need to minister to mortals on earth. In doing so, you will become more equipped to join the celestial beings in heaven, or Shamayim, as we call it here, and make your final placement. But first there are a series of tasks you must complete at the academy. GAA is built as a four-year program, though you may repeat a year as often as necessary to master a task. During your first and second years, you are only Guardian Apprentices, or GAs. We will be reteaching you many of the concepts and principles you learned in Shamayim before you were born but have forgotten through mortality. You will notice that your memories start to come back, but it could be a full decade before you remember everything from your first existence."

None of that applied to me. I was not created in Shamayim. I had no memories to recover.

"The second year are allowed to watch what goes on on earth and learn how to travel there, but you won't go to earth until your third year.

"During your third year, you should be assigned to your first ward, and then you will become a Guardian in Training, or a GIT. You will be mentored and guided. You might recall the temptations you had during your mortal life; our job as Guardians is to be the protector and the guide, helping mortals make the correct decision. If it is possible, we often save them from an untimely death, though you will learn it's not always possible to do so.

"The fourth year is a mere formality; you will receive a new assignment, and this time you will not be mentored.

Classes will continue in between your Guardianship, and you will become a master in your field and perfunctory in other fields. Should you decide to continue as a Guardian, after you graduate from the academy, you will continue with your ward until the end of their earthly days. From there, you have choices: you can take another assignment, or you may choose another profession."

Professions. Assignments. Guardians. The words swirled around me, and I grasped at their meanings, trying to clutch the intangible. Angels got to choose what they wanted to be? There were options? How could one make such a decision? There were no choices in Sheol, no consequences for me to weigh. I felt overwhelmed by the idea of making a choice for my existence. What if I chose the wrong thing?

"Now, a little about your field. In a moment we will move all of you to the manifestation room. This is a room full of Light and energy. Your spirit will be a magnet to these energies, and you'll discover a propensity for a certain gift. That doesn't mean it's your only gift, and it might not even be your strongest. However, each of the three GAA campuses specializes in teaching skills for one of these gifts. Depending what you manifest, you could stay here at Yishuv or go to the Academy at Zion or the Academy at Sinai.

"About this time, there's always a student who wants to know what happens if they drop out of school." She smiled at the angels around me, but they looked as nervous as I felt, too uneasy to return her warm expression. "You'll soon learn that everything is about choice here. If you do not wish to continue at GAA, you are free to go. We'll show you your options and let you choose what you do next with your life."

I snorted and rolled my eyes, sinking lower in my seat. Yes, heaven was all about choice. The choice to choose them or choose eternal damnation. I could just imagine what the options would be for any student who tried to leave the academy early.

"However, most of you will want to stay. The academy is a spiritually fulfilling and emotionally connecting place. You'll make friendships here that will last you throughout eternity. You'll come to understand yourself and the universe around you in ways you didn't know possible.

"Oh, one last thing." She looked out at everyone, and suddenly from behind her back, golden wings sprouted. A murmur rose up from the students, and even I had to admit they were impressive. The tips of the wings sparked and glowed, and she opened and closed them for effect. "I'm sure you've all noticed your new wings."

She'd broken the solemnity, the fear that paralyzed them. Some titters and chuckles echoed from the seats.

"Each of you has a set of black wings, symbolic of your decision to follow the decree from Shamayim and go to earth. When you finish your second year and become a GIT, you'll receive a set of white wings. Your assignment and other humans won't see these wings, and once you graduate from the academy, you can make your wings retract at will. The white wings will be your last set. Though you have these beautiful wings, let me remind you of one thing: flying is not allowed on campus, except at the Skyball pitch. We are not owls, to spend our time flapping about."

She smiled to take any sting from her words, and others laughed with her.

"A few of you, one, maybe two, may end up becoming one of the heavenly hosts. You will understand why as you finish your education."

I understood why, and my heathen ichor boiled in my veins. Because war was an eventuality. Sheol knew it. Apparently heaven did too.

I immediately banished the thoughts. The angel beside me could invade my mind, and I needed this guarded and private.

"If you feel the call to join the heavenly army, if you have a desire to serve in such a capacity, please let us know.

"After you manifest today, a master from your particular campus will find you and take you home. This campus, the academy at Yishuv, is home for all Empatya angels. The academy at Zion is for the Metamorfozahs. And the academy at Sinai is for the Teles. Don't worry if none of those terms mean anything to you; by the end of today, you'll understand.

"Your campus is your home, and the angels you meet today are your new family. You will take your meals with them, have classes with them, spar with them, and room with them. They will not take the place of the familial bonds you had with your mortal family, but they will fill a spot you didn't know was empty. So get to know your fellow angels, and don't be afraid to open up to them."

I studied this woman as she spoke, noting the other angels standing silent guard behind her. Their expressions were calm and benevolent, yet somehow the sight of the six of them, endowed with heavenly power, sent chills down my spine.

They could destroy me in a matter of moments. They could tear me apart limb by limb until every atom that made up my essence was scattered to the universe.

It had been done before.

CHAPTER TWO

The woman finished speaking, and the lights went on. I shrank even lower and considered crawling out along the floor. I thought they would notice me, but the students did not disperse at once. They formed groups of three or four and talked, their faces glowing, their mouths turning upward in smiles. How did they seem to know each other? Weren't we all first years?

"They've been trickling in from Gehenna for several weeks," Barachiel said, and I scowled. "The students gather here until they manifest and are sent to their official campus. First years cling to each other. You're all in this together."

"No, we're not," I breathed, and then I winced. I shouldn't have said that out loud.

He stepped into the aisle. "Come, Jez."

I darted to the archangel's side. I wished he would pull those massive wings out again and shield me from view.

He crossed the grass courtyard quickly and led me into an x-shaped building with arching entryways. He pulled open a heavy door, and we stepped into a hallway with marbled flooring. The air inside felt slightly cooler than outside, but without the mild breeze.

"This is so . . . modern," I said, thinking of the grand palaces I'd witnessed on earth. "I expected something more . . . ancient." And less comfortable.

"GAA looks and feels this way because it is what the students of this generation are familiar with. It has looked and felt very different in times past." He pushed on a door in the hallway and ushered me into a room.

A woman turned from where she stood examining the top of a desk, and I recognized her as the one who had spoken to us moments before in the auditorium. "Ah." She came toward me, a welcoming smile on her face. "Jezbathasat. We are honored to have you here."

I examined her closer now. She stood regal and tall, even with her golden wings tucked out of sight. If I had wings like that, I would never hide them.

But I had no wings, none at all, not even the black wings of a first year.

"Thank you for meeting us," Barachiel said. "I know you prefer to be present during the manifestations."

"Remiel and Sabriel are both present, as well as the eldermasters from the other academies. They can handle it just as well." She faced me, her expression kind. "Welcome to Yishuv."

Her kindness was not unexpected, but I did not know how to respond. I understood fear and formality, not gentleness. I inclined my head. "Yes, my Liege."

She gave a soft laugh. "I can see it will be an interesting journey for all of us. I am Archangel Selaphiel, master of the Human Relations class."

Another archangel. But I'd known that after I saw her golden wings.

"Selaphiel," Archangel Barachiel said, "could you find something for Jez to wear?"

Selaphiel looked me over, her eyes falling on the dark tattoos embracing my arms. "Of course." She opened a drawer of her desk and dug around for moment before pulling out a long-sleeved jacket made of some kind of animal skin. "Will this do?"

I took it from her, fingering the supple, black material, surprised and pleased she hadn't gone for a different color. I could not keep myself from asking, "You keep a supply of these in your desk?"

Her eyes sparkled. "Manipulating material to produce what you need and when you need it is a skill you will learn also."

I was definitely intrigued. This was not a skill available to the Forsaken in Sheol. This was probably yet another reason Hasatan wanted me to come here.

I slid my arms into the jacket, marveling at how the material fit to my skin as if it were made for me. Perhaps it had been. I exhaled, my shoulders relaxing. With the tattoos covered, I might not stick out quite as much.

"It's time to meet the other new students," Selaphiel said. "Like you, those just arriving are unsure of where they are and why. They do not have any knowledge beyond their recent deaths and earth life."

That certainly encouraged me. I knew more than these new recruits did.

"To begin with, I'll take you to the manifestation room, and you'll be separated by your powers."

"I don't have any powers," I began, but Selaphiel cut me off with a shake of her head.

"You don't know your powers yet, and neither do they. You will be on equal footing."

"I'm a Forsaken," I said, annoyed she seemed to have forgotten. "I'm not gifted like they are. I'm not endowed with Light. The only reason I can tolerate being here is because he —" I jerked my head at Archangel Barachiel— "is shielding me with his Light."

The two of them exchanged a look I couldn't decipher but didn't like.

"Eldermaster Barachiel has reason to believe there is Light in you. It's just been concealed by Darkness for so long, you don't know it's there."

"It's not," I retorted, the anger rising in me again. Wait — had she said Eldermaster?

"Calm down," Selaphiel said, reaching for me.

"Don't touch her," Barachiel warned, intercepting her hand. "It is forbidden."

Archangel Selaphiel withdrew, confusion flickering on her face.

Surely she knew this. The law forbidding touch between spiritual beings was created long before I was.

She gave me a soft smile, keeping her hands where they belonged. "You will not be as out of place here as you fear."

"I fear nothing," I said, but it was a boldfaced lie, and my face flamed. These mind readers would know it. "Do they all have wings?" I demanded, turning to another painful topic. Because that was the biggest thing. I couldn't hide my lack of wings.

"They all have their first set of wings, yes," Selaphiel said. "But none of them know how to use them, and many of them will spend the first few weeks trying to hide them."

I had never wanted wings as desperately as I did now. The Fallen had wings before they came to Sheol, but their wings were torn from them when they fell, leaving only shadow wings in their place. But the Forsaken and others like me who had never gone to earth to receive a mortal body had no wings. And we never would, because the time to make the choice to go to earth had passed.

"Come this way," Selaphiel said.

Barachiel stopped her before we exited. "Jez, remember you are not to go to Shema," he warned. "The amount of Light in that room will be too much for you."

I nodded. I hadn't planned on going anywhere that contained a concentration of Light, anyway. But that led me to a question I had.

"How do you keep so much Light in Arcadia?" I asked. I knew it was just another dimension of earth, and earth could not retain Light. "How do you keep other demons out?" I tried hard not to flinch at the word, as I was considered a demon.

"We have a generator. It receives Light directly from Shamayim and maintains a shield around the campus, much as I'm using my Light to shield you from the Light of Arcadia, except in reverse."

A shield within a shield. So much to wrap my mind around.

"And we keep the location of Arcadia, and the campuses in a particular, a carefully guarded secret," Selaphiel added.

Barachiel went one way, and Selaphiel guided me from the room. We walked down the corridor and out a door at the back of the building.

"Did you say—you called him Eldermaster," I said, trying to sound bold even though speaking to her took tremendous courage.

"Barachiel is not only an archangel," she said, crossing a dirt path and leading me to another large building, this one with a tall, arched roof. "He's the Eldermaster of the academy at Yishuv."

I should have known. As if being an archangel wasn't enough, he had the most power of all the master angels at this campus.

"Here's the Manifestation Hall," she said, coming to a stop. "It's also the greenhouse."

I tilted my head to examine the building. She opened the door, and I kept my head back as we entered, taking in the tall ceiling full of large windows curving over us. Though tall enough for multiple stories, it only contained one.

Hundreds of other adolescents crowded the room, looking a lot like me in their mortal clothing. A few glanced at me, but not with any more curiosity than they eyed each other.

"Join them," Selaphiel whispered, inclining her head toward the group. "You are one of them."

I moved closer, my eyes captivated by the black wings sprouting from the shoulder blades of the nearest girl. I looked over her in her earthly apparel, all the way down to the pink shoes.

She saw me staring and shot a glance at her wings as well. "I keep forgetting they're there," she said in a hushed voice. Leaning toward me, she said, "Did you hide yours under your jacket? I tried to pull my shirt over them, but they won't fit." She blinked, blue eyes wide. "I guess we're dead.

One second I was cruising in the car with my boyfriend, and the next, I was in—what did they call that place? The waiting place."

"Gehenna," I supplied.

"Yeah! I was there, being told all kinds of crazy stuff."

I nodded. "Yeah." The word stuck to my tongue. Communicating with other beings wasn't something I had much experience with. Not unless I was tempting them to commit a sin.

She offered a fragile smile. "I'm Kenzie. At least—I was. They told me I have a different name here. I can't remember it." Her smile wobbled, and liquid shone in her blue eyes.

I studied her. She seemed distraught. That never bothered me before. Why did it now? "I'm sure they'll remind you."

"What's your name?"

"Jez."

"Is that your earth name or—"

"My real name."

She nodded. "Jez. Do you think my boyfriend's here? No one will tell me if he died also."

"I—I don't know." Her questions were making my head ache, and I didn't want to talk anymore.

"Welcome, new students!"

Our eyes were drawn toward the front of the massive room, where Selaphiel and Barachiel and several other angels stood in a line, smiling at us. While she was dressed in typical modern earth clothing, others were dressed in loose robes or form-fitting apparel.

"You may call me Master Selaphiel. I know you're still accepting where you are and what this means, but let me reassure you, your life is far from over. There is so much to accomplish as a heavenly being, and many of you will find missions and journeys to fulfill in this part of your life. This is in reality your third existence, and as such, we will use that word more often. We have gathered you here in this room because it is thick with life and creative energy. Perhaps during your mortal existence, you sometimes felt like you could do more. Like you could be more. You sensed a power deep within you, urging to get out. But you were restricted to the limits of a physical body in a physical realm.

"The energies in this room will encourage your gifts to manifest. Discovering where your talents lie will help us know what campus to assign you to. However, as you develop your potential, you may find you're better suited for a different course. If at any time any of you wish to exit GAA, we will honor your choice and discuss your options with you.

"While you are a student here, there are many regulations we expect you to adhere to. None of these are meant to restrict your freedom, but to keep your future choices open. When you arrive in your dormitory, you will find a bag with your school supplies on your desk. You will be given a special book, called an agenda, particular to you and your needs at the academy. Study the rules because ignorance is not an excuse for infractions. If you choose not to abide by the regulations, you also choose not to continue as a student here. Not everyone graduates, and that's okay. There are many roles in Shamayim and many ways for you to serve in the Kingdom without a formal education."

Right. I sneered. Did they really think they had a choice? If they didn't adhere to the commandments of the academy, they'd join the Fallen in Sheol. I personally knew hundreds of angels who had suffered this fate.

"Whichever campus you're assigned to, there will be a second-year student to help you learn the ropes of the academy. This student is referred to as the Team Lead, and they'll help you understand everything expected of you here at the academy as you transition to this new existence. You'll stick together by dorms but begin to separate out based on your specializations, which you won't discover until later. And the academy masters will help you with you gift."

"Gift?" The girl called Kenzie ran her hands together in nervousness, but my eyes were drawn to her wings, which fluttered and touched their tips together.

"Now," Master Selaphiel continued. "Each one of you close your eyes and draw on your earthly memories. Find something or someone that represents love and light and hope to you. Think on that memory. Let it grow within you until it fills your entire being."

I looked around at the other students with their eyes closed. There was no need for me to do this exercise. I had never experienced love or joy or happiness. Not that I was unhappy or discontented. I simply was.

Not the case for these students. Their faces showed various emotions, from rapture to pleasure, even to tears. A shower of sparks sprouted over the head of a boy, and he opened his eyes with a gasp.

"Did I—?"

One of the master angels had already descended to him, smiling and nodding.

"Congratulations. You are an Empatya. You'll stay here, at Yishuv. This is your campus."

"What does that mean?" a girl said, looking more alarmed than excited.

"His gift lies with emotions."

Another girl gave a cry as rose petals formed in midair and dropped around her feet. "These are the petals from my *quinciñera*! How can they be here?"

Another angel, this one dressed in loose pants and a tight long-sleeved shirt, stepped up to her and placed a hand on her shoulder. "You're a Tele. You'll learn more about your gift at the campus at Sinai. You are able to accomplish things with your mind. I'm a master from that campus, and I'll lead you there once we've found all the other Teles."

Around me, students were discovering their powers. One boy transformed into small dog, yipping and wagging his small tail.

"Metamorfozah," a woman master said, smiling at him and patting his head. "You'll accompany me to the campus at Zion."

I swiveled, marveling, and I noticed I wasn't the only one doing nothing. Another human boy stood a few paces from me, his eyes narrowed, peering at the excitement and wonder around us as if it were all a trick.

Yet I could see his power, even if he didn't. Darkness radiated off of him like the sun during an eclipse, brilliantly hidden and deceptively blinding. It called to me, drawing me toward him. Without even meaning to, I moved his direction.

CHAPTER THREE

His eyes lighted on me, and his head turned slightly to watch my approach. Did he see the same Darkness in me?

"Who are you?" he asked when I halted inches from him. "Are you a teacher?"

I shook my head. "No. I'm a new student. Like you."

"Where are your wings?"

I stole the first lie that came to my mind, thanks to the girl called Kenzie. "I hid them beneath my jacket."

His lip quirked upward, amusement sparking in his eye. "So you're not any more excited to be here than I am."

It wasn't a question, and I didn't deign to answer it. I stepped closer still. "I can see your power." It called to me, beckoned me. It felt familiar to me in a way that was almost comforting. I closed my eyes and inhaled, and when I opened them, I saw an aura around him, a redness so dark it blended with the shadow peeling off him.

"Is that yours? To see other people's gifts?"

I shook my head. "I don't know."

"Jez. Kerubiel." An angel stepped toward us.

The boy glared at the approaching angel. "My name is Ryan."

The angel did not miss a beat. "Ryan was your earthly name. Here you are known as Kerubiel. It was your name before your birth, and you have returned to it."

Kerubiel/Ryan opened his mouth, but before he could say anything more, the angel continued.

"I am Master Cassiel. Have you discovered your powers?"

"No," Kerubiel/Ryan said, and the air between him and the angel darkened. "I don't belong here. I have no powers."

"Darkness is all around you," I said before I could stop myself. "Can't you see it rolling off you?" I gestured at the space near him.

The angel looked at me with a slight smile on his lips. "That's right. Kerubiel is a Shadow Shade. But that's not his gift."

"A Shadow Shade?" I leaned forward. "What is that?"

"Shades can create Light or shadow. It's a part of their being, and they are rare. Only one or two exists in each generation."

"He can actually create Darkness?" I knew demonic angels that could create an illusion of Light, or the perception of Darkness. But to make it appear out of nowhere—how was that possible? "What about me?" I asked. "Am I a shade?"

Cassiel studied me. "You see the shadow emanating from Kerubiel?"

I nodded.

"What happened when you thought of one of the times in your life when you felt loved?"

I stared at him as if he were crazy. Didn't he know where I came from? In case he'd forgotten, I scoffed, "I was never loved."

Sadness crossed over Cassiel's face. "You were not the first, and you won't be the last. Think of something that makes you feel comfort."

I remembered the moment when I felt the Darkness seeping from Kerubiel. That sense of familiarity. "Color," I said without thinking. "I saw a color around him."

Cassiel's face brightened. "What color?"

"Red. And then gray."

"You have the gift of discernment. You are an Empatya."

"Oh," I said, a wave of disappointment washing over me. "I can see colors?"

Kerubiel snorted. "Awesome power."

His color had changed again, to a rusty, muddy hue. My own face warmed, surprising me by my reaction. Why should his opinion matter to me?

Cassiel faced him. "And you are gifted with the ability to make others feel what you feel. You are also an Empatya."

The boy looked like he wanted to argue. But the fight seemed to go out of him, and the colors around him faded from dark red to a muted gray, barely discernible against the black surrounding him.

Cassiel pointed across the room. "Barachiel is the Eldermaster for Yishuv. Master Selaphiel handles room assignments for the girls. Go tell her, and she will assign you a room. Come, Kerubiel. I will take you to your room."

The boy didn't correct Cassiel this time but allowed him to guide him toward a gathering group of students. "Have fun coloring," Kerubiel called to me over his shoulder.

He mocked me. But even so, I took a step in his direction, a part of me yearning to follow him, to curl up in his Darkness.

I shook myself and continued toward Selaphiel. I would see Kerubiel again.

The girl Kenzie was also in the group of students who gathered around Barachiel.

"Welcome to the Academy at Yishuv, angels," he said.

Angels. The word brought an unpleasant tingling to the back of my neck, and I ground my teeth together. No one had ever called me an angel before. I wrapped my arms around my body, cupping the elbows of my long-sleeved jacket. I wasn't one of them, and it wouldn't take long for them to figure it out.

"All of you are what we refer to as Empatya, or empathic angels. Each of you has a gift rooted in emotion, whether you can create emotions, share emotions, feel emotions, or see emotions. That doesn't mean it's your only talent. You'll discover many others as you go through your academic learning, especially the ability to manipulate the elements. It turns out that nature is the earth's way of expressing emotion, and so Empatyas are frequently skilled elementals, as well. Even in the areas where you are not strong, you'll be required to take classes and become at least basically proficient.

"Our dorms are located to the left of the administration building. Inside your room, you'll find your school uniform. I know it will take a few days to get used to your arrival here at GAA, so put the uniform on when you feel ready. Until then, you may wear what you are comfortable with."

My heart gave a little patter of relief. I could keep this jacket on and no one would remark about it. I could even continue to pretend my wings were tucked up inside the black material.

"You will also find in your room your school supplies. Please familiarize yourself with your schedule and the campus. Step forward when I call your name. I will be assigning you a roommate." He consulted an open book in his hands, and I wondered how he'd already gotten the names of the Empatyas written within.

"Daniel."

After a moment's pause, a boy clad in tight blue slacks and a looser shirt stepped forward. He tossed a lock of thick black hair from his face.

"Eremiel."

This one took even longer to come forward, and the boy's face was nearly as red as his hair, but he joined Daniel.

I scrutinized them as they faced each other. Daniel looked a few years older than Eremiel, who looked like he'd just crossed into adolescence, maybe fourteen or fifteen. Neither seemed extremely comfortable to be here.

Barachiel handed each of them a small white rectangle. "You're in room two-nineteen. A map to the dormitory is on that paper, and your room number, if you forget." He turned back to us, not watching as the boys slowly walked away, shooting glances over their shoulders. But then, Barachiel had done this before. He must know they had nowhere to go except to their dorms.

"Iblis."

No one stirred, and Barachiel's eyes scanned the group of us before landing on someone to my right.

"Iblis," he repeated.

"Oh!" The girl Kenzie jolted forward. "I forgot. I forgot that's my new name." Her pale skin also took on a pink tint, and a yellowish color emanated from her skin, coloring the air.

I touched my own face, curious by her and Eremiel's apparent physical reactions. Pink skin, red blush, yellow aura. While my body was the same now as it had been in hell, I had very little experience with emotions. There had been no need. My actions were chosen for me, and I was guided and instructed on what to do and how to act. There was no room for thought or feeling.

Except the ever-present anger and resentment that surrounded everything and everyone in the lower kingdom of Sheol. The unfairness over being cast out sent my skin broiling, and I wondered if I wore the same colorful expression of those emotions on my cheeks.

"It's your old name, and you'll get used to it soon enough," Barachiel said to her, his tone kind, as always. "Jezb—Jez."

Something cold slithered through my veins at his almost-slip, and I lifted my chin, glad he'd caught himself. My name gave away my lineage, and I'd prefer to keep that under wraps as long as I could.

But also I felt a smug reassurance as I stepped forward to stand next to Iblis/Kenzie. Even the archangels weren't perfect.

Iblis/Kenzie's face had split into a smile so wide it looked painful. She reached out as if to grab my hand, but I jerked back before she could, and her smile dimmed slightly.

"Roommates," she said, her voice breathy. "I'm so glad. At least it's someone I know."

"Yes," I said, clutching my hands together. Why had she tried to touch me? Didn't she know it was forbidden? Had no one told her? I glanced around at the new angels beside me with a sudden dread. Maybe none of them knew. I would have to be on my guard.

"You are in building Alef, in room one-oh-two." Barachiel handed us each the white rectangle, and I noticed he, at least, was careful not to touch me.

He had already turned away to call the next students, and I turned the rectangle over in my hands, studying it. A map of campus was imprinted on one side beside circular symbols, and it was hard and cool to the touch. The other side held the school emblem, the golden hexagon with the creation symbol inside.

"Come on, Jez," Iblis/Kenzie said.

I lifted my eyes and realized she'd taken several steps toward the exit. "What is this thing?" I asked, following her.

She walked faster, as if eager to leave the Manifestation Hall. "Looks like some kind of card." She turned it over in her hands. "It says GAA on it and has our room number. Maybe it's like a student ID card."

"It says GAA?" I murmured, studying the symbols while hurrying to keep up with her.

She stopped and gave me a longer look. "Can you read?"

I shook my head. "I never learned." The Forsaken did not read. Even Fallen who learned to read on earth lost the ability to distinguish between the symbols in Sheol.

Her eyes went wide. "You must have had a very sheltered life!"

"You could say that." I was beginning to get a sense of what my learning curve would be. Not only did I have to keep up with the angels and their studies, I needed to quickly educate myself on earth-life, as everything at GAA was tailored to imitate the mortal experience the angels had just left behind.

I felt sweat break out along my hairline, a physical reaction I knew was due to stress and not outside conditions.

I had never sweat before. My body, though only a spirit, was created after the likeness of mortality, with ichor instead of blood running through my veins. I was as capable of any body function as a physical being. But I didn't know what that mean, not really. I'd never had the need to experience most body functions.

Including sweating.

Iblis/Kenzie led the way as if she had already memorized the campus. Three multi-story buildings with windows on every floor surrounded the x-shaped building, which I realized must be the administration building.

"Are those the dorms?" I asked, pointing.

"Yes."

In front of each dorm was a plaque, again with large letters on it. I assumed it must announce the names.

"This one's ours," she said, heading to the one on the far left.

I recognized the GAA symbol on the plaque, but the symbols beside it were unfamiliar. I paused to trace my fingers over them, wishing I could decipher them through touch.

"How did you discover you're an Empatya?" she asked, waiting me to join her on the sidewalk.

I left the plaque and pressed my lips together. "The boy next to me. I saw him ringed in shades of red and gray."

"Me too. I mean, something similar. I saw colors leaping around the girl — who had actually become a squirrel — beside me. I wonder what the colors mean. That boy, Daniel — he made fire come out of his hair. So they said that makes him an Empatya also." She pulled open a rectangular door, and we both stepped inside the building.

Inside stretched a hallway lined with doors. A staircase beside me indicated more hallways and doors above us. The floor and walls were a soft gray, almost white, the doors a light blue.

The whole effect was ethereal, as if we'd stepped out into a hallway in the clouds.

"We got so lucky, being on the first floor. We won't have to climb the stairs every day." Iblis/Kenzie counted two doors and paused in front of the room. The tall doors had ornate wooden panels, but there was no handle. Nothing to indicate how to open it. She pulled out her card and waved it at the door. She frowned and pressed it against the decorated wood.

"What are you doing?" I watched her curiously.

"I'm trying to open the door. I'm sure this card works like a key or something. But I can't figure out how to get it in . . ."

She pushed the card into the crack between the door and the wall. Nothing happened. She repositioned herself and pressed her hand against the wood as she studied it. Suddenly the door swung inward, and she gasped and jumped back.

"What happened?" I asked.

She narrowed her eyes. "Apparently we just have to touch the door. How do we close it?" She took a step back into the hallway, and the door swung our direction, closing in front of us. She gestured at me. "You try it."

I stepped forward, hesitant, and pressed my hand to the wood.

Again, the door swung into the room.

"Ha!" she crowed. "How neat is that? Just our touch opens the door!"

"Neat," I echoed.

"Maybe we'll want to climb the stairs for exercise." She looked thoughtful as she stepped into the room. "Or do we even need to worry about physical fitness anymore?"

I followed her and did a little spin, taking in the two beds, each beside a desk with a wardrobe against the wall. A bookshelf against the far wall separated the beds. One window lit the room from above the bookshelf.

"This must be the bathroom." Kenzie/Iblis disappeared into an adjoining room. "That's odd. There's no toilet or shower. Just a sink and a mirror . . . Oh!" She came back out, her eyebrows raised. "We don't need toilets anymore, do we?"

Toilet. The word meant nothing to me. But I was perturbed by one thing. "What should I call you?" I couldn't keep thinking of both of her names in my head.

The girl paused, tilting her head so the light brown hair cascaded to the side, an uncertain expression passing over her eyes. "I guess I'm not Kenzie anymore. I'm Iblis." She sighed. "They told me that was my name before I was born, that Kenzie was only my earth name."

I nodded. This was true. Her mortal parents had named her after their own desires, making her more of a creation after themselves by giving her a mortal name. Not that they could have known her spirit name. "So Iblis, then?"

She chewed on her lower lip. "I hope I start to remember this place. Right now it feels so foreign." Her eyes welled up with tears. "I just want to go home to my mom."

That feeling swelled in my chest again, a strange desire to help her, to ease her pain. Was it because she was an Empatya? Was she pushing her feelings onto me? "Things will be fine here. It's just going to take time." I hoped the sentiment applied to myself, as well. I sat down on the bed, running my fingers over the soft coverings, and considered the bench I'd had in Sheol. Resting wasn't really a thing in the lower kingdom. When I did grow too weary or too wasted to fulfill an order, I was allowed to sit on the bench. But it never rejuvenated me. I required the essence of a mortal to do that.

Not now. I would have to find another way to get my nourishment. Barachiel had told me I wouldn't have the same yearnings and cravings here, that the Light would counteract them. I hadn't believed him until now, when I realized I wasn't aching with need.

"I've never had a bed before," I said softly.

"What was that?" Iblis tilted her head.

I hadn't meant to speak out loud. It would lead to questions, questions about my life before here. Where I was kept locked and concealed in the Darkness except when needed to carry out a command.

Until Hasatan let me out and told me why I was created. Then he gave me a single command and let me loose.

And somehow through all that, I ended up here. An unheard of impossibility, a Forsaken at GAA.

CHAPTER FOUR

"Jez?" Iblis asked softly.

I slowly lifted my head and met her clear blue eyes. Her expression reflected the same emotion I'd been feeling in my chest, and only now did I think of a word for it: compassion.

I shook my head. I had no place for these feelings, no way to categorize them, so I tucked them away. "And you? Tell me about your earth life." Even as I said the words, a yearning desire, the hunger that I kept repressed, opened up like a giant cavern inside of me.

All who chose to follow Hasatan were denied the opportunity to go to earth. And I, an abomination in both kingdoms, was never even asked who I wished to follow.

Iblis had those black wings, the symbol of her choice to follow the Chosen before she was born. She didn't even remember making a choice, but there it was. The proof.

"Well." Iblis gave a little laugh. "I was born in Connecticut, in Southington, a little town outside the capital. I've got two brothers, I'm the youngest. My mom and dad work for the local newspaper, my mom's an editor and my dad's a writer. I'm on the volleyball team. Was." She whispered the last word. "Do you think I'll still be able to play sports here?"

"I don't know anything. This is all new to me as well." I wanted to ask her more questions, questions about earth, her family, her body. What it had been like to touch other people. My fingers traced each other, a haunting longing in the touch. The only being I would ever feel was myself.

Iblis went to her bed and picked up the uniform, a short, pleated apron that looked to go around her waist instead of slacks. It had a matching white tunic, but instead of a drawstring to tie it together, it had a row of white buttons.

"It seems so odd. Here we are, dead, but everything still feels so . . . alive."

"I think it's because you didn't understand what life is," I said before I could stop myself. "Being mortal didn't make you alive. You have always been, and you still are."

She nodded. "I'm starting to see that now. This name doesn't feel genuine, but it's actually the real me." She scooped up her uniform in her arms and headed for the room attached to ours. "I think I'll go change."

I stared after her. She was coming to terms with this so quickly.

I ran my fingers over my own uniform, laid out beside me on the bed. I felt the soft fabric beneath my fingers, the texture of the cloth. I noted with relief that the tunic was long-sleeved. If I ever did decide to put on the uniform, at least it would cover my chains.

Not that I could hide them forever. Perhaps it would be better just to show them and get it over with.

The door opened, and Iblis stepped out. The tunic was tucked into the skirt. A strange piece of fabric designed to match the skirt hung from her neck. She still wore the pink shoes from her earthly clothing, but everything else was changed.

"What is this?" I asked, eyeing the odd fashion statement.

"Oh, it's called a tie. It's pretty common with private schools back home. But this is home now, isn't it?" She got a quizzical look on her face.

I shrugged, not ready to commit to Arcadia as my new home.

But there was a growing part of me that wanted to fit in. Experience what it would be like to be a normal angel, just like them. Before they discovered my true identity.

For as long as I could.

Unlike my roommate, I did not change out of the clothes I was wearing. They were all I had ever known, and they fit me like a glove. They represented the person I was when I came here, and I wasn't ready to let go of that. It frightened me to think I might become like one of the heavenly hosts.

Instead I stepped over to the bookshelf and tilted my head, studying the spines of the books. The markings were shimmery and metallic, almost as if someone had painted fire onto the books.

"These must be for our classes," Iblis said, joining me. "Such interesting titles! *Ancient History of the Titans*, *Numbering the Stars*, *Understanding Quantum Physics*." She let out a gasp. "You know what this means? All the secrets of the universe — all of those unanswered questions — we get to know them! That's what we're doing here!"

I could only stare at her, not sure what kind of understanding she'd just received that hadn't already been obvious. "He is not going to tell us his secrets," I said, unable to keep the derision from my voice. "He keeps that knowledge to himself and a precious few others." I could name names, but I chose not to.

She gave me an odd look, like what I said didn't quite match up with her expectations. Well, I would happily enlighten her with the truth behind the stories she learned here at the academy. But I would have to earn her trust first.

A knock sounded at the door, and we both turned and looked at it.

"Come in," Iblis said, speaking first. Which was good, because I had not even been sure of the proper response.

The door opened to reveal Barachiel. He paused in the threshold and nodded at us.

"I see you've found the books. And Iblis is in uniform." There was no mistaking the approval in his eyes. "I have an agenda for each of you. You will find your class schedule inside." He held a small brown book toward Iblis.

"Thank you," Iblis said, accepting it. She opened it, and her eyes went wide. "What kind of book is this?"

"It's your personal assistant here at the academy. It functions like a book. It also functions like the tablets you're familiar with from earth. And like a computer, with a messaging system to both your teachers and your fellow students. Jez?"

I turned to see Barachiel holding another book out to me. My face warmed. I'd been so caught up in watching Iblis with her book that I hadn't noticed my own. I shook my head, not extending my hand to take it.

"I can't read," I whispered. Had he forgotten that small detail?

"I know. The situation will be rectified. Take your agenda, please."

I heaved a sigh and snatched it from his fingers. When I opened it, it was my turn for my eyes to go wide. Instead of unfamiliar letters, a gray screen glowed back at me. "There's nothing here," I said.

Iblis peeked over my shoulder. "How interesting! Mine has a list of my classes. Yours is blank."

A single line scrawled across mine even as I stared.

"'Please go to the library to meet your tutor for lesson number one,'" Iblis read from behind me. She pulled back to peer at me, then turned to Barachiel. "I thought we had classes together, but my first class is Intro to History. Jez won't have classes with the rest of us?"

"Even as first years, you won't take all your classes together, though you will see familiar faces everywhere you go. But Jez will have private classes to begin with. Then she will join the rest of the first years for more advanced learning."

"Oh." Iblis nodded, an expression of understanding crossing her face. "She needs remedial help."

Remedial help. I didn't like the sound of it. Judging from how Iblis said it, it couldn't be a good thing.

"Be on your way, then," Barachiel said.

I gave a start. "Wait, just like that? I have to go meet this tutor?"

Even Iblis looked surprised. "We don't get a day to adjust?"

"You won't need it. Everything here will feel very comfortable to you very quickly."

I had my doubts about that.

"I guess I'm on my way to Intro to History," Iblis said, consulting her book again.

I felt a surge of panic as Iblis started out of the room. I barely knew her, and I wasn't even sure I liked her, but I didn't have anyone else. "When will I see you again?" I asked her.

"I don't know. Do we have any classes together?" She looked at Barachiel.

He nodded. "The first years will meet together for After-Death Counseling starting tomorrow. Jez will be there."

"But I didn't—" I began, and then I cut myself off. I wasn't ready to reveal that info about myself.

"A part of everyone died to come to GAA, Jez," Barachiel said, his blue eyes piercing me.

I took a step back, feeling the meaning behind his words. Perhaps he was right. In a way, a part of me had died.

Or had it? Maybe I just carried hell around under my skin.

"But that's tomorrow," I said. "What about today?" Maybe I wouldn't see Iblis until we returned to our rooms. Which was when?

"All of the academy takes meal time together," Barachiel said.

"Meals!" Iblis' entire face lit up. "We get to eat! Oh, that makes me so happy!"

She actually clapped her hands. The exact picture of joy. I looked at Barachiel in confusion. "But . . . our spirits require no nourishment."

"Our spirits require as much nourishment as physical bodies do. We just require spiritual nourishment. The food we serve in the cafeteria is created to resemble mortal food.

Not only does it satisfy an emotional need, but it is imbued with charity and sacrifice and love. Thus it has a substantial amount of Light, the substance that enables all beings to exist in Shamayim with the Father," Barachiel said.

"I love food," Iblis breathed. "I'll see you at dinner, Jez!"

With that she went down the hallway, a skip in her step, as if she'd forgotten her recent death and sudden arrival at GAA.

"How can she be so accepting of all these changes?" I asked, watching her go.

"The emotions of sadness and loss and despair only linger in mortality. In this second existence, the understanding that pain and suffering are fleeting and temporary enables us to process them quickly and move on to the more agreeable emotions. As celestial beings, we still feel those emotions, but we know how to channel them so they don't consume us. Except during grave circumstances, when even knowledge of eternity cannot erase the emotional pain of certain events. Her spirit is already attuning itself to the celestial atmosphere. She will adapt quickly and be a brilliant pupil."

"Well." I looked down at my screen, feeling stupid for asking. Then there was me. The angel so behind I couldn't even go to normal classes yet. "Who is this tutor?"

"His name is Maalik. He's a Year Two, and he's the Team Lead for your dorm. He is one of my best students, one who greatly understands the challenges of mortality and adjusting to academy life. I've assigned him to you as a tutor."

"A tutor? Is that normal?"

"Every year a handful of second year students are selected to mentor those incoming first years with additional needs. It's not abnormal. However, given the unusual circumstances of your arrival, I felt it necessary to brief him about you."

"To brief him—did you tell him?" A cold shiver of fear rippled down my spine. So it was already over, before it had even begun. Everyone would know.

"Maalik's soul is honest and integral. He is someone you can trust. However, I did not tell him who you are."

Jezbathasat. He didn't tell him my lineage. I exhaled in relief.

"I told him where you came from."

I jolted. That was almost just as bad. "You told him I came from Sheol? That I am a Forsaken?" That would be enough to make this angel hate me. We were sworn enemies.

"You can expect he'll have many questions, but it will be up to you to answer them. It is your choice what you reveal or don't."

Choice. I gritted my teeth. So far it didn't seem like all it was cracked up to be.

"Follow me," Barachiel said, stepping out of the room. "I'll take you to the library."

The library was beyond the dormitories, continuing in a diagonal line behind the tall buildings. If the administration building were a sun, the dorms were the planets, circling it, and the outer buildings were moons. The cosmic similarities were not lost on me.

The library was the tallest building on campus, the one I had spotted from a distance when we entered Arcadia. Spirals reached into the heavens and disappeared into the clouds. We stepped inside, and I paused in the spacious entryway to admire the grand, sweeping structure lined with bookcases. Even craning my head back, I could not see the tops of them.

"Wow," I breathed.

"Every book ever written is stored here," Barachiel said. "You can find information on any subject."

I fixed him with a steely glare. "Any subject?" I knew for a fact that heaven withheld critical information from its followers. If they knew the truth about the war, they would have made very different choices.

He held my gaze. "Any subject. There is nothing you know, or think you know, Jez, that cannot be taught or explained further." He turned his head, and so did I. "There is Maalik."

Several desks lined the interior of the library, and sitting at one of them, directly in front of us, was a boy.

How had I missed him? His golden brown eyes peered at us, studying me intensely. His brows furrowed as if in disapproval of what he saw, and the magnificent black wings behind him fluttered before folding inward and resting against his back.

"Maalik." Barachiel led me forward. "This is Jez. She is the one you will be teaching to read."

Maalik's eyes glanced Barachiel's direction before landing on me again. Scrutinizing me. As if trying to discover my secrets. I pulled my jacket closer, afraid he would somehow see the chains that bound me to the underworld wrapped around my arms.

"Maalik," Barachiel said, a tone of warning in his voice. "Remember your training."

He looked up again and nodded, this time focusing on the archangel. "I will heed your words."

Barachiel nodded. "I will leave you to it. Bring her to the new student orientation in two hours."

Maalik's eyes flitted to mine again, and I saw in them irritation that I'd been left to his charge. My face burned, an unpleasant sensation I was becoming all too familiar with.

"Yes, Eldermaster Barachiel," Maalik said.

Barachiel swiveled and left the library. Maalik gestured to the chair opposite him at the desk.

"Sit."

I was not obligated to obey him, and I felt a surge of resentment toward him. I considered refusing. I considered running after Barachiel and telling him I'd changed my mind about all of this.

But there was something in Maalik's eyes as he appraised me, something like smugness. Like that was what he expected of me.

I pulled out the chair and sat down.

We both stared at each other for a few moments, then Maalik's eyes turned down to the book in front of him. He leafed through the pages. "So," he said, quite casually, "you're one of the Renegades."

I glared at him, the lusty emotion of hatred firing through my veins. I knew this feeling. It was the one that fed and fueled me, got me through each day of my existence. It was the one I whispered into the souls of mankind, prompting them to heinous deeds of Darkness. Weak. These self-righteous, condescending, arrogant angels from God's side had nicknamed all of Hasatan's followers Renegades, simply because they had chosen a different path. And because of it, they were condemned to Sheol, condemned to seek their sustenance from the follies of men.

I might not have been at the First War, but I was condemned right along with them.

"You hate me," he said, with such certainty that I reared back.

"How can you—?" I began, fearing he was also reading my mind, and then I remembered.

We were Empatyas. He could probably read my emotions as easily as he could read a book.

I lowered my gaze and took several deep breaths, trying to control my feelings. He waited without saying a word. I finally lifted my eyes, but this time I studied him, trying to get an emotional reading off him. I could not even discern a color. Why was that?

"Did Barachiel tell you I'm a—Renegade?" I forced the word out. We did not call ourselves that. We called ourselves Forsaken. Because we'd been cast out, abandoned, left to fend for ourselves.

And we had fended for ourselves. The best we could.

Maalik's eyes remained stern as he stared at me. "He told me you could not read because you've spent your existence in Sheol. You have no wings. It was easy to put the pieces together."

So Barachiel had not told him even that much. I exhaled and ran my finger over the wood grain of the desk. For a moment, I wondered if the furniture was brought from earth or if angels also had the skills to work wood.

"Are you?" he asked, driving my attention back to him.

"Am I what?" I said, matching the poisonous tone of his voice.

"Are you a Renegade?"

He couldn't begin to imagine my existence. How would I survive Sheol if I wasn't able to pry the darkest emotions out of a soul? I was a Forsaken from the moment I was created, existing as a shadow among humanity, bringing out the vile and wicked tendencies of mankind.

I wasn't given any other option.

CHAPTER FIVE

"Do *you* hate *me*?" I couldn't meet his eyes when I asked the question. Something within my chest trembled, and I willed myself to be still. His reaction to me was what I could expect from every angel who learned the truth.

He sighed. "Why are you so intent on destroying humanity?"

I couldn't even think of a response. Then my eyes flew to his as I burst out, "What? What makes you think I am?"

He blinked. "Aren't you?"

He thought I wanted to destroy humanity? Why would I want to do that? What were they to me? Nothing. Their short, brief lives would end and be snuffed out before I'd even finished maturing. They held no power over me.

"No," I said.

"Well, maybe not you, in particular," he said, and his shoulders relaxed slightly. "But your kind."

It wasn't that the Forsaken wanted to destroy humanity. They just wanted a piece of it. They wanted to feel what humans felt. And feed off those emotions.

Sometimes, I admitted, human souls became casualties.

Luckily I didn't have to explain that, as Maalik kept talking.

"And why do you get to come to GAA when no other Renegade gets to? What makes you so special?"

I couldn't tell him that. So I said, "I don't know."

He gestured to the book in front of him. "I've been reading. Looking for other examples, other cases of a Renegade attending the academy. I can't find any account or history of it. It's as if you're the first." The wings came out again, fluttering, and I took it to be a sign of agitation. "Why?"

I could only shake my head.

The wings opened all the way, and I tried not to stare at the impressive span as they flapped once before folding against his body. The envy sprouted in me like a budding plant, and I wanted to see them again. I wanted to touch them.

You can't touch.

The rule was seared into my very being, and I pushed down the forbidden desire.

He watched me a moment more, but when I said nothing else, he must have concluded I didn't know. Pressing his lips together, he pulled out what looked like a book ripped in half, long with white, blank pages. He placed beside it a marking utensil.

"Barachiel has asked me to bring you up to speed. He said even you don't know how much you don't know. So I'm supposed to stick to you like glue for the next few days and help you understand everything you see and hear."

We could start with him. I heard his words, but half of what he said didn't make sense to me. I slowly shook my head. "I don't know what you're saying."

His brow creased. "What did you not understand?"

"What is up to speed?"

He blinked, and then he let out a short laugh. "You really don't know anything. Who did you spend your time with, the hell hounds?"

"I was left alone in a dark room for most of my existence," I said, lashing out at his humor. "Except for when I was called forward to fulfill my duties."

That cut off his laughter. His expression grew somber, and I knew he was imagining what evil duties I might have been fulfilling.

Let him imagine.

"Up to speed means I'm going to teach you what all the other kids here know so you don't stick out like a sore thumb," he said shortly.

His terminology was still foreign to me, but I got the gist. "You'll teach me what I need to know to fit in."

"That's right. And I also have to teach you to read." He lifted the book of white paper. "Do you know what this is?"

"Paper," I said. I did know some things, at least.

"It's a notepad. We used them on earth to learn how to read and write." He put the notepad down. "Why can't you read?"

"I was never taught."

"It's more than that, though. Are there no books in hell?"

I was silent a moment, but then I figured I wasn't revealing any big secret. "Inhabitants of Sheol can't comprehend written glyphs. *He* will not allow it."

"He who?"

"You know." I pointed my finger toward the heavens. "*Him.*"

Interest sparked in Maalik's eyes. "Why?"

"I can't believe you didn't already know this," I sneered, unable to resist the jibe at his self-righteous attitude. "Because he plays favorites, and we are not them."

Maalik leaned forward on the desk, his expression darkening. "That's not it."

"How do you know?"

"Because I know The Father, and that's not how it works."

"Really?" I challenged. "You've met him?"

"Well, no . . ." Maalik faltered. "Not yet. I will after I graduate, though."

"Then your knowledge of him is less reliable than mine." I lifted my chin. "You've been dead for how long?"

"Four earth years," Maalik said. "But—"

"So you've been here for four years. I've been simmering in Sheol for the equivalent of ten earth lifetimes. I think I'm the more reliable source on the matter."

"But you've been in hell," Maalik fired back. "Your information is tainted. Your whole world view is distorted and black."

"No, it's not," I returned. "I see things how they really are, not through a holy, glorified view."

"That's impossible," Maalik said, and finally a color appeared around his body, a vibrant red pulsing around his being. "You are tainted and distorted. Everything you perceive will be the same." He stood up, grabbing the notepad and pulling it to his body. "I cannot teach you. I will tell Barachiel to find someone else." He pushed away from the table and strode toward the door, his wings flapping in rhythm to his rapid footsteps, his feet practically gliding across the stone floor.

And all I could think was that I wanted to glide my fingers along the edges of those feathers.

"Hello, first years!"

The angel that came into the classroom smiled at us behind the podium that was taller than she was. She grabbed a stool and pulled it over, then stood so she could see over it. "Ah, that's better!"

I didn't want to like her. I didn't want to like anyone, not after that horrible encounter I'd had in the library with Maalik a few hours earlier. But her tiny stature, quick smile, and bright pink hair made it hard to dislike her.

"I'm Master Nuriel," she said. "Most of you won't see me again until you're a fourth year because I teach advanced classes. But I also get to do the new student orientation."

She smiled again, her white wings fluttering like a butterfly's behind her. She reminded me more of a mythical pixie than an angel.

"You've discovered your gift by now and been assigned to a dorm. Hopefully you are feeling more comfortable here at Yishuv. There are just a few practical things I'd like to go over with you." She glanced down at the podium and cleared her throat, then looked up again.

"By now you've been to your dorm. We have three dorms on campus: Alef, Hesed, and Emet. The three dorms form a triangle around the quad. The boys' rooms are always on the left side of the building and girls on the right. Your classes are arranged by year and then dorm, so you will see the angels from your dormitory more often than those from the others.

"Master Selaphiel already told you flying on campus is not allowed. Sometimes your wings will control you more than you control them, and we understand that. But intentionally is prohibited on campus, so please — don't do it. Use your legs. Remember the blessing of having a body, even if it's a spiritual one."

She consulted the podium again.

"Many of you come to us with vices from mortality still affecting your mental state. You will be assigned special classes to help you with these vices, as they are much harder to control in this existence than in your last, but controlling them is essential. Whatever weaknesses you did not overcome in mortality must be conquered now. Most especially the vice of lust." She grew very serious, taking the effort to meet the eyes of nearly every angel in the room. "You will learn more about sacraments in your advanced classes, but steer clear of the carnal desires. It is not done here. There can be no accidents. Later you will learn about Bindings and the important nature of these feelings, but for now, just know that you must not give in."

I tilted my head, intrigued. Lust was a physical appetite, and I'd assumed it required a physical body. How could angels feel that? Was it simply a leftover memory from their mortality?

"We do play sports in this existence." That warm smile flashed again. "You'll learn more about Skyball later, but we encourage you to attend the games and participate on the team if you feel so inclined.

"And finally, Shema." Her smile became more reverent. "Shema is the evening devotional we hold every day. It's when a conduit opens to Shamayim, and the Light of the Father descends upon us and nourishes our souls. You are invited to come, to lift your voices to him and get to know the Father who you once knew so well. The Light will help you remember your previous existence, and each memory will fortify you as you go through your studies and recall who you are.

"That's all. Shema begins directly after dinner in the auditorium. Thank you for your attention."

Master Nuriel stepped down, and the other angels stood. Curiosity and an eagerness to experience Shema reflected in their voices.

Not me. I already knew I'd be staying as far away from the Light as possible.

I didn't know what else to do with myself, so I returned to my room. I sat down on my bed and stared at the glowing screen in my hands. The gray page flashed a message at me, but I couldn't read it.

I was used to being alone with nothing to do and nothing to hear except my thoughts. But I'd never had so many thoughts to ponder before, and my mind found it overwhelming. I lay back on my bed and stared at the ceiling, at the light placed there as if to mimic the sun. As if one could capture the glory of the sun and place it in a small container to light the rooms.

I wasn't sure I'd ever used the word glory before. Definitely not to describe the sun. But why not? The brilliant orb was glorious.

The thought made me sit up, and I stared at the door. Light. Light was glorious.

A shiver ran through me. I was changing. Without even meaning to, I had started to see Light differently than yesterday, when Light was still something to be afraid of. Before Barachiel brought me here under his protection, where I could face the realm of Arcadia without being burned to ash.

I stood up and walked into the adjacent room, the one I hadn't yet explored. A reflective glass steadied itself on the wall, which I found surprising. Vanity was one of the biggest sins of humanity, and these mirrors only perpetuated the mortal tendency to admire oneself. What other purpose could it serve?

But my thoughts quickly redirected when I caught a glimpse of myself.

I knew I had long dark hair because I'd gripped it in my hands before and held it before my face. But the only time I'd spent on earth had been as shadow, and I'd never seen my reflection. It had never even occurred to me to wonder what I looked like. Now I stared back at the image in the mirror with astonishment. My eyebrows were slanted upward at the ends, as were my eyes, which were so brown they were almost black. I wondered who created my features. I trailed my fingers over the high cheekbones and touched the corners of my face, intrigued.

This was me. Jezbathasat.

A familiar knock at the door brought me out of the bathroom. "Come in," I said, imitating Iblis' response earlier.

The door opened, and I wasn't the least bit surprised to see Barachiel there.

"It didn't work out with Maalik," I said. "He got up and left."

"I have spoken with Maalik, and he regrets his behavior," Barachiel said. "But you also should not have spoken the way you did."

"What?" I scoffed. "I upset his sensitivities? The truth bothered him?"

"The problem is, Jez, that you don't know what is truth and what isn't. Until you learn, your best course of action is to keep silent and observe."

I didn't like his insinuation. The implication that my understanding of the universe might be incorrect didn't settle correctly with me. "That's how all of you are," I said, my ichor growing hot again. "You think you know everything. Any opinion that differs from yours, anyone who threatens your authority, any truth that might show you what you really are, you stomp on it, you shove it down, you stifle it as soon as you can. Your followers only come along blindly because they don't know any better!"

Barachiel did not move or say a word while I raged. Only after I paused to take a breath did he speak.

"Are you done?"

"No." But no more angry words came to me. I needed him to fight back for me to keep going. Relenting, I leaned my head against the wall. "Yes."

"As I said, Jez, keep your mind open to learning new things. No one here will tell you what you should or shouldn't believe. But the truth will reveal itself."

Ugh, how his smug confidence made me want to hit something! I was quite certain the truth would reveal itself, and not in the way he expected. I had always assumed the archangels were involved in the Great Deception, but it only took a day with Barachiel to know he was sincere in his mission. No, the deception began higher up, and the guilt lay with those of higher powers.

"Tomorrow you will meet again with Maalik after your first class. May I see your schedule?"

I turned to my bed and picked up the book. He opened it and touched the gray page. Lights flickered as something else crossed over the page. He handed it back to me.

"I've changed your settings so your book will not show you words but images. The building you see on the screen is your next destination. When it's time to go somewhere else, a new building will appear. Once you've learned to read, your screen will resemble those of the other students. But you won't have regular classes until you've mastered that skill."

I could only stare at my book. The gray page was gone, replaced by a glowing, flat replica of the long, squat building behind the Hesed dormitory. "How did you do this?"

Barachiel smiled. "Technology, Jez. Heaven has always implemented the technology that mortals are just beginning to understand. But we introduce it in degrees to the students, giving them what they are familiar with before moving on to more advanced objects."

Technology. I didn't know the word, but I could see the definition clearly in front of me. My sense of injustice bridled again. What right did heaven have to keep this from Sheol? Why were we stripped of our powers except in certain spheres, trapped in unpleasant realms, and forced to use the minimal of elements? Why couldn't we have this same technology?

I tailored my thoughts, cutting back the most rebellious ones and working hard to avoid any inclination of my intentions from creeping in.

Shamayim would pay for forcing the inhabitants of Sheol to live in the Darkness.

CHAPTER SIX

I walked alone from my dorm toward my next destination, which Barachiel told me was the cafeteria, a place of comfort and familiarity to mortals who would gather in such places to socialize and eat. Other students began to emerge from various dorms and buildings, moving in the same direction as me.

"I wondered if I would see you again."

I turned slightly, not expecting anyone to talk to me.

Sitting on top of his dorm sign, his wings opening and closing as if they had a mind of their own, was the Shadow Shade angel.

"Kerubiel," I said, his name coming to me.

He smiled, but it was a dark expression. It didn't light his face the way Iblis' did when her lips curved upward.

It drew me toward him.

"What did they say we are?" he asked as I stepped closer. "Empatya angels?"

"Yes." I stopped a few feet from him.

"So you see emotions." A color like brown and green swirled around him, rippling and rolling off his shoulders and wings. "What am I feeling?"

"I don't know," I said. "I haven't attended my classes yet."

"Ah." He stepped off the sign and closed the distance between us, his eyes, so blue they were nearly black, swallowing me in their depths. His hair curled in loose waves against his head. "So you're a rebel also. Already skipping classes."

A rebel. A renegade. That was what the angels called us. "Yes. That's what I am," I said. For some reason it didn't bother me to tell him. I knew he wasn't going to hate me. If anything, his attitude indicated it was a desirable trait. That filled me with a sort of confidence that made my heart swell.

"Going to dinner?" He nodded his head toward the long building in front of me, where the students were clustering together as they entered the doors, an air of joviality and companionship emanating from them.

"Yes."

"Well, let's go then, Jez."

He knew my name.

We walked together toward the cafeteria, his wings opening and closing at random times.

"Can you control them?" I asked.

He paused and glanced at me, then continued forward. "Where are your wings?"

I halted mid-step, my veins flushing ice cold. I'd given myself away with my question. I considered lying. But I wasn't sure what to say. So I kept silent.

He waited a moment, but when I said nothing, he said, "I can't control them yet. They just sort of do their own thing. I guess I'll learn how in class."

So there was a class on that too.

"I've heard that sometimes angels get them torn off," he said softly.

A little shudder ran through me. "You've heard that?" I'd seen the marks on the backs of the Fallen, ones who crossed a rule or boundary and were thrust down to Sheol. Only shadow wings, a dark memory of what used to be, remained. They were angels who had already received their white wings. I could not begin to imagine the pain they must go through at the physical loss of such beautiful appendages.

He was looking at me again, a deep blue-green color seeping out of his skin. I struggled to maintain eye contact, distracted by his aura. I met his gaze and saw the question there.

"No," I said, answering it. "That's not what happened to me."

"But something did," he said, with the tone of one who knows. "Something damaged you."

"How do you know that?" I breathed. "You can't see colors."

"I don't need to. I recognize a kindred spirit."

Something inside me seemed to wake up, as if a light turned on in my chest. "Have you been damaged?"

"Over and over again." He took a step closer, his dark eyes capturing mine. "There's no fixing me. GAA is not the place for me. I don't belong here. Somehow I think you don't either."

I flinched, taking a step back and looking away. I felt as if he could peer into my soul and uncover my secrets. And I didn't want my secrets uncovered.

"Kerubiel," a girl called.

We both turned to see two angels standing by the cafeteria, the girl waving at Kerubiel. Neither had donned their uniforms.

"I'll see you later, Jez."

Kerubiel's smile was both intriguing and disarming. I stared after him, confused by the emotions tumbling around in my chest.

"Don't get too close."

I whirled around as Maalik came up behind me. His face remained stern, his eyes unreadable. No colors swirled around his visage now.

"What do you mean?" I stared at him.

"I see the effect he has on you." He didn't release my gaze. "He's playing your emotions."

I had no context for his words, but they made me defensive all the same. "I don't know what you're talking about."

"Maybe you don't." He finally looked away. "Our dorm sits at Table D, if you would like to join us. There is no obligation." He continued into the cafeteria with several other students.

No obligation. Was that a reminder that I had a choice? Or his subtle way of telling me he didn't want me there?

Maybe I was catching on to human nuances after all.

"Jez, there you are!" Iblis stepped to my side, her face flushed. "That class was so interesting! I can't believe I went through my entire mortal life without knowing anything about heaven or angels or demons!"

She reached for me again, and I flinched, rearing back before she got too close.

Why hadn't they told her touch was forbidden? That should have been the first rule explained in their classes.

But also, if she knew who I was, where I came from, she wouldn't be so keen to be close to me.

My reaction did not go unnoticed. She frowned, some of the glee going out of her face. "What's wrong?"

So many things. But I started with, "Why would you presume to touch me?"

"Well." She shrugged, still looking confused. "We're friends. I was excited to see you, to find out about your first class."

"First of all," I said, my incredulity ringing in my voice, "you can't touch me."

"I can't touch you?"

I wasn't done. "And you don't know me. Yet you assume a closeness to me that I don't reciprocate. I'm not looking for friends. I'm just trying to get through each day."

"Okay," she said in a more subdued tone. "Sorry for being presumptuous." She turned away, a gray color pulsating around her person.

I didn't have to attend a class to know what it meant.

I shuffled into the cafeteria behind her, wrapping my arms around my waist as if to shield myself from the onslaught of emotions and expectations of the students around me. Iblis paused to speak to Maalik at what could only be Table D. Maalik looked up and met my eyes, but I turned away, avoiding his gaze. Instead I found an unoccupied table and sat down.

Iblis moved past the table into a line of students. I watched them, curious in spite of my dismal mood. The students walked through a set of doors and came out the other side with a tray in their hands. They dispersed from there and settled into different tables, their expressions almost uniformly joyful and glad.

Except for one group of students.

Kerubiel stepped up to a table surrounded by angels who shared colors of brown and gray with hints of blue in their auras. He held a tray of food in his hands just like everyone else, and they welcomed him, greeted him with smiles and head bobs. They wore the purple color of the Emet dorm to the right of my own. Their moodiness hung over their heads, a feeling of brooding pouring off them. They seemed magnetized to each other, sucking one another into their auras.

I stood up, suddenly knowing where I wanted to be. I didn't bother to grab a tray of food before sitting down next to Kerubiel at the table.

"Jez," he said, giving me a slightly startled look.

The chatter at the table fell silent, and the others stared at me. An odd feeling came over me, making me want to jump up and run away.

"Who is she?" the girl who had beckoned to Kerubiel said. She glowered at me as if I were the enemy.

It hadn't occurred to me that I wouldn't be welcome. "Can I sit here?"

Kerubiel faced the others. "She's all right."

"She can see color," a boy with fair hair and splotchy skin said. Red and a brilliant shade of yellow spiked off his body. "We don't mix with them."

"How do you know I see color?" I asked.

"Because you keep looking past us instead of at us," the girl said. "It's easy to spot."

"She's not like the others," Kerubiel said. "She's an outsider also."

"Well, then. Welcome." The boy held his hand out to me. "Might be nice to have someone who can read feelings on our side."

I shrank back from his hand. Was this a test?

"Man, this food is great." Kerubiel redirected the conversation, taking their attention off me. "Like manna from heaven. Too bad we're expected to be vegetarians now."

They laughed and grumbled, and the conversation resumed. Only then did Kerubiel turn to me.

"You aren't going to eat?"

I shook my head. "It's not necessary. And I never developed a taste for it."

"You are one odd soul." He eyed me as he bit into what looked like a ball of rice. "I can't wait to learn more about you."

A shiver of something almost predatory and delicious crept down my spine. I held onto the heady feeling, relishing it.

Maybe not all of these new experiences would be unpleasant.

Iblis did not bring up our interaction when I saw her in our dorm room later. Actually, she did not say a word to me. She changed out of her uniform and disappeared into the bathroom, where she mumbled to herself about not being able to find a toothbrush. Then she came back out, climbed into her bed, and turned out the light.

As if I were not even there.

I lay in my own bed and stared into the darkness. But even with the lights out, it wasn't completely dark. Not like in Sheol. I could still discern particles of Light and energy around me.

Spiritual beings did not require as much rest as mortals did, but we still required some. But resting reminded me too much of being secreted away for most of my existence, hidden from the prying eyes of heaven.

The worst part had been the loneliness. Wondering when someone would come see me again. If anyone would.

Iblis said not a word from her bed, and I finally identified the colorful emotion swirling around her: Rejection. Wounded pride. Hurt. Because of me.

I didn't have to fix this. But if I didn't, I would lose my best chance at a friend and companion.

"Iblis," I said quietly.

"Hmm?"

Not a conversational response, but at least she hadn't ignored me.

"I am sorry." I waited, but silence met my proclamation. "I offended you, and I did not intend to. I—" I hesitated, not sure what words should come next. "I've never had a friend before," I admitted. "Or even someone to spend time with."

More silence met my words. Then I heard the bed creak, and she pushed up on one arm to peer at me across the room. "That doesn't make any sense. What kind of life did you have?"

"I didn't." I sighed. "It was a terrible existence. I've been alone for a very long time. But I think I would like—" I paused, feeling the rapid pulsing of ichor in my veins. "I would like you to be my friend."

"Considering we share a room together, it would be nice." She reached over and switched the bedroom light back on. "Why didn't you sit with us at dinner?"

How could I explain that one? "I think I fit in better with the other angels."

"Maalik said to beware of them," Iblis said. "He said there's a darkness around them, and the darkness often leads angels to become Fallen."

Maalik. The name sent a spike of indignation shooting through me. "Maalik doesn't know everything."

"No, but he's pretty smart. He's the Team Lead for our dorm. He's been here a few years already."

How did she know all this? "What classes did you have today?"

"Just Intro to History. Tomorrow I have the art of language, some kind of therapy class, and human relations. You?"

"None. I have to master basic principles before I can attend classes with everyone else. But I get to go to the therapy class."

"Oh. That's interesting." A moment of silence followed, and then Iblis said, "Can I help with anything?"

I sensed it was a genuine offer, and it rubbed me in an uncomfortable manner. "No. Maalik is helping me. He's my tutor."

"Maalik is your personal tutor?" She sounded impressed. "Then I'm sure you'll catch up soon enough."

"I'm sure," I said.

We drifted into silence. I didn't feel completely at ease, but at least I didn't feel so isolated.

Natural sunlight streamed through our dorm room window in the morning, waking us both. The sleep rested my mind, and I climbed out of bed feeling refreshed and ready. Ready to tackle whatever was coming my way.

Iblis donned her uniform again, carefully settling the school badge near her left collar. I stood up and picked up my agenda, checking what building I should be going to. The cafeteria.

"Jez?"

I looked at Iblis, who smiled at me gently while pulling her long golden hair to the side and weaving it.

"You haven't changed your clothes since we arrived," she said. "You don't want to go out today in the same thing as yesterday."

"Why should that be a concern?" I asked.

"Well, the clothes are . . . dirty."

I glanced down at them, grabbing the fringes of my skirt and looking for signs of soil. Then I frowned at her. "They are not dirty. They are as good as they've always been."

"They're the same, at least. You don't want to wear the same thing two days in a row."

I had worn them my whole existence. I sensed that would be the wrong thing to say, though. "You are wearing the same shoes."

She looked down at the pink shoes and laughed. "It's okay to wear the same shoes every day. These are my favorite."

"These are my favorite. And I have no others, so this it will be."

"You have your uniform."

I glanced toward the wardrobe filled with proper uniforms and academy attire. I was no more ready to don them today than I had been yesterday. "What's wrong with this?" I asked, almost challenging her to find something offensive with my jagged skirt and tight black jacket.

"You're dressed in leather. It makes you look like some kind of rebel."

Leather. I fingered the soft, supple material of my sleeve. So that was what this was called.

"You could at least take the jacket off. It's not cold here."

"No." I pulled the jacket closer to me. "It stays on." Perhaps forever. Without it, all my secrets would be given away.

"Fine." She shrugged. "Sit with us at breakfast?"

Her invitation resonated within me. Was this what it meant to have a friend? "Okay."

I walked with Iblis back to the cafeteria and followed her through the line, where she loaded her tray with what appeared to be mortal food. I found this silly at best and deceptive at worst. Why encourage the pleasures of gluttony?

"Aren't you getting anything?" Iblis asked me.

I shook my head. I remembered what Barachiel had said, about the food being imbued with Light. I didn't know what would happen to me if I ate, and I didn't want any more Light near me. "I don't eat."

"Here." She picked a small rectangular container with a brown square and set it on her tray. "I'll get that for you. You have to try it."

I did not comment.

We left the food line and went over to Table D, where I spotted Maalik and several unfamiliar faces.

"Everyone, this is Jez," Iblis said, introducing me. "She's my roommate."

The faces turned toward me, taking me in, confusion and questions in their eyes as they studied me.

"But if she's your roommate, she's also a first year? In Dorm Alef?" The girl who spoke frowned at me as she did.

"Yes, that's right," Iblis said, nodding.

"Why haven't we seen you in any classes?" a boy asked.

"Weren't you sitting with that Shadow Shade yesterday?" another boy asked.

"She looks like a Shadow Shade," a girl murmured.

I stiffened, regretting my decision to pursue a friendship with Iblis and sit with my classmates. It was clear they also saw I didn't belong here.

"Jez's previous learning didn't prepare her enough for the academy," Maalik said.

I tilted my face toward him, surprised he came to my defense. Or had I missed a human subtlety and he was actually putting me down?

"I'm tutoring her privately until she's ready to join us in classes," he continued. "But she's one of us."

That seemed to settle it. The students shrugged and relaxed and went back to their conversations.

"Here," Iblis said, putting the brown square in front of me as she sat down.

"Thank you," I said to Maalik as I also sat, though I wasn't sure why he deserved my gratitude. For whatever reason, his words had calmed them, put their worries to rest.

"Have you eaten food before?" he asked, quietly enough that I hoped Iblis, on the other side of me, did not hear.

I shook my head. He was the only angel among my peers who knew where I'd come from.

"Try it." He nodded at the food. "It's good."

I stared at it and then back at Maalik, lifting an eyebrow.

"I'm sorry for yesterday," he said. "I—reacted. I'm still learning to control my reactions."

Still learning. So he didn't know everything, and he readily admitted it. Some of my misgivings smoothed down.

"Try the food," he said again. A smile stole across his lips. "Trust me."

I stared at him. Did he know that Light wreathed his face when he smiled? Or was that part of my gift, to be able to see it? His eyes flickered from the square in front of me to my face, the color of his irises more golden than brown. His gaze captivated me. I forced my eyes away, a tingling energy pulsing over my skin.

I didn't know Maalik from Adam. But for some reason, I did trust him. I picked up the brown square and placed it between my lips, then took a nibble.

CHAPTER SEVEN

A shocking sensation of bitter and sweet spilled across my tongue, accompanied by a sticky, crumbling sensation unlike any I'd ever experienced. It dissolved into a pleasing taste of . . .

I had nothing to compare it to.

Nothing happened to me, either. No Light burned through my veins, eradicating my essence. I wasn't consumed with guilt or pain. Perhaps the Light in the food was not that strong.

"What is it?" I asked, pulling it away and staring in wonder.

"It's a brownie," Maalik said, satisfaction in his voice. "It's chocolate."

"It's the perfect dichotomy of bitter and sweet . . . as if together they make a whole." I took another bite and was again enthralled by the sensation.

"The bitter makes the sweet sweeter." Maalik stood, empty tray in his hands. "I believe you're joining us for group therapy at the Gabriel Building this morning."

I eyed Iblis' tray, wanting to snatch up another food item and try it. A new world had been unveiled from before my eyes, and I wanted to dig in with both hands.

How like heaven to keep something this wondrous from us.

"Group therapy?" I asked. "What is that?"

"I read about it last night," Iblis said. "We all recently died and left behind everything we thought we knew about existence. Group therapy is supposed to help us connect our mortal life experiences and our deaths with our current life. And because we get to hear about what our classmates went through, it helps us become more united."

I looked at Maalik. He knew I hadn't died. I didn't have life experiences to share.

"We've all experienced some kind of death," Maalik said, not lowering his eyes from my gaze. "We've all ended one life and begun another."

So that's what he thought this was for me.

I would have to try the other foods later. I stood when the others stood, and we left the cafeteria as a group. The upper year students dispersed to go to their classes while the beginning years moved toward the domed building lit on my screen. I lingered behind the group, fearful of accidentally bumping another student as we made our way toward the Gabriel Building. They clustered together in a mob, and I wondered how they kept from touching.

The Gabriel Building was located adjacent to the library behind another dormitory. At the threshold of the building, the students from my year stopped, looking as uncertain as I felt. Except Maalik, who pushed his way past everyone. I was certain he bumped at least one or two arms, but I had to be wrong. He didn't flinch, and the fires of heaven didn't rain down on him.

"It's this way," Maalik said, pausing to wait for us. "You'll know the way next time."

"Why are you coming?" I asked, letting everyone else pass in front of us. "You're not a new arrival."

"I'm the Team Lead for our dorm," Maalik said. "It's my responsibility to orientate all of you. I also need to get to know each of you on a personal level."

"Why is that?"

He gestured me forward. "Come along, Jez, and learn about mortality."

We entered a room with chairs set up in a large circle. A wingless man with a head full of curly red hair stood in front of a chair, smiling warmly and inviting each student who entered to have a seat.

"Are you an angel?" a boy with dark hair and dark skin asked.

"I am, Leike," the man said.

"Then where are your wings?"

"I've learned to control when they emerge."

This created a small stir among the new angels, who must not have known the wings could be controlled. A few heads turned my direction where I sat in between a small blond girl and a large red-head boy.

Well. Kerubiel thought my wings had been torn off, and my classmates thought I'd learned how to retract them. I sat up straighter.

"Now that we're all here," the man said, "let me introduce myself. I'm Master Eleleth. I've been teaching at

GAA for eighty-five earth years. I died two hundred years ago, during an outbreak of the Spanish Flu. I was fifteen."

I leaned forward, enraptured in spite of myself. I didn't know about life on earth. I'd never spoken to a newly dead about their earlier existence. When I went to earth as a shadow, my focus was on my human target. The earthly surroundings were as dark and hazy to my eyes as I was to a mortal's eyes.

"I grew up in Ireland, the oldest of six children who learned how to plow the fields and grow crops to make money for our landlord. My father died three months before I did. When I died, I left behind my mother and five small siblings. They were left to fend for themselves." He paused. "Their story did not have a happy ending. While I attended GAA as a student, my brothers and sister were starving, trying to take care of the land and crops with no man in the household. My eleven-year-old brother became the male head of the household. When he couldn't bring in the cash crops necessary to pay for our piece of the land, the landlord sold my siblings off one by one to pay the debt."

Soft noises came from various chairs in the circle. I glanced around and realized a few of my classmates were crying. Some cried quietly, eyes focused on Master Eleleth, a dignified, resigned expression on their faces. Others buried their faces in their hands, shoulders shaking as if his story had somehow personally wounded them.

This I could not understand. Why did they cry? Was it for Eleleth's siblings? That made no sense. All of this happened so long ago, none of the students had even been alive then. Whatever suffering they might have experienced was long over.

"I kept an eye on my family and did what I could to intercede on their behalf. As soon as I graduated from GAA, I asked to be my brother's Guardian. By then he was fifteen, the same age as when I died."

I held my breath, strangely caught up with his tale. Was he allowed to guard his brother?

"And then what?" Iblis asked, looking as engaged as I was. Tears glittered in her eyes, and I wondered what part of his story resonated with her.

Eleleth's lips curved upward in a smile. "My request was granted. I protected him from evil and outside influences as much as he allowed me. He went on to get an apprenticeship that brought in enough money for him to support a family. He had a stable life, and eventually he had the means to seek out my other siblings and help them where he could."

"A happy ending after all," another angel said. But his tone wasn't pleased. He sounded bitter, frustrated.

Eleleth focused on him. "Happiness is often a matter of perspective, Jerahmeel. Before I invite each of you to share what you wish of your deaths and mortal existences, please feel free to ask questions."

"What happened to your mother?" Jerahmeel said, his voice aggressive. He tossed a lock of sandy blond hair behind his head, his blue eyes glittering. "You didn't mention her in all of this."

"I couldn't help her," Eleleth said calmly, not acknowledging the anger behind Jerahmeel's words. "She became ill and died only a few years after I did."

"And how is that fair?" Jerahmeel's eyes flashed, and he clenched his fists together. "Where is the happy ending for her?"

"What you perceive as an injustice is only the middle of a story. My mother's mortal life ended, but her eternal one had just begun. She lived a faithful life and passed through the gates of Shamayim without resistance."

That brought a soft murmur from the class.

"Have you seen her?" a girl asked. "Can we see our family members?"

"Is my boyfriend here?" Iblis asked. "He was in the car with me . . ."

"My brother died from cancer two years ago," a boy said. "Is he here? Can I see him?"

Eleleth held up a hand. "Your family members who have passed on are most certainly here. Children go straight to heaven and finish growing and learning under the tutelage of angels. Adults are held in Gehenna before moving on to their eternal reward."

Or punishment, as it might be, but Eleleth didn't say that. And neither did I.

"Inhabitants of Shamayim are allowed to descend and visit you on breaks, but you cannot visit them until after graduation." His eyes focused directly on Iblis. "Your boyfriend is not here. He did not die in the car with you."

"Oh." She gave a little gasp, and I wasn't sure if she was relieved or disappointed.

"Now, please. Not only will you learn from each other in this exercise, but you will take the first steps to let go of your mortal self and mortal existence as you embrace this stage of your lives. We will go around the circle. I ask each of you to share as you feel comfortable, but please be open with your classmates. It is how you will become a united group."

I shifted in my chair with sudden anxiety, clutching the bottom of it tightly. What story could I tell? What fabrication could I create to make them think I'd had a normal earth life also?

But Maalik would know. He would know I was lying. And lying would not be allowed.

Eleleth turned to the boy on his right. "Israfil?"

Israfil, a young man with ebony skin and black hair, cleared his throat. "Well, my name is Israfil, and I'm an alcoholic."

The students tittered with laughter and Israfil grinned, though I failed to see the humor. His smile dimmed.

"Really, I'm not. My name was Ethan, and I had cancer. I lived in Maryland with my mom and dad and sister. I knew I was dying." He hesitated. "I actually saw my own guardian angel when I was passing on. He told me not to be afraid. And then he stayed with me until I arrived here."

"I didn't see a guardian angel," a girl said, cocking her head with a puzzled expression on her face.

"Not everyone has an assigned angel," Eleleth said. "Some people only need an angel during times of duress. Most people see an Angel of Mercy at the time of their death, come to guide them during the moment of their passing. But everyone is administered to from time to time during their mortal existence." He focused on Israfil again. "How has the transition gone for you?"

Israfil shrugged. "Honestly, probably better than for others. I knew I was dying. I was kind of looking forward to it. And this is a heck of a lot better than hanging out on clouds strumming harps."

Again the students laughed, and I shifted in my seat. I should know the context of his jokes, but I didn't. They had all shared an experience together, a mortality, but I could not relate. They'd even shared the same historical time period on earth.

Eleleth looked at the girl next to Israfil. "Dara?"

The girl cleared her throat and gripped the edges of her chair. Her long black hair draped over one shoulder, her sweeping eyelashes nearly brushing her ivory cheeks as she lowered her gaze to the floor. "I grew up in Tokyo."

"Wait," Israfil interrupted, staring at her. "How do you speak English so well? You don't even have an accent."

"I—" She paused, blinking at him. "We learned English in school. But I'm not speaking English."

"How can I—" Israfil began, and Eleleth chuckled.

"You are all speaking Adamaic, the first language, the language of the heavens. It was the first thing your spirits learned when you were created, and your intelligences reverted back to it instantly when you arrived in Gehenna."

"Oh." Dara nodded.

"So right now I'm speaking Adamaic—not Hebrew?" a boy with deep-set eyes and hollow cheekbones said.

"That's right," Eleleth said. "Continue, Dara."

She cleared her throat again. "I grew up speaking Japanese. But I could get by in several languages. I'm an only child. One day I was walking to school with my friends when there was an earthquake." She blinked, and twin rivulets crept down her cheeks. "A piece of the building beside me collapsed on top of me. My hips were crushed. There were men there, men who tried to help me, but they couldn't." She choked on her words, her chest heaving as she sobbed. "I wanted so desperately for them to save me. I had such plans for my life. To be a doctor, to travel. And now it's all over. There's nothing left for me."

My heart twisted within me, an agonizing twinge welling up inside. Why did her story hurt?

"It's not over," Maalik said, his eyes on Dara with an expression of complete sympathy. "That life is over. Your new life has just begun. That's how you have to look at this. It's just the beginning. You're still going to do amazing things."

Dara held her hands out in front of her, her wings flapping in agitation and creating a small wind tunnel around her. The hair lifted off her shoulder, swirling above her head. "I'm never going to help people with these hands."

"Empatyas are very powerful angels, Dara," Eleleth said. "You will learn how to use your powers. Empatyas can accomplish many tasks, including healing. Your true nature will reveal itself."

"What if our true nature isn't a good one?" Jerahmeel said. "What if we use our powers for evil?"

Eleleth swiveled his face toward Jerahmeel, but instead of fiery anger in his gaze, his eyes held infinite sadness in their depths. "Some people do choose to use their powers for ill. That is their choice. But there is no place in heaven for those who do."

But there's a place in hell for them. A short bark of a laugh escaped me, and I pressed my hands to my mouth, silencing the offensive sound. At least my thoughts had stayed put.

"What about you, Jerahmeel?" Eleleth asked. "Would you care to share your story?"

Jerahmeel sat up in his seat, rocking the floor with his toes. Gray and red colors swirled vibrantly around him. I was sure I wasn't the only one who could see them. What did they mean?

"My story? I grew up in the inner city in L.A. My dad ran off when I was six. My mom worked the streets. And I joined a gang when I was fifteen so I could provide for my two younger brothers. But I didn't have no guardian angel." He glared at Eleleth as he spoke. "I made my money thieving and breaking into houses. And one day the owner of the house pulled a gun on me and shot me. And there ain't no one protecting my younger brother now. I'm here instead of there. So what's happening to them? I'll tell you what. They're starving. My brother is probably initiating into the same life I was trying to save him from. Instead of taking one for the team, I let them all down. All because someone here didn't think I deserved a guardian angel."

Each word left his mouth punctuated by a flash of red, and a spattering of soundless colors escaped as well. Black and gray.

Silence met his story, and then Eleleth said, "Your mortal suffering must have felt very great. But that time is over now. Now you—"

"That's bull—." More soundless colors emitted from Jerahmeel's mouth, and I realized suddenly that he was speaking in forbidden expletives. Arcadia did not allow that type of language, and thus we saw their meanings without hearing the sound.

My curiosity piqued, and I studied Jerahmeel more closely. What sort of angel was he?

I waited for Eleth to reprimand him or chastise him, but he didn't. He stood up, that same calm look on his face, and said, "Thank you for sharing, Jerahmeel, Dara, and Israfil. That concludes our class for today. We will meet again next week. Everyone will have the chance to tell their story, but you will find it becomes easier as you adjust to life as an angel. I will see you soon."

Was it over already? It felt like only thirty minutes had passed.

Master Eleleth left the room first, and slowly my classmates stood up and followed, whispering to each other while they clutched their agendas to their chests. I paused to open my book and check my next destination.

"Ready?"

Maalik's voice next to my ear startled me, and I jumped, dropping my schedule.

"Sorry," he said, bending to grab it at the same time I did.

I withdrew my hand quickly before our fingers touched. Alarm spread through me at his lack of caution, at the lack of caution of all of the angels. I had felt the searing agony of spirit matter brushing spirit matter before, and I had no desire to experience it again.

"Ready for what?" I asked, and I couldn't help noticing that my voice had a tremor in it.

"Our study session."

He held my agenda out to me, and I took it. Opening it up, I saw that, indeed, the library was my next destination.

Wonderful. I couldn't wait to spend time with this arrogant angel who judged me when he didn't even know me.

CHAPTER EIGHT

I left the room ahead of Maalik, though he caught up to me outside and matched my pace. His wings folded up against his body, the feathers quivering in the breeze, and I stole glances at them.

"What's it like?" I asked, somewhat timidly. "Having wings?"

"It's one of heaven's greatest gifts to those who chose to follow the Firstborn."

The words were a simple statement of fact, and yet they held a stinging rebuke. I bit my lip and resolved not to say anything more unless required of me.

I got to the library door first, and I pulled it open, then ducked through it and hurried to a table in the center of the building, not waiting for Maalik. I was seated and staring blankly at the aisle in front of me when he settled down across from me.

He dropped a fat book onto the table. "You haven't forgiven me, then."

"For what?" I kept my eyes ahead.

He heaved a sigh. "I already apologized for losing my temper with you, but I'll say it again. Sometimes my mortal emotions return to me and conquer my mastery. I'm still learning."

I finally looked at him, and his calm demeanor irritated me. Such arrogance. "I made you so angry you lost control? It doesn't take much to rile you up, does it?" Why was I goading him again? I wanted to ruffle that emotionless exterior.

He didn't rise to the bait. Instead he steepled his fingers and met my eyes. "Did you have any questions about the things you heard in the TLG meeting?"

"The what?"

A trace of a smile crossed Maalik's lips. "The Transitional Life Guidance meeting. The one we just walked out of?"

"Oh." My face warmed, and I pulled on my dark hair. "Our therapy class? I didn't know it has a name."

"It does. Do you have any questions about it?"

The light brown of his eyes had somehow swallowed me up and distracted me. I blinked and then remembered his question. "Yes, actually. There were several things I didn't understand."

"Ask."

Where to begin? "Jerahmeel. Was he using forbidden language?"

"Yes. It's a normal reaction for many angels when they first arrive in Arcadia. They're frightened and scared, and that's one of the only ways they know how to lash out."

"So there's no . . . punishment for such behavior?"

Maalik shook his head. "Each of us is learning in our way. We give each other space for making mistakes."

"But . . ." This didn't fit my understanding of heaven at all. "Doesn't each error count as a black mark on his soul?"

"Errors are just another stepping stone in the school of life."

No, that didn't make sense. "There is a judgment," I said, wondering if Maalik didn't know. "The angels who have not lived out life according to heaven's rules and expectations are sentenced to hell and imprisonment. Jerahmeel used the forbidden words. He's broken the law and is subject to the judgments."

"It doesn't work that way," Maalik said. "First of all, I'm not his judge, and neither is Master Eleleth. Judgment is withheld until after our probational period is over."

"Mortal life was your probationary period. Now it's time to see who you really are."

"You are misinformed."

"No," I said. "You don't understand."

"Jez." He held up a hand. "There's no need for us to argue over this. One way simply is, and we will both in time see which way that is."

His logic infuriated me. I pressed my lips together, angry at his self-righteous attitude.

"Other questions," he said, redirecting the conversation. "Was there anything else from TLG that you weren't sure about?"

I tried to remember. "Jerahmeel's earth life. He said he was in a gang. Please explain this term."

"Gangs are a problem on earth. It's like having two sides in a battle, except the sides are small and the war is one they create, like who owns this street or who can shop at this store."

"I don't understand."

"You know battle." His eyes peered into mine.

"Yes." I glared back.

"Gangs are like armies, fighting each other. But they have no real cause."

"Then why do they fight?"

"To show who is more powerful. Who has the most team members."

"And this is a bad thing?"

Maalik nodded. "Gangs operate outside the law. They follow a leader, and if that leader tells them to steal, they steal. If he tells them to kill, they kill. He's in charge of them."

This I could understand. "They have no choice?"

"They do, but at great consequence. Really, they give up their choice when they join a gang."

I nodded. "And his mom? Working the streets?"

Maalik rubbed the skin between his eyes. "She sold her mortal body for other people to use for their own pleasure so she would receive material goods."

I needed no further explanation to understand the severity of this sin. I wondered if she'd given into a shadow and chosen that life, or if she'd been so desperate that it felt like the only option. Sometimes shadows weren't needed.

She, on the other hand, would have become an instrument for the shadows to use to ensnare the souls of men. "So she will go to Sheol when she dies."

Maalik shrugged. "I am not her judge."

"But you can still say," I needled, annoyed by his answer. "She is breaking some of heaven's most serious laws. The penalty is damnation."

"It's not so cut and dry as all that, Jez," Maalik said.

"Yes, it is," I said. "I have met many women in Sheol who are there for the same sin. That's the punishment."

"I'm sure you have. That doesn't mean every prostitute goes to hell."

"Why would they not? That's the law."

He sighed. "Some of these things you will just have to learn with time. I can't explain them to you."

"Then what good are you?"

He rubbed his nose, looking more weary than ever. "Any other questions?"

"No." I waved him off. "I doubt you could answer them. I'll figure things out on my own."

"Do you have to be so difficult?" he growled. He opened the thick book in front of him. "Before we get started on your reading lesson, I wanted to tell you I did some research."

I couldn't care less what he did. "Good for you."

He glowered, a hint of fire in his golden eyes. "I found out why you weren't allowed to read."

I stared at him, wondering what would come out of his mouth next. I knew he was going to tell me what he found out, whether I wanted him to or not.

He turned to a page near the middle. "It says here that Renegades and the Fallen are not allowed to read so that mortals can have safety in recording their private thoughts, dreams, and fears without concern of being overheard. Prayers that are written or uttered in the head are confidential, and demons cannot take that information and use it against a mortal."

I narrowed my eyes. "Says who?"

He closed the thick book in front of him. "Says Master Remiel, the author of 'Living among the Fallen: A Discourse on Demons.'"

"Never heard of him," I scoffed.

"You will." A smirk crossed his face, a single crack in his calm facade. "He teaches here at the academy."

"Great." I kept my face blank, trying to appear entirely uninterested. But my heart raced with trepidation. What kind of stories had been written about us? "That doesn't mean he knows what he's talking about. That's not why we can't read."

"Why, then?" he said, lifting his chin.

"It's a punishment from *him*. One more thing to make us inferior and keep us from improving our station in Sheol."

"Improving your station?" Maalik repeated. "You can't improve your station. No demon can suddenly elevate who they are. They can't become Light when they've been full of Darkness, or change their nature and become—"

He drew up short, cutting his words off so abruptly it was as if he sucked them back into his mouth. He looked at me, and I met his gaze without flinching.

"Well. I suppose the truth will come out." He looked away, not referencing his other words. He pulled out the notepad he'd had last time. "Let's get started here."

I watched him as he bent over the paper, my heart in my throat. I'd seen writing and symbols before, but the lines always squiggled out of my view, blurring and morphing so I couldn't focus on them. What would Maalik do when I wasn't able to learn the writing? Why was Barachiel even putting me through this?

Using a pen, Maalik drew two lines that connected at the top, as if to make a triangle. But instead of connecting them at the bottom, he placed the third line in the middle of the two connected lines.

"Can you see this?" He lifted his eyes to mine.

"I . . . can." I furrowed my brow, a bit surprised that the lines stayed in place. A surge of hope flared in my chest. "How? I've never been able to discern the symbols before."

Maalik tilted his head. "Because you are . . ." He hesitated. "You were . . ."

A demon. He didn't want to say it, and suddenly, I didn't want him to, either.

"I still am," I said shortly. "I can't suddenly change my nature and become Light."

I threw his words back at him and felt a satisfying pleasure when his cheeks turned pink.

He swallowed and said, "You've been given enough grace to live in Arcadia. Why, I don't know. But that grace allows you to perceive the writing and symbols."

Grace, he said. Not Light. Because Light came from within the soul, and we both knew my soul was black.

"It's fine," I said shortly. "Let's just do this. What is it?"

"It's an A." Maalik's tone was hesitant, as if he still lingered on the thoughts of what I was or had been. "You hear it in words like 'apple' and 'acronym.'"

Apple. I was familiar with that one, at least. I wasn't there when Adam fell, but many of the Fallen shared the theory that the forbidden fruit was an apple. "How do you spell 'apple'?"

Maalik made a few more symbols after the A. "This is a 'p.' It makes the 'puh-puh' sound."

My eyes traced the lines, absorbing the new information. "There are two of them." I mouthed the word "apple," trying to hear an extra "puh" sound.

"Yeah, it's kind of redundant. You only hear one of them. I'm teaching you English, right, because that's what I know.

Barachiel said in the end it won't matter; as long as you can read one language, you'll be able to interpret the others. But you have to know how to read one first."

"Oh." I kept my eyes on the symbols. "And then?"

"That's an 'L', followed by an 'E.' It can be tricky because the sounds are reversed, but—"

"Write another one." The letters had engraved themselves in my mind with an astonishing clarity, and I hungered for more.

"Okay." Maalik wrote on the pad, then turned it around for me. "This is the letter 'B'. You hear it in 'baby' and 'body.'"

Baby and body. Also important words. "Write them."

Maalik obliged, making the symbol for B, followed by an A, then another B before adding an upside down triangle-shape with a tail.

"Buh-ah-buh-" I tried.

Maalik shook his head. "Here the 'A' makes a different sound. It's what we call a long 'A', like in 'ate.'"

I tried again. "Buh-ay-buh—" I knew the word and the last sound, which meant the fourth symbol sounded like —"Ee."

"Good job." Maalik beamed at me, looking both impressed and proud. "You're a quick learn."

"It is easy." And my soul hungered for it. I soaked up the knowledge like a sponge, feeling as blank as the notepad before Maalik wrote on it. "Teach me more."

"It's good you want to learn," he said, and his smile seemed genuine. "Knowledge is the only thing we take with us when we die. So the rest of us have an advantage on you.

We're bringing all of our earth knowledge with us. It's a lot to learn, but we can catch you up to speed."

The next half hour flew by as Maalik taught me the entire English alphabet with coordinating words.

A bell chimed, indicating the end of our study session. Maalik put the notepad into a bag and added the thick book to it.

"You did well today, Jez. Your eyes have been opened." He nodded his approval. "Maybe we will make an angel of you yet."

His condescension grated on my nerves. I stood also, grabbing my book tightly. "Maybe I don't want to be an angel."

Something glittered in his eyes, something like satisfaction. "Then why are you here?"

He had me there. I turned away, holding my agenda to my chest, and stomped out of the library ahead of him.

By the time I stepped into the cafeteria, the tables were buzzing with conversation and laughter. I picked my way through the students and almost avoided Table D. But as I was about to bypass it, I realized that to earn my classmates' trust, I'd need to associate with them as often as possible. Appear like them.

"Jez." Iblis swiveled to face me as soon as I sat, her face bright. "The first Skyball game is tomorrow night. Want to go together?"

"What in the sky is Skyball?" I'd heard the term during orientation, but it meant nothing to me.

"Oh, you missed lunch today! The older students were telling us all about it. It's a combination of basketball and football, but of course there's flying and stuff to make it more interesting!"

I nodded along as if I understood her, but I didn't. I gathered that it was a sporting event, but I didn't know what kind. "I'm surprised they have that here," I said. "Sporting events are when humans tend to be the most irrational." They were prone to anger and impulsive actions when their blood ran hot at such activities.

"Right, well." Iblis shrugged. "Apparently that's why only third and fourth years can be on the team. First and second years haven't learned to control their emotions yet." She gave an eye roll.

"I see."

"So you want to go with me?"

I may as well. Besides, I was intrigued. How did angels play sports? Had they really mastered the part of themselves likely to cheat or become angry?

Iblis put away her tray and walked along with Dara, the two of them chatting nonstop. She didn't seem to remember me, and I lagged behind, unsure if I should catch up or sit by myself.

"Jez. Long time no see."

I turned at the sound of Kerubiel's deep voice. My eyes took in his dark clothing, this time paired with one of the academy's jackets, the Emet dorm symbol emblazoned in gold across the lapel. "You're wearing the uniform," I said.

"Surprised?" He arched an eyebrow. "I guess eventually we all cave to the desire to fit in." He shoved his hands in his pants pockets. "Going to the game?"

I was still mulling over his words. Was that what I was doing? Trying to fit in? "Yes. It appears everyone is heading to the game."

"You don't sound too thrilled."

"I don't understand sports," I admitted. "And I don't know anything about the game . . . or the games it's based on."

"Because your earth life was so sheltered."

"Sports were not a part of my previous existence."

"Well, I used to play basketball once upon a time. I can tell you all about it."

The thought of sitting next to Kerubiel during the game appealed to me. His shadow enveloped me, draping itself over his surroundings as he walked. For once I didn't feel I had to pretend or change. If there was Darkness in me, it found acceptance in Kerubiel.

Iblis turned around, catching my eye. "Jez! Come on!"

I faced Kerubiel. "Maybe next time. I told Iblis I'd sit with her."

His eyes appraised me, the blue color bright enough to swallow me. "Next time, then." His gaze slid from my eyes to my mouth, and a slow grin spread over his face. "I'll hold you to it."

He strode away, his wings folded against his back, and I stared after him, a little breathless. Something tingled in my chest, a longing that I couldn't begin to define.

CHAPTER NINE

"Jez!" Iblis beckoned wildly. "Don't make me come get you!"

No touching. I wrapped my arms around myself as a reminder and climbed the wooden stairs to sit beside her.

The stairs led us up and up, past the supports keeping the platform of rising steps high in the air. Three other platforms also dotted the field. Angels who had mastered flight flew to their seats while the rest of us climbed the stairs in the back. To our left sat the library, with its tall towers disappearing into the cloudy atmosphere.

"There." Iblis pointed, her arm crossing in front of my face. "Can you see that hoop perched on the exterior wall of the library?"

I zoomed my gaze onto the building and saw a hoop extending outward from the tower. "Yes."

"That's where the players put the ball."

"Ah." My eyes lowered from the hoop to the ground beneath it, and the familiar bitterness crept into my chest. This game could not be played by those without wings.

Somewhere a whistle blew, and two rows of angels dressed in tight blue or green uniforms walked onto the grass in front of us. Each row held three people, and they came to a stop facing each other.

"Those are the players?" I guessed.

"Yes."

Master Sabriel, the woman who taught our Creations class, stepped onto the field next. She carried a large orange ball in her arms.

"She must be the referee," Iblis breathed, her tone excited.

I suppressed a smile. It was already starting. How would my classmates resist the impulsive emotional rush of the game?

A whistle blew again. Master Sabriel held the ball up, and then she threw it at the ground. The moment the ball hit, it bounded upward, flinging itself into the atmosphere.

Instantly, the two rows of players took flight. I found myself rising to my feet, my eyes wide as I watched the outcome. Who would get the ball?

Two players from each team stayed back while the other three players zipped into the sky. I could see them perfectly from where I was, as my vision was much clearer than that of mortals. The ball rocketed skyward, and I caught my breath as the blue-clad angel flapped his wings in the wind and bolted after it.

"They can fly so fast!" I whispered.

His arms wrapped around the ball, and he held on as if it fought him.

"Yes." Iblis had also stood. "That's another reason why only third and fourth years can try out for the team. You have to have control of your wings first."

The angel barreled toward the hoop, and I watched intently, waiting for him to throw it in.

But before he could, a flash of green shot down from the sky and wrapped itself around him. I gasped and leaned forward as if it would give me a better view. Around me, the students screamed and cheered, emotion thick in the air. Another flash of blue and green joined the huddle, and the group of angels with the ball seemed to come to a halt.

"What just happened?" I cried.

"They tackled him!" Iblis shouted.

"That's allowed?" I could make out the shapes now of four distinct angels, except now they were falling, falling toward the ground with their arms around each other, all grappling for the ball.

"It's a game!" Iblis said. "They're not going to hurt each other!"

That wasn't what I'd meant at all.

The first angel broke free, but only for a moment. A moment was all he needed, however. He reared his arm back, the one holding the ball, and threw it.

Away from the hoop.

I furrowed my brow in confusion until I saw his teammate, the one who had been waiting near the ground, soaring upward. She caught the ball in her arms. At the same time, the huddle seemed to realize the ball was gone and broke apart.

The angel with the ball didn't hesitate. She bolted forward. The angels flew at her, but before they could converge, she tossed the ball to another angel, one I hadn't even noticed.

Apparently neither had the others, because he had a clear shot to the hoop. And he tossed that ball, his muscles bulging as he put his force into it. The ball flew through the hoop and then lost all momentum. It sank slowly back to the ground while the angels followed, patting each other on the back.

My classmates cheered. And so did I.

Iblis explained more of the game to me as we walked back to our dorm hours later.

"They told us all about it at breakfast. I don't quite get it, but there are three players on each team, and only one of them can score. They all learned different roles and have to stick to that. And they're allowed to use their gifts."

"How did they learn to do all that?" I couldn't stop marveling at their speed or their coordination.

"Grigori—he's a second year—said most of them played sports on earth. It was their talent. Skyball is an opportunity for them to continue their talent here at the academy."

"That's kind of cool," I admitted. "What happened after they scored?"

"The ball is degravitized when the game starts, and the angels have to keep it from zipping off into space. If it does, the team who had the ball last automatically wins. But as soon as they score, the ball falls back to the ground until the next play begins."

"And the scoring?" I knew the green team had won, but I wasn't sure how. They hadn't put the ball through the hoop as many times as the blue team.

"That I'm not entirely sure on. But I think the farther away the player is from the ball, the more points they get for scoring."

"I never knew it could be so much . . ." My voice trailed off because I wasn't even sure what to say. The emotional rush I had gotten from watching angels I didn't even know try to slam the large orange bar into a certain location was rather bewildering.

"Fun?" Iblis grinned at me. "Have you ever had fun before, Jez?"

"No." I said it emphatically and without hesitation, and the smile wiped from her face. And then pity replaced it.

"Oh, Jez. I'm so sorry. Do you want to talk about it? Do you wanna share what your home life was like on earth?"

"No," I said again, and I regretted answering her truthfully earlier. Now she would wonder. Now she had questions that a moment ago she hadn't had, all because I didn't think before I responded.

"Well, welcome to your new life!" She clasped her hands together, and I knew she really wanted to clasp her hand with mine. "You're about to experience all kinds of fun."

I paused a moment, and then I asked, "What about you? What was your earth life?"

I wasn't just asking to take her attention off me. I was genuinely curious.

She lifted a shoulder. "You already heard about my death, my brothers, my family . . ."

"What about the boy who was in the car with you? The one you kept asking about?"

"Jason." Her face took on a happy glow. "My boyfriend." And then the excitement went out of her. "Do you think he still is? How long will he mourn for me before he moves on?"

"That depends on the person," I said. "Some people linger in mourning for too long, wallowing in despair. Others seem to brush it off and keep living without too much thought."

She tapped her fingers against her palm and stared unseeing into the horizon. "It's not that I wish he was dead," she said quietly, "but I wish he was here. I miss him."

"Why?"

She turned to me and blinked, looking surprised by the question. "Don't you miss anyone?"

"No." Again, I winced, kicking myself mentally for the honest answer. I missed the Darkness. I missed inhaling the lecherous thoughts of a weak human soul, of tasting the delicious decision to commit a sin.

Something twinged in my chest, something uncomfortable. I frowned. Why would thinking of Darkness make me uncomfortable?

"Well, I miss Jason," Iblis said, turning away and continuing the walk back to campus. "I want to see him. Even if he's forgotten me. But I hope he hasn't."

"What happened in the car accident?"

She shook her head, not looking at me. "I'm not sure. It was February. The roads were slick, and I remember Jason loosing control of the car. I don't remember anything else. When I opened my eyes, I was in Gehenna. Except I didn't know that then, of course." Now she turned my direction.

"What about you?"

I should have seen that coming. I'd opened myself up for a question-and-answer session. I hadn't died. I had nothing like that to share. "Same. I was in Gehenna, and Eldermaster Barachiel came for me."

"The Eldermaster came for you?" She lifted both eyebrows.

"Did he not for you?"

She shook her head. "The woman—I guess she was an angel in disguise, but I didn't know—told me it was time to go. She told me to walk out the front door and I'd be where I needed to be. So I did—and I was here. An angel greeted me and showed me to the assembly hall."

"She must have made a portal with the door."

"I guess so. I don't really know what that is."

Heaven's throne, I'd done it again. I pressed my lips together and resolved to be silent.

The next morning, my schedule directed me to a building on the outskirts of campus. I made my way over there and spotted several other students heading that direction. Not all of them were from my dormitory, either. I noticed the color scheme of the sweaters and ties changed with each dorm.

Sweaters and ties. How quickly I was learning their terminology and culture.

"Well, well, if it isn't the elusive Jez."

I looked up to spot Kerubiel a few paces in front of me. He stood still, other than his wings, which opened and closed in a slow motion.

"You're here," I said, and something pleasing spiked in my chest.

"Looks like our dorms have this class together." His eyes scanned me from head to toe before landing on my face again. "Still not in uniform?"

"You either," I replied. He wore the same baggy slacks and the tight black T-shirt, which only called more attention to the magnificent wings spreading out behind his shoulder blades. This time he'd left behind the academy jacket.

"Yeah, not happening. This isn't my place. I might wear the jacket sometimes. It's kind of cool." He fell into step behind me.

His words resonated with me, but I couldn't let on that I didn't belong here. "So what do you intend to do?" I asked.

He glanced around and then leaned in close to me. "I'll learn what I need to, stick to this charade as long as I can. Then I'm out of here."

A shiver ran through me at his words. No angel was required to stay at GAA, but there were consequences for leaving. "Where will you go?"

He didn't answer. Which either meant he didn't know, or he didn't want me to know.

He was not forthcoming about his plans, so I let the topic drop. For now.

"What class do we have in here?" I asked as we stepped through the doors into an open arena.

"Weapons." A glint entered Kerubiel's eye. "This is a very important class."

"Welcome, angels." A woman with flaming red hair stood in front of us, her legs spread apart in a defensive stance, a long bo in her arms. "I am Master Ingram. Please put your bags down on the floor and gather around me, and I will explain the purpose of this class."

I gathered in with the others, my gaze going around the room and studying the various weapons on display. Daggers lined an entire wall, and above them pointed stars and sabers dangled in threatening manners.

A shudder ran through me. I hadn't been created at the time of the First War in heaven, but I knew about it. I knew how the heavenly host descended upon hell with their cursed daggers and blades of damnation, destroying the Fallen with single blows and changing the nature of the Forsaken into weak and lustful demons. It had been an unprovoked massacre, a merciless show on heaven's part of what happened to any who disagreed. The very thought stung my eyes, and my hatred for these angels stirred within me. I wrapped my arms around myself and glared at the master angel in front of us.

"We will start with the daggers. This is a weapon of necessity for angels. Every one of you will be trained to handle a dagger, though some of you will have a better affinity for it than others."

"Why?" a girl spoke up. "I don't understand. We're angels. Isn't this life all about peace on earth and goodwill in heaven? Why would we need weapons?"

Master Ingram gave a patient smile. "That is the goal, but we have still not attained it. The war between heaven and hell wages on. We fight for the souls of humanity, and we fight for our future, and we fight for the souls of the redeemed. That said, any time you leave on a mission, you will take a dagger with you. It's not necessary to carry one around on campus, but you want one whenever you leave the safety of heaven or Arcadia."

I tried to reign in my breathing, but my thoughts were growing dark. I took a few steps backward, breathing heavily, trembling from head to toe.

"Who do we use these weapons against?" a boy asked. "Humans?"

Master Ingram's eyes were somber. "We will discuss the use of the weapons and the consequences in greater detail. You will be given your own dagger especially for your use, and eventually you will carry it always. But that will not happen until you have passed this course and understand not only when and how to use it, but what will happen when you do. For now, everyone step over to this wall."

I moved even farther back as our two groups crowded around the wall of weapons.

"Today we will practice bo work, because the bos are a fantastic weapon for incapacitating a mortal threat. They don't work so well against Temptare, but we'll get to that. Before you select a bo, however, I would like you to get a feel for the daggers. Please pick a dagger."

I didn't move except to clutch my arms tighter. Such weapons of hatred and destruction. I felt it vibrating in my soul. How could these angels not feel it?

"What do angels need weapons for," I said, my voice hard and cold, "when the Five Point exists?"

My question caused all heads to turn my direction, brows furrowed, eyes wide and quizzical.

"A Five Point?" a boy I recognized as Daniel said.

"Why don't you explain the Five Point?" I breathed, glowering at the master angel.

"The Five Point is something we will discuss later, when we learn hand-to-hand combat," the angel said, not taking her gaze from mine. "Students, go ahead and touch the daggers, but do not remove any."

Still glancing over at me, the angels studied the daggers, forgetting me as they touched the sharp blades and admired the shimmering, shiny handles.

I needed to touch them also. It was imperative I act normal and proceed with the plan. But dread snaked up through my feet, paralyzing my legs.

Ingram shifted sideways and maneuvered her way around the students, her eyes glued to me. I took a few more steps back when I realized she was coming my way.

"You're Jez," she said when she reached me. Her eyes remained hard, and her mouth didn't pull up in greeting the way the other master angels' did.

It wasn't a question, but I nodded anyway. She frightened me. All she had to do was pull out that dagger and stab me in the forehead, and I'd become a substance-less wraith. It couldn't kill me, but it would take time to gather my essence together from the dust and reform myself, and each moment of that separation would be an eternity of agony.

"You won't be receiving a dagger," she said.

I reared my head back, surprised. "Why? I thought I was to have the same experience as the other students. I thought I was to be treated the same."

She pursed her lips together, her eyes tightening. "Eldermaster Barachiel would like you to transition here a little longer before we ask you to take up arms."

I understood what she didn't say. He didn't trust me. He wanted to see where my loyalties lay before handing me over a weapon that could injure his precious students. A dagger could not kill a being of Light, but it could put one out of commission for awhile.

Well, I couldn't say I blamed him. But I'd been lied to. "So I'm not to be treated just like them, then," I said bitterly. "I'm already being set apart as different."

"I am sorry it feels that way to you," Master Ingram said, the perfect manipulative, diplomatic response. "I will tell the students we are pursuing a specialized program with you for now."

I laughed, seeing how she distorted the truth to tell the other students a story while not making it a full-out lie. "Just tell them I chose not to attend the class. Then you won't be lying." I picked up my book bag where I'd set it on the floor and turned around, stalking out of the room.

CHAPTER TEN

"*Jezbathasat.*"

The name whispered across my consciousness, rousing me from my dreamless sleep. I blinked and stared up at the darkened ceiling of my dorm room, a shiver running through me.

"*Jezbathasat.*"

Hasatan was calling me. And I could not resist his call.

The academy had been in session for six weeks. I had been expecting this call for weeks now. He would want to know what I'd learned.

I climbed from the bed and tiptoed to the door, careful not to wake Iblis, where she slept soundly on her bed. What did she dream of? Her home on earth? Anticipation for her life in heaven? Her boyfriend Jason?

My dreams were empty, as my existence thus far had been.

"*Jezbathasat, come to me.*"

The call echoed in my mind and through my soul, heard not by my spiritual ears but by my inner soul. The chains around my arms burned and tightened, demanding, and I shrugged out of the leather jacket, freeing myself from its confines for the first time in days. I breathed a soft sigh of relief, enjoying the reprieve the freedom brought.

The chains glowed on my flesh, hot against my skin. I opened the door and slipped out, letting the fiery chains guide me from the dorm. Their intensity increased as I crossed the courtyard, and I gasped against the searing pain.

"I'm coming," I said, pleading in my voice. I wrapped my hands around my forearms. "Stop. I'm coming."

The pain lessened but did not stop. I glanced back at the dormitory as I crossed the quad. Should anyone glance outside, they would see me sneaking away from the academy. But I doubted any of Barachiel's perfect little angels would be awake at this hour.

The fountain in the middle of the quad sprang to life, the water turning a bright blue. A circular well opened in the fountain, growing in circumference, and I recognize the portal. Fire flickered in the blackness in its depths. The rift would carry me back to Sheol, back to Hasatan. He could not ascend, but I could descend.

Yet I hesitated. Would I be able to return? Barachiel had shielded my soul on the journey to Arcadia, had guarded me until we reached the academy and I could face the Light. What if the journey back held similar dangers for me?

"Descend."

He would not wait any longer. My feet moved forward without my telling them to, and I stepped through the rift.

I felt it when I stepped away from the academy's influence. The shadows of Arcadia suddenly felt more oppressive, deeper and bigger. I took a deep breath, feeling as though I were closer to home. At the same time, a sense of loss drifted over me.

I only had a moment to reflect on it before a sensation of falling ripped at my hair and my clothes, and I screamed. My arms flailed out to my sides. I longed for wings to lift me and carry me back—

Back? I didn't want to go back. This was home. This was where I belonged.

What felt like an eternity was only a moment, or was the moment really an eternity? In a flash it ended, and I stumbled as my feet hit hard ground. I caught my breath and hunched over, breathing hard, shaking from the experience.

It wasn't my first time to travel by portal. But I hated the way it made me feel after.

I could see nothing in front of me but blackness. I blinked, but my eyes were not adjusting. "Hello?" I hesitated to put a hand out, not sure what I would find.

"The daughter returns."

I turned to my left as a ball of fire appeared. I bowed my head. "I am here."

The fire stopped, and even with my eyes averted, I could make out the dark humanoid shadow within the flames. But I couldn't see him, and I'd never looked directly. It was easier to focus on the Fallen behind him, dressed as mortals but with ethereal, shadowy wings behind them. I could tell from the solidness of their forms that they'd recently fed. They had mortal ties, which meant they were some of the strongest Fallen in Sheol. I wondered briefly why he'd brought them.

"Report, child," he said. "What have you learned?"

"I can see things differently," I said softly. "I am learning to read."

"Good. Your eyes have been opened. That will be a valuable skill. What else?"

"I know how they keep demons out."

I felt his smile even though I could not see his face. "Excellent. How is it done?"

"They have a generator used to dispel Light over the campus and keep it shielded. No demon can cross it, even if they knew the location of the campus."

Hasatan nodded. "Find the location of this generator. I'm certain an infusion of Darkness would destroy it."

I knew just where he intended to find that Darkness, also. I felt the power coursing through my veins, replenishing here in Sheol. My appetites were returning, my longing to inhale the misery and sin of mankind.

"You are hungry," he said. "Your form is fading."

How quickly whatever Light they'd put in my drained away. "But there is not time for me to go to earth and feed."

"I keep souls here for that purpose. Tell me what else you've found, and I'll find you nourishment."

I craved what he offered. "There's a weapons room."

"Did you find the daggers?"

I nodded. "Yes. The room is full of daggers and swords used to fight against us."

"Did they give you one?"

Something tightened in my chest. "No."

"Why not?"

The chains on my arms lit up as if on fire, and I screamed, shaking my arms in a futile attempt to rid myself of the pain. Just as quickly as it had begun, it stopped.

"Do not wait for me to ask, Jezbathasat. Give the complete answer the first time. Did they give you one?"

Panting, I shook my head. "No. I have not earned their trust."

"But you will."

I nodded. "I will."

"Very good. I will summon you again. You must tell me the moment you have their trust. Recruit them, by avarice or cunning. Some will look evil in the face and gladly embrace it. Some will turn their face away from the blatant evil but will allow a blind eye to pass over the smaller infractions. Find their weaknesses and exploit them."

Why? I wanted to ask. But I didn't dare. It was never up to me to ask the questions.

Not even the one I really wanted to know.

"Have you learned anything else?"

"No. My classes haven't started yet. I'm being taught to read first." I shouldn't do it, I shouldn't ask, because the answer was always the same, but the words were slipping past my lips before I could stop myself. "Has my mother returned?"

"She is your biggest weakness, isn't she?" He sounded amused, his tone taking on an almost fatherly quality. "She has not returned."

I nodded, masking my disappointment.

I could barely remember my mother. But sometimes I felt an aching and the distant shadow of a memory of comfort and goodness and something else, something less tangible but more genuine. I'd started asking Hasatan about her after my first feeding because my longing for her grew strongest after I'd gorged myself on human iniquity. He told me she'd vanished and to forget her.

But I could not let go of the feeling that someday she would return.

He turned slightly, and two Fallen appeared, dragging a howling soul between them. The face was distorted by agony so I could not tell if it had been male or female.

My hunger returned in full force, gaping wide, scratching at the chance to add to this soul's misery.

But something in me revolted. Some new part of me, some unusual part, and I felt a sudden, keen sense of mourning.

"Feed," Hasatan said, and I had no choice.

I stepped forward and dug into the soul, prying open the secret sins, sucking up the regret and weaknesses. The Darkness in me sighed in contentment, and I moved back, strangely sickened by my actions.

"Go now," Hasatan said, and it was not a suggestion. "Find angels you can turn to my side."

My feet were already turning, leaving the safety of Sheol and heading back to a place where I didn't belong.

"Is there no other way?" I asked as my body pivoted.

"There is no other way. I know Barachiel stressed upon you how you have free choice now and can make your own decisions." His words were laced with derision, and I felt it also, the foolishness of handing free choice to weak, controllable beings such as myself. "Be strong, my daughter. Remember who you are."

The chains around my arms tightened, the pain marking my soul. "I will not forget."

It was still night when I returned to Arcadia. The moon shown brilliantly overhead, so close I thought if I jumped high enough I could touch it. I rubbed my arms, feeling naked and vulnerable without the jacket to hide my chains. I felt like a ticking time bomb. I had started to make friends and feel connected. But the moment they found out who I was, they would cast me out. Send me back to Sheol.

Back to my home. I frowned. That was where I wanted to be. Wasn't it? I'd felt so sure of that a moment ago when I was near my father and felt the weight of his Fallen. But now, standing in the soft grass of Yishuv, the gates of the academy open before me, the light of the moon cascading over my hair and shoulders, I no longer felt the desire to return.

I didn't like the doubt that wormed its way into my heart. Sheol was what I wanted.

I re-entered my dorm quietly. Iblis still slept. I reached for my leather jacket, but my academy uniform caught my eye. Normally it hung in the wardrobe, but here it was on my bed. I touched the long sleeves of the jacket with the academy symbol on its lapel. I slipped it on, tracing my fingers over the emblem of the universe with the spirals circling it. A tingling erupted in my finger tips, a pleasant warmth, as if the power of the universe were actually embedded in the thread.

I made note of the phenomenon and then whipped around as Iblis stirred in her bed.

"Jez?" she murmured, blinking as she looked up at me. "Why are you up?"

I moved over to the window and looked outside, where the rising sun had started over the edge of the meadow and appeared behind the tree line. Reds and oranges and pinks colored the clouds, and I let out a soft breath. "I never noticed how beautiful it is." The same colors seemed to erupt in my chest, and I looked down, expecting to see shades of red and orange flowing from my skin.

Iblis rose and stood beside me. "It's nice not to wake up with morning breath," she said.

I couldn't relate to the comment, so I kept quiet. Which was fine, because she kept going.

"Where did you come from, Jez? You say the strangest things sometimes. It's like you didn't have the same experiences as the rest of us." She gave me a searching look, her eyes flicking over my face. "You can talk about it, you know."

"No, I can't." I wrapped my arms around my waist, feeling the weight of the chains on my arms. The weight of my mission. "My life was not like yours."

Her lower lip pushed outward, and for a moment I thought I'd wounded her with my words. But then she said, "I'm so sorry. I wish everyone got to experience a happy life like I did."

My gaze moved to her wings, the majestic black appendages folded tight against her back. She was learning control.

I would never have those. She didn't know how lucky she was.

"Let's go to breakfast," Iblis said, stepping into the dressing room. Her voice carried into our sleeping room. "And this time you're going to eat."

I smiled at that. Only a few weeks into my academic training, and I had to admit that food was a welcome pleasure. I even had a preference for yogurt and granola.

The two of us set off toward the cafeteria, meeting up with others from our year. Iblis greeted them cheerfully, and they responded in kind. A few even greeted me, though they eyed me like I was a curiosity. Dara stepped in beside Iblis, and the two of them chatted about the previous day.

"Eremiel!" Dara said, calling out to an angel in front of us.

The redheaded angel slowed, then turned around, a smile lighting his features. "Dara," he said, just as the raven-haired girl flung herself into his arms.

I stopped mid-motion. He didn't hesitate to wrap his arms around her, tucking her in close to his body in a way that looked both invasive and welcoming. My eyes grew wide, and I waited for the wrath of heaven to fall upon them, for them to begin screaming as the slow burn of flesh on flesh melted away their bodies, or to turn them into ash and damn them to Sheol as Fallen.

Instead, he put her hand in his, and they continued strolling toward the cafeteria.

As if it were nothing.

As if they hadn't just broken the cardinal law of heaven.

My legs trembled, and I thought I might collapse.

"Jez?" Iblis reached a hand out toward me, but I backed away, and she withdrew. "Are you all right?"

Thoughts tripped around my brain with lightning speed, questions, confusion. "Dara and Eremiel . . ."

Iblis smiled. "Yes. I think they like each other. It's kind of nice. I was worried after we died—"

"They were touching." Touching!

"I know." Iblis lowered her voice. "Do you think he's kissed her yet? I don't even know how that works here!"

"It doesn't!" I blurted out. My whole body shook as one of the building blocks of my celestial understanding trembled. "Spiritual beings aren't allowed—" I cut myself off before I said something foolish.

I needed to talk to someone who would understand. Maalik. He was the only one who knew my secret.

I whipped away from her and raced into the cafeteria, searching out the brown-haired, olive-skinned angel. I found him at the head of Table D, laughing as he used his fork to stab pieces of fruit off another student's tray.

"Maalik," I said, jerking to a halt in front of him, my book bag banging against my thigh. My chest heaved, and I struggled to pull oxygen into my lungs, my spiritual body imitating the same reaction of a mortal one. But this was a first for me. I'd never run somewhere in a panic before. "I need to talk to you."

His light brown eyes roved over my face, and he stood, the carefree expression of moments ago morphing into something more concerned. "Of course. What is it?"

"Somewhere in private." I clutched my bag to my chest to keep it still and strode through the cafeteria, leading us out the back door, to the gardens that framed the cafeteria.

The sun was full in the sky now, shining down with a gentle warmth, and the fragrant scent of flowers filled the air.

Maalik crossed the patio and stood behind me. "Jez? What is it? Has something happened?"

"Yes. No. I don't know." I turned around, letting my gaze travel from his face to his wings and landing on his hands. My own fingers twitched, wanting to test what I'd just seen. Maybe in my wildest dreams I'd imagined stroking my fingers over his wings, but I'd always known the reality was I couldn't. I took a deep breath and lifted my eyes to his face again.

"I just saw two angels. They were — *touching*."

CHAPTER ELEVEN

I cringed as I said the word, feeling as if I were about to condemn them, as if I brought the guilt of the act upon myself. I watched him, waiting for his response.

But Maalik only blinked, his brow furrowing slightly, and said, "I don't understand."

I clutched my own fingers to keep them still. "She ran up to him, and he put his arms around her. Their bodies were adjacent, there was no space between them. His flesh — his flesh was on hers!"

A small smile crossed Maalik's lips, though he still looked mildly bewildered. "I know what touching means. I'm not sure about your reaction."

"It's forbidden," I whispered. "The laws of heaven condemn physical contact."

Maalik studied me a moment, and then he moved over to a stone bench beneath a tree with long, sweeping branches. He sat and patted the spot beside him. "Come and sit."

I shook my head. Fear vibrated through my core. Would he try and touch me next? Was this a trick? An illusion created by heaven to have reason to condemn me as a demon?

Maalik sighed. "Fine. Jez, I don't know what you've heard, or what you've been taught, but it's wrong. Heaven does not condemn physical contact."

"Yes, it does," I said immediately. "The act of touching, or of taking pleasure from another being, is sinful, salacious, and evil. To reinforce this rule, all celestial beings are punished by burning, condemned to fire and brimstone, perhaps even turned to ash, for touching another."

Maalik's eyes did not break contact with mine. "You recited that as if you have it memorized."

"Word for word," I whispered.

His eyes narrowed, and a color erupted from his form, a deep purple, almost blue. "Jez, whoever taught you that . . . was mistaken."

My lip twisted at his euphemism. "You mean they lied to me. Intentionally deceived me. No." I shook my head. "There is no need for lies or deception in Sheol. The path is laid before us. We don't have to weigh pros and cons to know the way to go. There is only one way. Heaven uses lies to manipulate, not Sheol."

"Touch is one of the Father's greatest gifts. It's why we all were so eager for a physical body. There is pleasure in it, yes, but there is also comfort, and strength, and unity. It's a blessing." He held his hand out to me. "Come here. I'll show you."

"No!" I bolted backward, terrified he'd jump up and force me. "No!"

"It's okay." He lowered his hand. "You don't have to." His eyes crinkled slightly. "It's not flesh on flesh, you know.

We don't have bodies. We are spiritual beings. But even our spirits can touch."

"No, they can't!" I blinked back tears of frustration, desperate to right this confusion.

"But you saw it. How can you deny what you saw?"

"Because I've tried it!" I clenched my fists tightly, unable to stop the shaking that rattled up my arms. The memory was seared into my mind, and it flashed before now as clear as if it happened that morning. "My mother—she knew it was forbidden to touch me, but one time she did it anyway." It was one of the only memories I had of her. I squeezed my eyes shut, feeling again the fire that lashed across my body where her spirit caressed mine. My screams had merged with those of the damned, and she'd made it worse by trying to comfort me. My eyes snapped open, and for a moment all I saw in front of me were the flames of hell. "I never saw her again."

And that was when the chains came. Whipping out of the ground, wrapping around my arms and torso, tightening until I couldn't breath. They melted into my skin, tying me to Sheol. The constant reminder of where I came from and who I was.

"Your story does not make sense to me," Maalik said, but he didn't say it in a challenging way. "Was your mother a Fallen?"

I shook my head. "I don't know. That is one of my only memories of her."

"How is it possible? What are you?"

I didn't know the answer to that, though I wished I did. So I ignored his question. "We cannot touch. The spiritual beings cannot touch."

"Maybe not in Sheol," he said, "but here, we can touch each other."

"No." I shook my head. "No." But the doubt crept in. I'd seen it happen.

It couldn't be. That beings in heaven would be allowed to touch, but those of us in Sheol deprived of that simple allowance—no, not even heaven could be so cruel.

Maalik stood, his aura color changing to a yellowish green. "Someday we will have to learn to trust each other." His wings opened and closed before withdrawing near his body. He strode across the patio to the cafeteria door in two steps, then let himself in.

Trust each other. Not in my lifetime. I could not trust anything that came from heaven.

And he certainly could not trust me.

I stayed outside pondering Maalik's words and what it could possibly mean until my schedule beeped at me.

Heaven's throne, that meant breakfast was over. And I had truly intended to eat.

I took a deep breath, then another, reminding myself that the physical reaction was not real. My lungs didn't cry for oxygen. I opened my agenda to see what class I had next.

This was a new building for me, located behind the library. For the first time, I noticed letters along the bottom of the picture of the building. I traced my fingers over the markings, but I couldn't remember the sounds for these letters.

I would have to face Maalik again before I did.

I swallowed down the bitter thought and went around the cafeteria, avoiding the other students. I saw as I approached the building that students from several dorms and years moved that direction. I avoided them as well, careful to keep my distance, now that I knew they believed they could touch without consequence.

My face felt hot and sticky. I ran my hand over it, surprised to come away with tears on my palm.

Why should I cry over this?

Why did it feel like my world was being ripped out from under me?

My schedule changed from showing the building to showing a hallway with one room lit up. I followed the instructions until I reached the room.

Inside, the room was set up in a rectangle. A white wall glowed at one end next to the master angel, a man with white wings and a head of hair to match, the color as white as snow.

He could have chosen to have any appearance from his mortal lifetime. Why would he choose white hair? He was not the first I'd seen to do so, but I didn't understand it.

Four rows of desks were set up facing the angel. I dropped into a desk and pulled my jacket close. Students wearing the colors of the other dorms came in and sat down around me, carefully folding their wings to avoid bumping the edges of the confined seats.

"Well, if it isn't Jez."

Kerubiel's rich voice drew a smile to my lips, and something fluttered in my chest. I raised my eyes as he lowered into the desk beside mine. His wings flapped once and then rested over the edge of the seat as he twisted toward me.

"You're in here also, huh? Figures."

I nodded. "Though I'm not too sure what class this is."

He opened his own agenda, and the light shown on his features as he read over his schedule. "Remedial Ancient History. Class description: a refresher course for those who have forgotten the basics of the first existence."

"I haven't forgotten," I huffed, annoyed that I had to take this class.

"Welcome, students," the master angel said, and I hushed as the power of his voice filled the room. "I am Master Remiel, and I will be your instructor for this class."

Remiel. Where had I heard that name?

"This class is to bring you up to speed on the basics of what happened in your life before you went to earth. Once you're caught up, you'll move onto another history class or even a cultural studies class. This class is especially geared to those who were not believers in mortality, so chances are what I teach you will be new to you."

"Life before earth?" a girl in a red sweater asked. I searched my mind, trying to place her dorm. Red was Dorm Hesed. The building on the right of mine, across the quad. "What do you mean by that?"

"Yeah," Kerubiel said, stretching his long legs out in front of him under the desk. "Pretty sure life started when we were born." He sort of sneered as he said it, as if about to catch Master Remiel in a foolish announcement.

Master Remiel only smiled, and I was sure he'd heard these same words from countless new students. "This class will be a lot to take in," he said. "That's why we break it down into smaller bits and only meet once a week, so you have a chance to internalize what you learn and do your own research. Who here knew you existed before you were born?"

I glanced around the room. Of the two dozen kids in the class, not a single one raised their hand. What the sky? May as well be me.

I let my hand slide upward, past my ear and toward the sky.

Master Remiel's gaze fell on me, and it seemed his eyes narrowed slightly. "Yes. It's . . . Jez, right?"

I nodded.

"You know about the prior existence?"

"Yes." I felt the other students' eyes on me, surprise and wonder and even disbelief oozing from them.

"What can you tell us about it? Anything?"

Oh no, here was where I drew the line. I shook my head. "All I know is there was life before earth." A lifetime of life. "And some angels chose to go to earth. Others did not."

"Yes, that summarizes things up." Remiel smiled, and he looked relieved I hadn't said more. "As Jez said, before you were born on earth, you lived in heaven, similar to how you are now. You were created, you grew, and you learned. When the chance came to come to earth, you chose to go."

Not all of us. But I kept quiet.

"You couldn't all go at once, so a time line was created, with the great epochs of earth time outlined. Each one of you chose when you would be born. I chose to be born two thousand years ago. When I died, I continued the learning I'd received before my birth. You chose to be born in a later period. You chose to descend to a world of many enlightenments, but also many trials. Because of that, your education in Shamayim continued right up until the moment of your birth, making your generation more prepared for earth life than any generation before it."

Nothing he said was a surprise, and I sat quietly, pretending this applied to me. Because it didn't. I hadn't sat in a classroom like this one for the past several hundred years, increasing my knowledge day by day. I'd sat in Darkness, often in pain, listening to the cries of the damned and the Fallen, or I'd descended to earth as a shadow, feeding off the iniquity of mankind and knowing every moment that it was heaven's law that decreed my miserable existence.

"So we just sat around going to school for thousands of years?" Kerubiel said. "That doesn't sound like me."

His comment was met by chuckles from other students who apparently agreed.

"Well," Remiel said, "the person you are now is the same person you were before. Your personalities don't change. But you had a broader vision before you went to earth, before the veil covered your mind and you forgot everything. Perhaps the person you became on earth is not who you originally intended to become."

Even I heard the insinuation in his words that perhaps Kerubiel had not lived up to his potential. He scowled, and the shadows around him grew. I cleared my throat, drawing the attention back to me.

Remiel looked at me, and I said, "Tell us about the war in heaven." I lowered my chin, glowering at him, and my fingernails dug into the surface of the desk I sat at.

"Ah. The war in heaven." Master Remiel did not lower his eyes, but faced me head on. "Who here knows about the war in heaven?"

"I think I may have heard something about it," a girl with a green sweater said.

"War in heaven?" A boy shook his head, his shaggy brown hair drifting around his shoulders. "How could there be a war in heaven? That's a place of love and peace and everything good."

"No, it's not." Remiel moved away from his table and waved his hand over the wall behind him. The wall changed to a display of a blue-green world floating in space.

"That's earth!" the girl said.

"This is earth, Zophiel," Remiel affirmed. "And in Shamayim, we are connected to earth, to its life, to its aging. We live in a separate sphere of existence, yet we are intricately bound to the planet. And angels are not perfect. We are not God. We still feel passion and rage and love and fear and devotion. Once we have returned to heaven after earth life, we have more control over those emotions, control we learned in mortality and continue to perfect in this existence. But before we were born, we were emotional infants in celestial bodies with heavenly power. And we thought. And we loved. And we disagreed. And there was war."

I sat, breathless and mesmerized, as captivated by this vision of heaven that Remiel painted as the other students. I had always imagined the angels as passionate beings, swayed by folly and illusion and desire, but I had never heard it explained so clearly. And by one of their own.

"What happened during the war?" Zophiel asked, her face flushed and her voice breathy.

Remiel focused his gaze on the angel. "You picked a side. Either the side of the Father, or the side Hasatan, the angel who rebelled."

Silence followed his pronouncement, a heavy, poignant quality to the air. Zophiel fingered her collar, then asked softly, "Which side did I choose?"

Remiel looked at each student, meeting their eyes. He flinched slightly when he met mine, but his gaze moved on quickly before anyone else noticed. "Which side do you think you chose?"

I shifted in my seat, not able to sit quietly any more. "It wasn't like that."

All eyes in the classroom turned to me. I waited for Remiel to silence me or tell me I had no place to speak here, but he didn't.

"What do you mean?" Kerubiel asked, his blue eyes steady on me. "What do you know?"

I swallowed, a little unnerved by the attention. "Technically we got to pick sides, yes. But it wasn't really a choice."

"How was it not a choice?" Zophiel asked.

I lifted my chin, daring Remiel to contradict me. "Because our existence was being threatened. Heaven pretended to offer us a choice, but if we didn't pick earth, we would lose a chance to get a body. We would be damned to Sheol for all eternity. We would never get our wings." I choked on the last words and shook my head, clearing the anger.

"It wasn't like that, Jez," Remiel said, his voice gentle. "The consequences for choosing Hasatan—"

"The punishments," I said, my hands shaking. "You—your kind—punished all of the angels who chose a different path."

"It was Hasatan—" Remiel began, but Kerubiel interrupted.

"Knowing all those consequences, why would anyone choose Hasatan?"

Kerubiel's eyes peered into mine as he spoke, and I had the sense he was seeing directly into my soul.

"We weren't told what the punishment would be for following Hasatan," I said. "We were told we got to choose. And those who chose Hasatan did so because they loved him. Because he offered a path of security and safety, with no lies, no manipulations, no hidden agendas." I glared at Remiel. "The same cannot be said for the agents of heaven."

My statement brought murmurs and whispers from my fellow students. Except Kerubiel, who remained silent, his gaze steady on me.

CHAPTER TWELVE

Remiel cleared his throat. "I appreciate the arguments Jez has brought to the table. Now let us discuss the fallacies in her statements."

I opened my mouth to speak again, but this time he spoke right over me.

"There were consequences for choosing either side. The pros and cons were laid out before all of us so we could make an educated, informed decision."

"The angels were not—" I began, but now Remiel steered his light blue eyes on me, and I fell silent.

"Hasatan deceived his followers. When Shamayim warned them that they would not to go earth and receive a body, that they would not receive their wings as a first inheritance, Hasatan told them that wasn't true. He told them it was a lie meant to frighten them, and he promised his followers that they would go to earth and get bodies, no matter what the Father said."

A shiver whispered down my spine at the power in Remiel's eyes. And something whispered through my soul, something that frightened me to my core. I quickly silenced it.

"So all the angels had a choice. Some chose to believe the Father. Some chose to believe Hasatan. Who is, Jez, the master of all lies."

No. That wasn't how it happened. The room spun, and I gripped the edge of my desk, taking quick, shallow breaths.

Remiel's gaze finally moved away from me, and I sank into my chair, trying to discern his words. It couldn't be true. Hasatan only wanted freedom and pleasure and progress for his followers. What motive would he have in lying?

A bell rang out across campus, echoing in the small room where the twenty or so of us sat.

"Class is dismissed," Remiel said. "I encourage each of you to spend time in the library, learning about the things I've taught you. Follow up with your questions. I myself have written several books on the subject of the heavenly war and life before the war."

Suddenly his name clicked, and I reared my head back. Maalik had been reading from his book.

I felt a surge of anger toward Remiel, heaven-bound and determined to indoctrinate the new angels with his theories and manipulations. And I felt angry at Maalik for buying into it, for believing the deceits so easily.

I pushed out of my desk with the other students. Kerubiel walked to the door ahead of me and then he paused, and I knew he waited for me.

"Jez," Remiel said, calling me back. "May I speak to you a moment?"

My footsteps faltered. I didn't want to talk to him. But it was against my nature to disobey. "Go on," I said to Kerubiel. "I'll catch up to you later."

He nodded and left, and I turned around to face Master Remiel.

"What?" I said, wanting to sound indignant. But my voice trembled on the word.

"Jezbathasat," he said, and his use of my full name silenced my outrage. "I know the pain and discomfort you are feeling as you encounter new truths here in Arcadia. But you will have to let go of the things you think you know if you are going to learn here."

"The things I think I know?" I sputtered.

"Yes." He offered a smile. "Your understanding of the First War and the events thereafter is not accurate."

"It's factual history," I said stiffly.

"It's not true. Keep in mind, Jez," and he lowered his voice, "you were not there."

I reared back and glanced around, afraid someone would be near enough to hear. But no, it was only us.

Of all the creatures created by God's hand, I was the only one not present during the First War.

Because I hadn't been created yet. Because I wasn't created by God's hand.

I didn't go to the cafeteria with the other students but instead went to the library. The quiet inside soothed the rush of confusion in my soul, and I wandered through the rows of books, wishing desperately that I could read. There would be nothing here written by a demon, but perhaps one of the Fallen might have written their story before being condemned. There had to be something here to shed truth on what I'd heard today. I fingered the spines of the books and lifted my head upward, watching as the shelves disappeared into the ceiling, so high I could not make out the end of it.

My schedule pinged, a soft chime that sounded pleasantly in my ears. I lifted the agenda and opened it.

The cafeteria building sat on the screen, lit up and indicating that was where I should be. But instead of the name beneath it, a small bar had appeared with a string of words inside. I couldn't read them, but I recognized the face in front of the banner: Kerubiel.

I raised my eyebrows, surprised, yet at the same time, not. Eldermaster Barachiel had said these books were also a way for us to communicate with each other. My father could summon me in my mind and speak to me when he wished, and yet I could not do the same. I had not learned to speak into a mind yet. And neither had the other students, which meant we needed a more technological means of communication.

But I couldn't respond. I couldn't even read what he'd written. Frustration crept across my shoulders, and I turned, making my way to the exit and heading for the cafeteria, where I assumed he was.

He met me halfway across the quad, a gentle breeze blowing his blond hair away from his face. "I wondered where you'd gone. Should've known it was the library." He tilted his head, his expression quizzical. "Master Remiel really got you riled up."

"I don't trust angels," I said without thinking. "You can't believe everything they say."

"Interesting," Kerubiel said softly. He slowed his steps, his hands dropping into the pockets of his black pants. "You say that as if you are not one."

I did not know what to say to that. I swallowed and glanced at him, saw the way he studied me. My face warmed, and I looked away.

"You didn't respond to my message," he said, and I faced him again, glad for the subject change. I opened my book, where his message still glowed.

"I can't read," I said. I held my breath, not sure how he would take my admission.

"You can't read?" he repeated, disbelief lacing his words.

I shook my head. "I never learned."

He made a noise in the back of his throat. "You are an interesting mystery, Jez." His eyes glowed with curiosity, almost a hunger, as if he could hardly wait to uncover my secrets. The expression left me both heady and weak.

He reached a hand out toward me, and I shied back.

"Chill," he said, smirking. "I'm not gonna touch you. Let me see your schedule."

"Oh." I handed over my agenda, embarrassed by the misunderstanding.

He opened it and scanned the image and message. "All I said was, 'where are you?' See here?"

He pointed out the symbols, and I leaned close, but not too close.

"Wh-wh-wh. Where. Are. You."

I nodded along as he read the words out loud, committing them to memory.

"So you could always respond and tell me where you are," he said with another grin. "But you could also press this button right here." He pointed to a red circle with a black dot in the middle of it, right underneath the message banner. "So let's say you're in class and you don't want to type back a response, but you want to show me where you are. You press this button." He pressed it, and somewhere on his body, his agenda dinged. He removed the book from within his shirt and opened it. "Now it shows me where you are."

He turned the book around, and I gasped to see a tiny image of my face floating on a map of the quad, right where I stood.

And with a sudden chill, I realized the angels knew where we were at all times and all moments. They could track us.

Which meant they knew I'd gone to Sheol last night.

"You okay?" Kerubiel asked, his dark blue eyes still focused on me.

I pressed a hand to my head, distraught and anxious. The archangels must be right now, at this very moment, discussing what to do with me.

But it wasn't the thought of being sent back to the underworld that distressed me. It was not completing my mission.

Failure was not an option. I'd been commanded, and I had to obey. Or the consequences to my soul would be dire. How long would I suffer? How long would I be tormented? A thousand years? An eternity? Two eternities?

"Jez?"

This time there was no mistaking when Kerubiel reached for my hand, and I slashed downward with such force that a physical wind blew up between us, blowing his hair away from his face and mine behind my head.

"No!" I cried. "You cannot touch me!" That law I would not break. I didn't care what the other angels did. I would not intentionally bring torture and condemnation upon myself.

The wind died down, the dark strands of my hair settling again on my shoulders.

"How did you do that?" he breathed.

"I don't know," I said, closing my book and holding it against my chest. "I don't know how anything works." Those, at least, were true words.

Up on the high tower, the bell tolled, signaling the end of lunch. Kerubiel lifted his eyes toward it and then looked at me.

"Time passes differently here."

"How so?"

"It seems we've barely settled into a place before the hour is up and it's time to move again."

I hadn't really noticed. But then, my perception of time would be different than his. In the darkness of Sheol, I had no concept of time. A year and a day and a lifetime all merged together. I aged and I grew, but sometimes it seemed to take forever, and other times it happened in a flash. So to have time act strangely wasn't a surprise to me. I shrugged. "Hours and minutes and days are mortal concepts. It's how humans try to interpret infinity."

Kerubiel fastened his eyes to my face, and I realized I'd done it again: made it sound like I wasn't one of them. I hugged my arms around my waist.

"Do you know—?" I sucked in a breath, gathering my resolve. "Do you know where the generator is?"

He tilted his head. "What generator?"

"The one used to put a shield of Light around Arcadia. Eldermaster Barachiel told me it's what keeps the demons out."

"No," he said, and I knew from the way he stared at me that my question raised a dozen others in his mind. "I don't."

I didn't like how his eyes probed me. "I have a class to get to," I said. "I'll see you later."

"Looking forward to it."

I glanced back at Kerubiel once as I made my way toward my next class. He stood with his hands in his pockets, gaze focused on me.

Or was his gaze focused on my back and my obvious lack of wings?

I looked away, my heart sinking. As desperately as I'd wanted to hide my differences, it looked like my secrets would reveal themselves, whether I wanted them to or not.

※ ※

I spent the next few days on edge, jumping whenever my agenda beeped at me, certain one of the archangels was going to summon me for disciplining.

But one week passed into another, and no one came for me. Was it possible my descent had escaped their notice?

The more I thought about it, the more confident I became. They might be able to find us at any given moment, but that didn't mean they sat around watching our every step. They had more important things to do.

Creation class was in the big green bubble building, the one we'd used as a manifestation hall. Normal classes were being added to my schedule every week as I proved myself capable of learning. I stepped inside and found the students seated in a circle on the ground, which consisted of soft green material that resembled grass. In the center sat a master angel in a belted tunic, whose white wings opened and folded as if attempting to lift her from the ground. Her eyes landed on me as I came in.

"Greetings, Jez," she said.

I nodded, wary of her, wary of anyone who knew who I was when I hadn't even met them.

A girl in the circle twisted around to see me.

"Jez," she said, her face morphing into a smile. She scooted over slightly and patted the spot beside me. "Come sit with me."

I exhaled, taking note of the sense of relief I felt at the sight of Iblis. There was a familiarity, a welcome feeling. I was wanted.

I settled in next to her. "You have this class too?"

She nodded. "I think we'll have most of our classes together when you join the regular curriculum."

A few more students wandered in and found places in the circle. I glanced around, noting that we were a mixture of our dormitory and the one beside ours, Hesed, donning red sweaters or red ties or a mixture of both. My dormmates, on the other hand, displayed navy and gold colors on their blazers and jackets.

Except me. I looked down at my black jacket and black skirt. In my closet was a navy tie like the one Iblis wore, and a navy jacket like the one Dara wore. Or even a gold-striped tie like Jerahmeel and Maalik.

A strange sense of longing to belong washed over me. I didn't have to fight this feeling. I was a part of this group, and remaining aloof would not help me accomplish my mission.

Yes. For the sake of my mission, I could try to blend in.

The master angel greeted each student by name as they came in and settled down. Then she closed her eyes and sat with her hands on her knees, her legs crossed, and said nothing.

Minutes passed by. The conversation I'd had with Kerubiel earlier about time became more poignant as I took note of its passing. We sat and did nothing. A few angels copied the master, sitting up straight and closing their eyes, breathing deeply.

Eventually she opened her eyes, and she looked directly at me. "I am Master Sabriel, and I will be your instructor for your Creation classes."

Creation. The power of life. Interest stirred in my chest, and I sat up straighter. This was a power not given to any of the demons. It was a power of the gods.

"Thus far, you haven't missed much. We're still learning to attune ourselves to the universe. Before you can begin to tap into this miraculous ability, this most noble of powers, you must feel the energy around you. This power does not come out of nowhere; it has to came from something. It exists in the force of the elements around us."

I let out a breath. "Is this something only Empatya angels can do? Since we also control the elements?"

Master Sabriel looked around at the students. "Would anyone like to answer that?"

A girl in a red sweater who I didn't know said, "Empatya have an easier time of it, but all angels learn how to tap into the power."

"That's right. Thank you, Harut. Whether you become a master at creation or not remains to be seen. You will become adept in all angelic abilities before you can graduate, though you will only become a master in one or two."

I blinked, remembering how the wind had exploded around me when I'd become upset with Kerubiel. Did that mean I might have a proficiency with air? Perhaps creating would also come more naturally to me.

"Please mimic my posture, Jez, and you'll find yourself catching on soon enough. Mimicry is the first step to mastery. Sit up straight, cross your legs, and rest your hands on your knees."

Mimicry was the first step to mastery. I pondered that as I sat the way she instructed. If I mimicked the angels long enough, would they forget I wasn't one?

Jerahmeel, the angel who continued to react with such anger in our TLG meetings, snorted and rolled his eyes. "This feels a lot like yoga."

"Yoga implements one of the ways to achieve meditation, which places mortals on a plane a little closer to heaven. It's one of the most spiritual experiences a mortal can have while still on earth, and many mortals manage to achieve high levels of elemental mastering while still alive."

"I love yoga," a Hesed angel said from my left. She closed her eyes and arched her back, lifting her chin and inhaling deeply.

"My girlfriend tried to get me to do yoga once," Jerahmeel said. Red and orange colors rolled off him in waves, and I wondered who else could see it. "I wasn't into it then either." He paused. "Of course, she's probably not my girlfriend anymore, is she? Hey, Mistress Sabriel, when can we see the people we left behind?"

Iblis glanced at me, and I returned her look. Jerahmeel had already asked this question in TLG. It didn't appear he was going to let it go until he got a different answer.

"It's Master Sabriel," the teacher said, unflustered. "We don't go by gender-specific titles here in Arcadia."

"Arcadia feels an awful lot like prison to me. When do we get to see our families?"

"Please speak with me after class, Jerahmeel," she said. Though her expression remained calm, something steely entered her eyes. "You're intentionally disrupting the ambiance I'm attempting to create here, but I'd be happy to answer your questions later."

"Sure you would," he grumbled.

Such anger broiled beneath his skin. I couldn't take my eyes away from the emotional anguish. It festered in him, popping over his flesh and releasing thick colors like exploding boils. I wanted to dig into them, to find out what brought out such emotions.

"Everyone, please close your eyes. Allow me to remove your struggles and the strains of adjusting to celestial life."

I studied Jerahmeel a moment longer, who showed no inclination of closing his eyes. I noted that he also did not wear his uniform. He was like a blustery storm cloud, ready to burst and flood the world with its contents. It wouldn't take but a little provoking to make him overflow. What sort of power did he conceal inside that spiritual body?

How long could his dark rage nourish my soul?

CHAPTER THIRTEEN

The thought surprised me. I'd just fed off a spirit, but suddenly I felt a stirring hunger. I shook it off and faced Master Sabriel, wiping any emotion from my face. I closed my eyes and took a deep breath, trying to find my focus. What sort of being would feed on the depravity of others? I'd done it my whole existence, but only because I had no choice.

So why did I desire to do so now? Was it in my nature as a demon to do so? Or was I weak because of the previous night? If left to my own devices, would I choose to relish the anguish of mortals?

The thought bothered me enough that my spirit trembled. I didn't want to be someone who enjoyed the suffering of others.

When had I begun to desire to be something different?

"Take a deep breath and hold it. Feel your lungs expand the way they did when you were alive. Your spiritual bodies are a representation of your physical ones, but without the handicaps or limitations that held you back. You might feel the urge to take a breath, but your cells are not screaming for oxygen. You can hold your breath forever."

I couldn't hold my breath at all. My spiritual lungs didn't know how to do such a thing. For that matter, what was breathing? I could speak on command, but I'd never considered the manual act of pulling air in and out of my lungs.

"Now exhale. With your eyes closed, visualize your breath intermingling with the atmosphere around you. Here in Arcadia, there is a higher concentration of Light. Try to picture it. Imagine the power as sparks of energy, beads of life pulsing near your ears, your eyes, your nose. Inhale again, and feel them enter your system.

"We've done this much before. It's time to expand your experience. Place your hands on the grass. Feel the sensation of life beneath your palms. Treasure it, honor it. Find the energy source in the soil that nourishes the plants. Don't rush things."

Nothing. I had nothing. I put my fingers on the grass, the stems tickling my skin, still attempting to breathe in and out as if it were something I'd done my whole existence. The grass clumped beneath my fingers, and I searched for energy pulses, for life, for anything.

"Picture your spirit reaching into the ground, finding that energy. Now pull the power from the ground. Coax it into the roots of the grass. Nourish them. Give them life. Feel them grow."

I heard a gasp beside me, and I peeked one eye open. The Hesed angel had dug her hands into the ground, and the grass around her fluttered upward, twining with her fingers, creeping around her wrists.

"I feel it," Israfil said, wonder in his voice, and I looked over at the Alef angel from my group. "It's like the embodiment of life itself."

"I can see the spark of life," another Hesed angel whispered. "They're just out of reach, but I see them in my mind. They're everywhere."

"Good," Sabriel said, smiling, and I snapped my eyes shut.

With more desperation than earlier, I dug my fingers into the grass, reaching into the root system, searching out the life source. Water, nutrients, sunlight . . . I gripped slippery green shoots in frustration and pulled.

They yanked out of the dirt, slender brown roots and all.

"Oh," I said softly, feeling morose sadness as I stared at them.

I hadn't given them life. I'd taken it.

I considered skipping dinner and going straight to my dorm, but the truth was, I wanted to put something tasty in my mouth. My heart hurt from the failure in Creation class, even though Master Sabriel gestured for me to stay in class after everyone left.

"Don't be too hard on yourself," she said, peering at my face even as I avoided her eyes. "This was your first time. The other students have been coming for a month, learning how to feel the energies for weeks before we attempted to manipulate them."

I nodded, wishing I could believe her. Wishing the only cause of my failure was my lack of preparation.

Now my spirit craved chocolate. My tongue, which had never tasted food until I'd arrived at the academy, had quickly grown accustomed to it. I knew the sweetness would soothe the aching in my heart.

At least I wasn't longing to devour Jerahmeel's essence anymore.

I delayed entering the cafeteria until the majority of the angels had gone in. Then I went inside and skipped getting a tray, instead grabbing two cookies and ducking back outside again, taking my cookies and heading to my room to sulk in peace.

My agenda dinged at me before I finished crossing the quad. I pulled it from my bag and wasn't surprised to see a message flashing at the bottom of the screen. But I was surprised to see who it was from.

Maalik.

What could our brave leader want with me? We hadn't spoken since our last tutoring session, nearly two weeks prior.

I couldn't read his message and couldn't respond, either. So I did the only thing I knew to do: I pressed the red locater button.

And then I stood there, waiting, two cookies in my hand, knowing he would find me.

He came out a moment later, pushing open the cafeteria doors and joining me halfway to my dormitory.

"Come to talk to me about the incident in Creations class?" I said. He wasn't in my class, being a second year, but I could imagine the report the other students had given him at Table D.

He paused. "Hello. How are you? I'm good, thanks for asking."

I blinked and shook my head. "I didn't ask."

"No," he said, and something like a smile creased his features. "I know. But you should have."

"Why? I'm not interested in your well-being. You are the one who contacted me."

"But you should be, Jez."

My temper rose, and I glared at him. "Did you need me for something?"

"No. But I did hear about the incident in Creations class. I wanted to make sure you were all right."

His words were concerned, but the stern expression on his face, coupled with his hands shoved deep in his pockets, did not fill me with the desire to share my innermost feelings with him. "I'm fine. Creating life is a new aspect for me."

One eyebrow lifted over his light brown eyes. "I suppose it is. Probably doesn't come naturally."

He was only voicing what I had already thought, but coming from him, an angel who thought himself superior because he had chosen a different side, rankled my ichor. I turned away and continued my march toward the dorm.

"Eldermaster Barachiel asked me to try to fit in another study session with you," Maalik said, matching my stride. "He said it would go a long way to easing some of the frustrations you're feeling."

These angels had no understanding of the concept of privacy. I rounded on him, fully annoyed. "And why would I want to do that? So I can sit there and be insulted by you, all in the name of furthering my education? So that Barachiel can listen in on my thoughts and feel self-satisfaction that he is so much more enlightened than I am? Maybe I'll find someone else to teach me to read."

"Why?" Maalik asked, something like wounded pride entering his voice. "We were accomplishing something. And it's more than just reading. There's so much you don't know."

"I can think of other people I would rather learn it from," I snapped.

Maalik's eyes hardened. "Suit yourself. See if someone else will be as understanding about what you are as I am."

"Ha!" I actually laughed. "This is what you call understanding?" How I longed to be able to take my finger and dig it into his chest. "You know nothing. But you think you know everything. One of us is unteachable, and it isn't me."

"So at least we're in agreement. This arrangement was never going to work."

Maalik did not even wait for me to come up with a retort. He pushed ahead of me toward the dorm. I considered chasing after him, furious enough to continue our argument, to make him recognize his arrogance.

But I realized how desperate that would make me look. His wings folded up when he opened the door, and I couldn't take my eyes off his retreating back. I felt a spasm in my heart, a mixture of envy and wounded feelings. What did I care what Maalik thought? I was making other friends.

I fumed through the rest of the evening, indignant over Maalik's insinuation that he was the only one who could teach me to read, the only one who would be willing to do so. Iblis sat at her desk with a small plant, humming as she caressed it. I couldn't help watching. Though her plant did not suddenly grow upward like the Hesed's plant in class had, it didn't die, either. Not like mine.

My schedule dinged. I chose not to look at it. I couldn't respond anyway.

"What do you suppose our families are doing now?" Iblis asked, startling me out of my reverie.

I preferred not to think about it, really. "I don't know. What do you think yours is doing?"

"My mom is probably sad," Iblis said, her tone wistful. "I hope my brothers are okay. One's in college and the other's married. I didn't see them much, but I adored them. And Jason—" Her tone became hushed. "I don't know how he is. I'm worried he blames himself. I'd like to see him."

I remembered Jerahmeel's desire to see his family. "You could ask. Find out how it works."

"I did, in Gehenna, when I finally accepted what happened. They told me I would see them when the time was right. Anyway, what's the rush? We have eternity." She smiled, but I sensed it wasn't genuine. "I would like to comfort my mother. I can't wait. Why can't we see them now?"

I shook my head. "I don't know." I had no reason to see earth. There was nobody there I was longing for.

Her agenda dinged, and she opened it up. "Oh. I got a message." She sounded surprised and delighted, and she glanced at me.

What? Somehow I sensed I was supposed to have a reaction here. I cocked my head and said, "Oh?"

It must've been the correct response. "It's from Barachiel. He asked me to tell you he sent you a message. He said you might need some help with it. Did you see the message?"

Now even Barachiel was getting in my business. Soon the whole school would know I couldn't read. "No, I'm good," I said. "I just haven't responded to him yet. But I will." When I was good and ready.

※ ≋

The next morning my schedule showed me to go to the library after breakfast. Kerubiel found me on the way and invited me to eat with him. Something about the Shadow Shade pulled me, and I followed him to his table without question. I sat with him and the other angels from Emet, the purple of their uniforms dark enough to swallow the Light in the room. Maybe that was why I liked them.

"She's not an Emet," one of the girls said.

I watched the dark colors spilling across the table at her words, a visible extension of her emotional projection.

"She's more like us than anyone else here. Trust me on this," Kerubiel said.

I gave him a startled look, not quite sure what he meant by that. But he just shrugged and went back to his food.

The others accepted me because Kerubiel did. So I tried not to worry about what he meant. Instead I cut my pancake into little bitty pieces, trying to avoid the sticky sweet syrup all over the plate. I decided I preferred yogurt.

When breakfast ended, I snuck away to the dorms and sat down on my bed instead of following orders and going to the library. It was the first time I'd chosen to disobey, and it gave me a strangely heady feeling, almost empowering. I sat on my bed in the empty room, wondering if I'd actually get away with it. What was everyone else from my dorm doing right now? What classes did they have while I was still learning to reading? Class had been in session nearly two months now, the weather changing into fall, and my schedule was only missing a few of the general education classes. Still,

I couldn't help wondering what they were learning without me.

I lay back on my bed and let time wrap around me the way it had so many times in Sheol, when agency was a foreign concept.

But time didn't seem to work as it had before. Instead of entering a semi-aware state, I felt more anxious with each passing moment. My agenda dinged, and I opened it up to see another message. This one was also from Barachiel, and it showed beneath the one he had sent me the night before. I squinted at it, recognizing the first four letters. "P-L-E-A." Another letter followed, but I couldn't remember what it was, and an E finished the word.

I might be able to figure this one out. I sounded out the letters PLEA. Only a handful of words could start this way. Plead. Please. Pleat.

Please. That had to be it.

He was issuing a request.

But the rest of the symbols I didn't recognize. I couldn't guess what he was asking.

The image of the lit up library on my screen dissolved, to be replaced by the administration building.

Ah. Now I understood. I hadn't gone to the library, and now I was wanted at the administration building.

I could only imagine what this was about.

You can refuse, I told myself. *You are not required to obey.*

But it was not in my nature to rebel. This recent act of rebellion, choosing to come to my room instead of the library, left my stomach queasy and my hands shaking.

Uttering a dramatic sigh that would have made Iblis proud, I shuffled to my feet and made my way to the administration building.

I had not been inside since the first day I arrived. As it had before, the screen on my schedule changed when I entered the building and showed me the path to take. I walked down the hallway, passed three doors, and then made a right. On my left was an open door, and I paused in front of it.

"Come in, Jez."

I did so, hesitant.

Eldermaster Barachiel slid from behind his desk, his wings hidden as he approached me. He looked like a human.

It occurred to me that so did I.

"Thank you for coming."

I narrowed my eyes. "As if I had a choice?"

"Here you always have a choice."

I gave a dry laugh. "We have different definitions of choice."

Barachiel sat down and folded his fingers together. "You have a different understanding of heaven. But that's not why I called you here. I am concerned about the altercation you had with Maalik."

I rolled my eyes. "It wasn't an altercation."

"You missed your lesson this morning."

I arched a brow. "Maalik said we were done. So I didn't go."

"Humans often say things in anger that they do not mean. Maalik is still learning to curb his passions."

"Oh, well." I shrugged and pleated my hands together. "It's probably for the best, anyway. We don't get along."

"He came to me when you didn't show."

"To tell you how unteachable I am?"

"He did say he cannot teach you."

This was sounding familiar. "Didn't he say that last time?"

"He said he unintentionally offends you at every turn and does not wish to continue to put negative feelings between you."

That stopped me. He had taken the blame upon himself instead of pointing it at me. I trailed my fingers along the wooden desk and frowned at Barachiel. "He said that?"

Barachiel sighed. "Jezbat—"

"Jez," I hissed, glancing around quickly.

"Jez. I know this is a difficult transition for you. But you face everyone with blades drawn, metaphorically speaking, and not everyone sees you as the enemy."

My thoughts flew to Kerubiel, who seemed to sense there was more to me than met the eye but accepted me anyway. "Maalik sees me as the enemy."

"He sees Sheol as the enemy."

"And I'm the embodiment of all he's been taught to hate," I said bitterly.

"We do not teach hate," Barachiel said. "And you are not that embodiment."

I stayed silent. The angels might not teach hate, but mortals learned it. The Fallen arrived in Sheol either lusty in their desire to take revenge on heaven and God, or terrified of what eternal damnation might mean. There was no love or curiosity or desire for friendship. Only hatred and fear.

"Try one more time," Barachiel said. "Give Maalik a chance. He is one of my very best pupils, and I have faith in him."

"This is the third time," I said.

"Give him as many tries as necessary."

I let out another dramatic sigh. "Fine. One more time. But if it doesn't work, I want another teacher."

"Agreed." Barachiel checked a large screen on his desk, his finger moving across it and scrolling it upward. "Your next class is Synergy. It will be outside at the Synergy Fields after lunch. I think you will enjoy this class. It's where you'll learn how to master your energy. The class only started this week for all first years, so you haven't missed anything." He looked at me with his piercing eyes. "Go be with your dormmates. Get to know them. The time for you to make your final choice will arrive before you know it, and the more educated you are, the better decision you can make."

I nodded and backed away, careful not to think until I'd escaped the room.

My final choice. To stay at GAA or return to Sheol.

I knew what was expected of me, but I wasn't sure I could do it.

CHAPTER FOURTEEN

The faces of the kids from my dorm were becoming more familiar to me.

Jerahmeel sat beside Iblis, who shared a pastry with Dara. Maalik, Daniel, and Eremiel sat talking together, while several other students I didn't know listened with riveted attention to Vanina, a girl with long blond hair and dark eyes and as subject to vanity as any Fallen I'd ever met.

None of them excluded me. They knew who I was by now, but there was no doubt from the way they shifted and turned ever so slightly away from me: I was different, and they felt it. I might be in their dorm, but I was the weird one.

"Jez." Dara caught my eye and held out a piece of pastry. "Would you like some? You're not eating."

"Oh." I'd forgotten to get a tray and go through the line.

Friendship. She's offering it to you over food.

Food came riddled with so many connections. Food was meant to create bonds between those who shared and ate together. And Dara was reaching out, making an offering.

So I pulled my lips up into a smile. "Thanks." I accepted the pastry, careful to make sure our fingers didn't touch. The sweet crumbs melted away on my tongue, and oddly enough, I felt a tiny bit closer to her.

Dara smiled back. Her dark hair was pulled up in a bun on top of her head, the navy sweater proclaiming her dorm. "I was shy on earth too. It was hard for me to make friends. It's definitely easier here, though."

"I didn't get the same experience," I said.

"Iblis told me. She said your earth life was hard."

My eyes went wide, and I shot a glance at Iblis, startled to learn they'd been talking about me. "You told her?"

"Should I not have?" Iblis furrowed her brow, looking confused. "Was it a secret?"

"Everything is a secret," I said, lowering my voice as the conversations around us died down and more eyes turned our direction. "If I tell you something, or you learn something about me, it's not for you to share with the entire group!" Good feelings abandoned, I shoved to my feet and stomped away from the table.

"Jez!" Iblis called.

I heard her jump up and run after me, but I quickened my pace, escaping the cafeteria ahead of her. My anger carried me, and for a moment, I thought I might be able to fly, wings or no wings. The water from the fountain flew upward when I passed and crashed down behind me, soaking the grass and stone pathways.

I took a deep breath, calming my fury. I may as well go to my next class and learn how to "master my energy."

I spotted purple sweaters as I approached, an indication that the Emet dormitory was also in this class. Other Alef students had arrived and seated themselves on the wooden chairs set up facing the tree line.

My eyes scanned the purple uniforms, looking for the boy who would not be wearing the school blazer.

There he was, still in his black earth clothing. Kerubiel fit in with the color of his dorm without even trying, the black blending with the purple.

"Jez," he said, fondness in his voice when I settled down in the chair beside him.

"Hi," I said, sliding a glance at him. A piece of hair fell in front of my face, and I tucked it away.

His eyes followed the motion, and then he gave me a slow smile. A smile that seemed to have a hidden meaning behind it.

If only I could interpret it.

"Welcome, angels."

I whipped my head forward, startled to see Barachiel standing in the midst of us. "Where did he come from?" I breathed.

"Beats me," Kerubiel said. "I didn't see him fly in." He squinted. "Can he even fly without his wings?"

Barachiel continued speaking. "In this class, you will learn to master the energy within you and use it to control the elements. Does anyone know what synergize means?"

Not a soul raised a hand. I certainly didn't.

"Synergize means the combined efforts of two or more beings to create a result. In other words, while you can use your energy to some extent on your own, the peak of your abilities comes only when you learn how to merge your energy with another.

"We won't get to that today, but know it's the end point of these exercises. We will begin with recognizing the energy you hold. The energy is within you, and you must learn to harness it. You will likely find one element in particular is easier for you to control. Some of them you might not ever control. It is rare that an angel cannot control any element; however, it does happen sometimes."

"What would that mean?" a girl from Emet asked. "That we don't have enough energy within us?"

"No. Just that you are unable to channel it."

"But don't we have to master all of our classes to pass them?" Iblis asked.

"Is school all she cares about?" Kerubiel murmured, and the Emet around him chuckled.

The sound wasn't friendly, and my defenses flared. Why did that bother me? I hadn't forgotten I was angry with her, but it still rubbed me wrong. "She just wants to do everything correctly."

"Yeah, we have a name for those people," Kerubiel said, and more snide laughter followed.

I turned away, huffy and annoyed for reasons I couldn't explain. In the meantime, another student spoke, and I missed Barachiel's answer.

"Please stand and spread out," he said. "Find a space around you where you won't bump into anyone."

I stood and took several paces away from Kerubiel, glad for the reason to put distance between us.

"Now extend your hand like this." Barachiel demonstrated, holding his right hand out chest high, palm down. "Look down at the earth in front of you. Close your eyes and imagine you can see into your heart."

I did as he commanded. I peered into my soul, searching for a heart. Did I have one?

"Physical body or spiritual, the heart is the center of your soul. See it beating. See the life force it sends rushing through your being with every second."

I let out a small gasp. Because I could see it. Tiny rivers of gold energy sped through me, dissipating at my fingers and toes, only to have another river of blue energy come sweeping back in, racing into my soul.

"If you haven't found it, keep searching. If you did, bend your fingers and dip them into that life force."

I bent the fingers of my extended hand as if brushing the surface of a gilded river. I opened my eyes, marveling when I saw the gold energy perched on the edges of my fingers.

Barachiel walked among us, his hands behind his back, smiling and nodding. "Good. As soon as you've pulled that energy to the surface, turn your palm right side up. Feel that energy at your fingertips. That's your life force. It will enable you to manipulate the air, move mountains, or call down the sky itself. By yourself, however, you will only achieve a portion of that power."

I turned my hand over, watching the orange energy flow across the back of my hand and over my palm. I had it! I had the life force! It sparked and shimmered, and I felt that this power was strong enough to accomplish any task.

"The life force energy will be used in almost all of your classes. You've already learned how to summon it, to some extent, in your Creations class.

"Now, there are a few rules you should remember when it comes to the elements."

I lifted my eyes and focused on him, drunk off the euphoria of having found my life force.

"You cannot coerce another being into sharing their life force with you to manipulate the elements. When you synergize with another angel, it must be a mutual agreement. You will channel your forces outside your bodies and work together to achieve a purpose. You will learn how to do this as a second year. And you cannot take the life force of a mortal creature, no matter how small or insignificant the creature might seem."

But we could. The Fallen did. They sucked up the life force of mortal humans and kept them as slaves, forming a symbiotic relationship: the humans got longer life while they served the Fallen, and the Fallen had a physical being on earth to do their bidding.

Perhaps what Barachiel meant was, to do so would tarnish our souls and banish us from Arcadia. From the academy.

In that way, we could not do so. At least, we could not if we wished to remain a student.

I shook my head, clearing it of the riddles and circular word choice. My eyes fell upon my hand, where the energy had grown into a shimmering ribbon of light dancing around my fingers.

"Please spend the rest of our class session familiarizing yourself with your life force. Discover how to tap into it and access it quickly, and make the action instinctive. When you need the energy, you don't want to think about how to access it. Let it go and then summon it back again."

I opened my palm flat and watched the shimmering orange life force return to my body, channeling back into a river of gold flowing in and out of me with each moment. I imagined dipping my finger into that river again, then scooping it up by the handful. The energy rocked its way to my palm and coalesced, glittering like a miniature sun.

"Amazing," I whispered.

Why did the Fallen need access to mortal energy when we held this much within ourselves? Could the Fallen not do this?

The answer came to me with certainty, even though no one had ever told me. The Fallen lost their life force when they descended to Sheol. That was why they needed to harvest the energy of mortals.

"Next time we will use this energy to learn how to manipulate the elements. Here's your homework assignment: go to the library and research the elements. Do not try to summon one; we will do that in class. But each element symbolizes a heavenly attribute. You might be able to interpret what element you will have the most success with based on your personality or life experience." Barachiel smiled. "But be prepared to be surprised. It's not always what you expect."

"Jez, please wait."

I was still marveling over my ability to access my life force. I turned my hand over and over, studying it, wondering. I glanced up at Iblis as she approached, only remembering after she reached my side that I was angry with her.

"Please don't be mad," she said, her blue eyes wide and woeful. "I'm sorry for saying anything about you to Dara. I just thought . . ."

She broke off, and I couldn't be sure what she thought.

"I'm not angry anymore," I said. "I'm unfamiliar with living with others. I simply assumed when you learned something about me or my life, you would keep it to yourself." I paused. "Is that unusual? Do people share information about each other with others?"

"Well, it depends." Her face flushed pink. "It's called gossip, when you talk about others, but usually that means you're talking negatively. Dara's my friend. She's nice, and we're all kind of family here. So I thought you wouldn't mind. But I was wrong, and I'm sorry."

"Why were you wrong?"

"It upset you. I shouldn't be the one to judge what of your personal business gets to be public knowledge. So I apologize."

"It did make me feel like I can't tell you anything about myself," I admitted. "But I thought maybe that is how this existence is. If I want something kept private, I must keep it to myself."

"No, no!" She reached for my hand, but checked herself and withdrew. I almost smiled. At least she'd learned not to touch me. "I'm trustworthy. Really. I won't say anything about you to anyone."

"There are many things about me I don't wish anyone to know," I said.

"Like that you don't have wings?"

I drew back, sucking in a sharp breath. "You—what?"

She gave me a smile. "There are a lot of things you can hide, but not your lack of wings." Her wings flapped open and beat the air for a moment, as if in agreement to her statement. "I tried to stuff mine under a jacket like I thought yours were. I couldn't."

"Maybe my wings are very tiny," I said, my voice small.

She looked instantly contrite. "I'm sorry. I didn't consider that. So you're embarrassed of your wings?"

"Yes," I said, my face flaming. I hadn't meant to tell a lie, but somehow the falsehood had happened, and I went with it. "Have other people asked?"

She nodded. "Yes. But not me. I heard them asking Maalik."

Maalik. My shoulders stiffened. If he felt my information was as public as Iblis did—but no, everyone would know about me already if he thought that way. "What did he say?"

"That you're a student here like everyone else, and they should ask you if they have questions."

"He said that?" A warm feeling simmered in my chest, and I glanced around, as if to catch a glimpse of him. But he hadn't been in our synergy class.

"So if they ask me . . ." She paused, her cheeks turning pink. "Do you want me to say anything?"

I exhaled, considering. It might be good if she spread the word. "Yes. Tell them I don't want to talk about it."

"You're sensitive about it." She gave me a knowing look, and then her brow creased. "I wonder why they're small, though? Do you think it has to do with how unhappy your life was?"

"Yes," I said with conviction. "I'm sure it has everything to do with that."

My schedule lit up the next morning after breakfast, highlighting the Gabriel building. "TLG," I muttered. Time for my therapy class. With any luck, Master Eleleth would continue to skip me. Even though I was one of the only students who hadn't gone, he knew my past. He wouldn't expect me to share that with the other angels.

At least, that's what I hoped.

Iblis had already left for breakfast. I lingered behind in our dorm room, examining my closet full of academy clothing. There were pants and sweaters, skirts and jackets. And of course the ties, navy or gold or both.

It was a much bigger assortment than necessary, as I had never felt the need to change my attire.

Checking the room one last time to make sure I was alone, I slipped off the jacket Barachiel had given me when I arrived at Arcadia. The chains lay quiet and innocuous against my skin.

I pulled one of the white blouses from the closet and held it against my torso. The material was foreign and unfamiliar. Feeling entirely at odds with myself, I slipped my arms into the long sleeves and buttoned it up over my black halter.

I looked at the ties hanging from a rack and fingered a silky navy blue one similar to the one Iblis liked to wear. But that felt like a bigger commitment, as if putting it on would signify I was all in, and I wasn't.

The white shirt didn't feel like enough protection, so I chose a navy sweater and pulled it on over my shirt. I did not change my skirt. This was enough for now.

I went down to breakfast, pulling the edges of the sweater around me subconsciously, suddenly anxious everyone would notice my change of clothes and comment. But nobody did. If anything, my fellow students seemed to smile at me a little bigger and include me a little more. I used my fork to cut my fruit into tiny pieces, and I took small bites.

Heaven truly meant to torture the Fallen by not including food in Sheol.

I watched as Dara and Iblis finished eating and carried their trays together to the window, where they were deposited. Then they hooked their arms through each other's, their wings tucked in against their backs as they made their way out of the cafeteria.

I stood up and put away my tray, then walked behind them, wanting to join them but feeling completely different than them. Other students came out behind me, and I considered slowing to walk with them, but I found I was more comfortable in the middle.

Perhaps my isolation was self-induced.

The chatter quieted it as we entered the Gabriel building. The voices turned to whispers and then to silence, and we clustered closer together, me folding in on myself to make sure nobody bumped me.

The room was set up as it had been before, with chairs in a circle and Master Eleleth already seated in one. It was a big circle, with maybe twenty-five chairs, but I was familiar enough with my year to know there were many more of us apprentices than merely twenty-five.

It was easier to share our personal lives in smaller groups.

"Good to see you all again," Eleleth said. "I hope in the weeks between the last time we met and today, you've had the chance to get to know each other more and feel more comfortable sharing the details of your lives."

I sat myself in my chair and focused my eyes on my hands. Maybe the rest of them had gotten more comfortable with each other, but I was still trying to figure out where I fit.

Eleleth's eyes went around the circle and landed on Maalik. "The first time we met, I started the conversation by sharing my story. I've skipped over Maalik because he's not a first year, but today, Maalik, as Team Lead for your dorm, I invite you to share yours."

I lifted my head and turned to him, as did everyone else in the circle.

CHAPTER FIFTEEN

Maalik cleared his throat and then bent forward, resting his elbows on his knees and clasping his fingers together.

"Yeah, sure, why not." He pushed his hands off his knees and leaned back, his wings opening to readjust before folding around the back of the chair. "My death was stupid, and it didn't feel fair at the time. I was a swimmer. I swam meets and competitions and was becoming good. But I overestimated my ability. When I was seventeen, I was at the lake with several of my buddies. We lived near Lake Michigan and went there a lot. Some of them were getting on a little crazy, and they weren't thinking right, and my friend did a backflip into the water. Except the back of his head hit the dock before he fell in and knocked him unconscious." Pain flickered across Maalik's features, and he pressed his lips together. "I thought I could save him. So I dove into the water. But instead, we both drowned."

"What a tragedy," Arella whispered.

"Yeah, it was. But then it wasn't." He shrugged. "I came here, and I can do so much good now. I'm really looking forward to becoming a GIT, to receiving an assignment. I can do more to benefit people now than I thought possible before."

His pronouncement was met with silence. Israfil ventured, "And your friend? Is he here too?"

"Yeah. Except he's a Tele, so he goes to the academy at Sinai. I've seen him a few times, at inter-campus games."

That brought a whole slew of exclamations and excited remarks.

"Are you angry at him?" Jerahmeel asked.

"How often do those happen?" Daniel asked.

"No, I'm not angry at him," Maalik said. "I was only angry with myself, when I realized what happened. But I'm not that anymore, either. We made our choices, and these are the consequences. I've told him that, too."

"You mean we get to meet the other students?" Vanina said. "When are the games?"

Eleleth laughed. "Are you already tired of each other? Eager for new faces?" But his eyes twinkled, negating any criticism from his words. "You will see the other campuses at various Skyball games throughout the year, and all three campuses gather together for the championship game before the Progression Ceremony in the spring."

"So are the Championship games like World Cup for soccer or something?" Israfil asked.

"Kind of," Maalik said, inserting himself in the conversation. "All of the campuses come here. The playoff between the teams lasts all day, and it's fascinating to watch how the different groups use their gifts to play."

"What do you mean, use their gifts?" Vanina asked.

I was glad she did, because I wanted to, but I doubted Maalik would answer me.

"Some of them are Metamorfozahs," Maalik said. "They can shape-shift. And they use that in the game. Some are Teles, and they can do things with their minds. It's fascinating to watch."

"Yes," Eleleth said. "Skyball is amazing. And you'll have chances to go to several games before the semester is over." His eyes landed on the girl beside Jerahmeel. "Arella. Could you share your story?"

We were done talking about the game, apparently.

Arella, a girl with short, black hair and dark, velvety skin, took a deep breath and sat up straighter. "Yes. I was born in Jamaica . . ."

My mind wandered as she told her story. I kept picturing Maalik's narrative: a bunch of teenagers messing around at the water, probably giving into the vice of alcohol, maybe even to lust. A shiver crept over my skin. Touch was forbidden for the spiritual beings, but the mortals engaged in physical acts whenever they wished. The resulting pleasure was a sinful act, an addicting release of hormones and chemicals that bound their spirits and made them more susceptible to temptations and wrong choices.

Which was why touch was forbidden. And why choices should be, also.

"Jez?"

Eleleth's voice jarred me from my introspection, and I snapped my head his direction.

"Your turn. Can you share your story?"

I stared at him blankly, unbelieving. He actually wanted me to speak? I glanced at the students to my right and realized I'd not even heard the past two stories. My mind had zoned out, and time had blipped by.

My classmates still stared at me. I licked my lips and cleared my throat. "What should I say?"

"Whatever you wish."

"How is this existence proving different from your last?" Maalik said, drawing my gaze back to him. He nodded at me, his brown eyes taking on a golden hue. "What do hope for your future?"

For my future. I took a deep breath, concentrating on Maalik's questions. He'd given me a focus, something I could truthfully address.

"I spent a lot of time in isolation before coming here," I said. "My education was lacking, and I didn't have the opportunity to develop my humanity." *At all.* "It's an adjustment, being here. I've learned more in the past two months than in the past year. I'm looking forward to feeling more comfortable with you. To understanding more about being . . . human."

I said the last word almost like a confession, admitting that I was something different than they were. Yet the girls stared at me with compassion in their eyes, and even the boys wore expressions of understanding that they hadn't before. My face warmed and I looked down, running my hands over my knees.

"Thank you, Jez. You add an unexpected element to our dynamic. It's a pleasure to have you here." Eleleth spoke without guile, and yet I thought I detected a note of amusement in his tone. His eyes flicked to the boy beside me. "Lieke? How about your story?"

Just like that, the attention moved off me. I breathed a sigh of relief and relaxed in my chair.

My agenda chimed, letting me know I'd just received a message. I slid the book open in my lap.

It was from Maalik. The little circle image of his face showed beside the message banner. But instead of a series of symbols I wouldn't be able to interpret, he had sent just one: the image of a yellow fist with a thumb poking up.

I didn't know what it meant, but it left me with a feeling of camaraderie. I leaned back enough to catch his eye. He gave a little head bob and then repeated the gesture with his hand: closing his fingers into his palm and lifting his thumb.

I imitated him, and he smiled. I pulled forward, feeling the edges of my own smile tugging at my lips.

"You did good."

Maalik spoke quietly as we walked across the quad together, approaching the library. TLG had concluded with Lieke, and my schedule had promptly shown me a new location: the library.

Maalik had slipped out before me, but I found him waiting for me outside the therapy room. He didn't say a word the whole way out of the building and halfway across the quad, and his words startled me from my own reverie now.

"What?" I asked, trying to find context for his words.

"With your story. Good job. You kept it real without giving too much away."

Thanks to his encouragement. I smirked. "I didn't want to scare everyone in the room."

"You wouldn't scare them. New apprentices don't know enough about the war yet."

"Because they haven't had the history classes that fill them with lies and falsehoods about Sheol and Hasatan?"

Maalik didn't answer. I mentally berated myself.

"I started another argument, didn't I?" I hadn't meant to. It occurred to me that I wanted my lessons with Maalik to continue. His confidence inspired calmness in me, and the hunger to learn what he knew roared like a lion inside me whenever he was near.

"No," he said, his voice level. "You don't know what you don't know. It's foolish of me to allow your ignorance to anger me."

Well, if those weren't fighting words . . . I pushed down my own frustration. "It's you who doesn't understand. You can't believe everything they teach you."

"Like you believe everything that's been taught to you?" he returned, some fire entering his tone. He held up a hand and shook his head. "Sorry. That's not what I meant to say."

To heaven with my resolution. My ichor warmed. "Let's have it out. Tell me what you really think."

"Jez, I remember."

His words stopped me. They didn't fit in the context of our conversation. I frowned at him, and he stopped in front of the library doors.

"You remember what?" I asked. A nervous energy thrummed through me, as if I subconsciously knew his next words would be important.

"I remember the war." He turned to face me, his eyes dark and haunted. "I'm not parroting words and events that someone put in my head. I remember. I was there."

My breath caught, and I was captivated by his expression. "Your memory has returned?" I knew when the angels went to earth, a veil fell over their souls, covering the part of them that thrived in heaven, darkening what they knew of life beforehand. It seemed another trickery from heaven to me, another unfair move meant to coerce more souls to become Fallen. Heaven preached multiplying and replenishing, but they wanted to populate Sheol and keep the streets of Shamayim empty, reserved for an elite few who saw through the deception.

But their treachery would be our gain. Because each soul who became a Fallen became a soldier in Hasatan's army. And he was waging war on the mortals, dragging them down to become more Fallen in an endless cycle.

Except it would end, and soon. Delivering the dagger would be the beginning. Hasatan would have what he needed to begin his New Rule. And God would pay.

That was the plan. But why did I suddenly feel sick, shaky at my part in it?

The war in heaven hadn't happened the way it was taught to the students.

But I knew enough of Maalik's character to know he wouldn't lie to me.

Question swirled through my head, but I had no right to know. I had no right to ask if Maalik lost people, what he remembered. What happened to him in the war. I shivered, understanding his deep-seated hatred toward me now.

I hadn't even been there. But I couldn't tell him that without giving away who I was. I also wasn't sure it would even make a difference.

"I'm sorry," I said instead.

"Are you?" His golden brown eyes were sharp and sad as he scanned my face. "Do you even know what you should be sorry for?"

It was a sincere, serious question, and my breath caught. For moment I was lost in the depth of his gaze, which seemed to be an open door leading straight into his soul.

"Yes," I whispered, captivated by his stare. Even though, really, I didn't know. "I'm sorry."

His eyes held mine a moment longer, and a sigh breathed from his lips, seeming to emerge from deep within his soul. "Maybe."

With that one word hanging between us, he turned around and opened the library doors.

I followed him, feeling an ache in my chest, as if I'd wounded him somehow and in doing so wounded myself.

The sensation puzzled me.

Maalik settled himself at the same table we'd sat at before, and when he looked up at me, his expression had cleared. "Let's see what you remember."

I sat across from him and watched him write the familiar symbols on the paper. "A. For apple," I said immediately.

One eyebrow shot up, and Maalik appraised me. "Nice. You remember. Try this one."

"B," I said as the rounded letters appeared. My heart soared. This made sense to me. "Like baby or beneath or bad."

"Great job," Maalik said. "Let's go through the entire alphabet now." He wrote out a series of symbols on the paper and then flipped it around to show me. "What do you remember?"

I studied them and then touched the familiar ones. "A. B. P. L. E. W."

"Can you make their sounds?"

"I think so." I attempted it, and Maalik nodded.

"The next one is C." He circled the semi-circle and then wrote beneath it "CAT." He smirked. "One of the first words kids learn in first grade."

"First grade?" I looked up at him.

"It's the schooling system used in most countries on earth. You're learning English, but once you learn how to read one language, you'll be able to learn how to decipher any language."

"Really?" I remembered him saying that earlier, but it meant more to me now. I'd go from not being able to read any to being able to read them all. What a talent . . . what an asset I'd be to my father.

"Yeah, but you won't take that class until next year. It's a more advanced class."

"Ah." I nodded my understanding, but my thoughts were already tumbling around the time line.

That meant I had to keep this charade up for at least one more year. I needed that skill set.

Maalik continued with the rest of the alphabet, and each letter that matched a sound was like a light clicking on in my head.

"You're doing a great job," he said after we'd done the last letter. "Let's put the letters together to make words now."

I watched as he wrote a series of letters on the notepad, then flipped it over.

"Ah-RR-Cah-ah-duh-eye-ah," I read, stumbling over the sounds.

"Okay, so, there are a few tricks you need to know. But you're getting it, you're doing great. First, when you pair an R with a vowel, it changes the sound slightly. So this becomes 'AR'."

"Like 'where are you,'" I said, remembering the message from Kerubiel.

"That's right. In that case, the E at the end was silent."

So many rules. But instead of confusing me, they fell into place like a puzzle, each having a spot that helped make the image into a whole.

"And the A here has that longer sound. So it's CAY instead of CAW. And the I sounds like an E."

"Arcadia," I said, suddenly recognizing the word.

"You got it."

Maalik's lips curved upward, and his praise warmed my chest. I lowered my eyes, wanting to please him again. Wanting to see that smile directed at me.

But I couldn't want that. Those were human emotions. I couldn't crave his approval and my father's also.

No man could serve two masters. Even I knew that.

"Try this one out." He wrote another beneath the first word.

I studied the sweeping curve of the J. "J-E-Z." I looked up at him. "That's my name."

"Yes, it is."

Why did it give me such joy to see my own name there? To know how to write it? I took the paper from him and slowly wrote out, "M-A-L-E-" I paused at the end, aware that two separate letters made the same ending sound. Which was his? I took a guess and added, "K."

"Almost."

The smile he gave me warmed me to my toes. He took the notepad from me, and I inhaled when his fingers nearly touched mine. An electric energy tingled around them, and I curled my hands into fists and put them in my lap.

"M-A-A-L-I-K." He turned the screen around for me to see.

Strange spelling, and it didn't seem to apply to the rules and pronunciation I'd just learned. And yet . . . "The name fits you."

"I do like it." He flipped the notepad closed and put it into his bag.

A curious desire to know more about him pulled through me. "What was—" I shouldn't ask this. It felt too private. "What was your earth name?"

He lifted his eyes from his bag, once again studying me in a serious, probing manner. "Maybe I'll tell you someday." He stood up, his wings opening and expanding behind him before retracting again. "We're done for today."

"We didn't even argue." I stood up, unsure how to describe what I felt. I had enjoyed my time with him, and it saddened me that we were through. "When do we meet again?"

"In a week, I think."

He walked toward the door, and I matched his stride. Maalik glanced at me.

"I like the uniform on you."

"You do?" I looked down at the white shirt and pulled my sweater closer around me. "I always feel like I don't fit in."

You don't belong here. His first words to me flashed through my mind.

"It fits you," he said, echoing my own words back to me.

He moved ahead of me in the quad, and I lagged behind, holding my sweater against me with one hand and clutching my agenda with the other.

The uniform couldn't fit me. I was black, and hollow, and ugly next to the rest of the students.

Could it?

No. I shook off the thought. No matter how hard I tried or what it might look like, I would never be one of these angels of Light. I belonged with the Fallen. I was created with the Darkness. Nothing could ever change that.

CHAPTER SIXTEEN

Maalik and I had studied through the designated lunch time, which was fine, since food was not a requirement. Next on my schedule was the building with the weapons room. Now I could recognize the letters underneath, and I sounded them out with some pride at my own ability.

"Ur-eye-el Ar-mor-E," I said. Oh! Uriel.

I knew all about him, of course. The archangel had been a captain in the First War, right up there with Michael and the Favored One himself. He was a master of weaponry and had sentenced many of the Forsaken — or all those who followed Hasatan — to Sheol. Unlike Michael, who preferred to place the Forsaken into heaven's prison, Uriel's blade cut them down where they stood. His blazing Sword of Truth became the stuff of legend, and the archangel was referenced with a mixture of horror and awe even today.

So it should not surprise me that the armory would be named after him.

I was several minutes early to class, and I entered the building quietly, not wanting to draw attention to myself.

The room was empty. The gray wall covered with daggers and sabers beckoned me forward, calling to me.

I was alone with a golden opportunity in front of me. This was my chance to take a dagger. I took a step forward and hesitated. A thickness grew in my chest, a warning that I shouldn't do this.

I shook it off. I had no conscience. Heaven's curse was a gift; those of us in Sheol felt no difference between good and evil. The knowledge was lost to us. We knew only pain and pleasure, punishment and reward.

So why was a little voice whispering in my head, telling me to stop?

I took five more steps forward, and the blades were within my reach. I could take one now, conceal it on my person, and take it to Sheol the next time I was summoned. There was no one around to witness my thievery.

The ichor pounded in my ears. *Do it*, I told myself. I reached a hand out, but I shook so badly I worried I'd cut myself. And while the blade would only cause a temporary wound to my classmates, as a demon, one scratch could banish me for decades.

What does Hasatan want with this? I hadn't bothered to ask, because I was certain I didn't want to know. I had heard enough to understand his plans to create a weapon that could be used against the angels of Light. Against my classmates.

My classmates. The statement hung in my head, drawing up images of Iblis and Dara and Maalik and Jerahmeel. Could I really be the instrument to bring about their demise? If I delivered one of these daggers to my father, even if I did not strike the blow, I would be the cause of it.

I took a step back before I even realized I had. My hand lowered, and I took another step, then another.

When I looked again, I was on the other side of the room, the tantalizing wall of weapons out of reach. Why had I backed down? Was I so weak? "There will be another chance," I whispered at them.

The door to the armory opened, and by the time Master Ingram entered, flanked by several angel students, I was seated on the windowsill, quietly and innocently doing nothing.

"Oh." Master Ingram paused, something like surprise crossing her features when she saw me. "What are you doing here?"

"I got here early," I said.

She just stared at me. "But how did you get in? The door should have been locked."

"Well, it wasn't." Heaven's throne, was it usually? My heart sank within me at the realization that this might have been my one and only chance to take a dagger.

"I thought Barachiel didn't want you in here."

Now my face warmed, and the other students peered at me with piqued interest. Suddenly I wasn't just an early arrival; I was a curiosity. "The class is on my schedule," I said. "I guess he changed his mind."

"Just one moment." She separated herself from the students around her and moved into another corner of the room. Her lips moved as she spoke toward the wall, but I couldn't make out what she said, nor did I see anyone with her. Then she turned around and came back, a grimace trying to pass for a smile stretched across her lips.

"Eldermaster Barachiel says you can stay. He wants you to learn how we fight." Her white wings gave a single flap behind her, the only indication that perhaps she didn't love this plan. "But he says you cannot touch the weapons. Not yet."

I nodded as if I didn't care. Barachiel was right not to trust me, but it still grated on my nerves. I hadn't done anything to make him doubt me . . . yet. "That's fine."

I didn't need her permission. I'd get my hands on a dagger without her help.

I didn't need to check my schedule to know dinner was next. I took my time leaving the weapons classroom, though not because I planned to sneak back in and grab a dagger. There were too many eyes on me right now.

First, I had to earn their trust.

But my soul was troubled, and I didn't want to analyze why.

Maalik stopped me as I neared the cafeteria.

"Come with me," he said.

I looked at him in surprise and peered around him toward the tables inside, where the rest of our peers were getting their food. I'd skipped the midday nourishment, and my body surprised me by letting me know it wanted an evening meal. "I was going to eat."

He held up his bag and opened it, revealing an assortment of baked goods. "I've got food for us."

There was a jovial sparkle in his eye, something playful in the set of his mouth. I tilted my head, trying to make sense of it. "Why?"

"I want you to see something."

I could refuse. But I had no reason to. Whatever Maalik's intentions were, they were not meant to harm me. "Okay."

"This way." He stepped past me and hurried down the path, leaving me to fall into his wake.

A few other students were on the same path, and we made our way across the quad to the Gabriel Building. We weren't the only ones, and I walked slower to avoid bumping into the other angels moving toward the building.

Maalik reached the entrance first, and he stepped to the side and waited for me, one hand clutching the strap of his bag.

"You all right?" he asked.

I eyed the contents of his bag. "I could use some food."

He pulled out a pastry and held it out to me. "Your soul is starting to crave the Light," he said, his eyes studying my face as I took it.

"What do you mean?" I took a bite and exhaled, feeling a sense of wholeness rush through my soul as I did.

"As angels, the energy we expend during the day and during our classes is Light energy, energy we receive directly from Shamayim. It's replenished during Shema and prayers, but it's also infused into our food. Everything we eat helps us restore our Light."

I put the roll down. "But I'm not an angel," I whispered, catching his eye. Only Maalik knew this truth about me.

"Maybe you don't know what you are."

I opened my mouth to protest, but he rode over me.

"You're surrounded by Light. You're consuming it. A creature of Darkness would be burned at its presence. You're not."

He seemed satisfied with his assessment of me, but I shook my head.

"Eldermaster Barachiel is shielding me. Only because of him am I able to withstand the Light of Arcadia." I hated to remind Maalik of what I was. But he could not forget. I was a creature of Darkness.

"Maybe," he said, but something about his eyes made me think his words were not entirely truthful.

The other students had disappeared inside the building, and Maalik bobbed his head. "Let's go in. You're going to like this."

"What is it?" I asked, but he just opened the door and led the way.

The auditorium was dark, but a spotlight shown on the empty stage. Maalik scooted into the empty row in the back, and I followed, leaving one empty seat between us. A prickle of nervousness crept down my spine. This wasn't Shema, was it? If he'd led me here to join in prayer and devotion, I'd have to leave in a hurry. No way my demon heart would withstand the outpouring of spirituality.

Before I could speak or ask any questions, two lines of students filed onto the stage. Instead of wearing their uniforms, they were dressed in the more traditional white gowns, their white wings open and brilliant behind them, creating the effect of looking like a large dove instead of a dozen individual students. The girls wore a white scarf knotted on the side of the neck.

What were they going to do? I leaned forward in apprehension.

A girl on the front row opened her mouth, and a single, high-pitched note pierced the air.

I caught my breath, hanging on the pure, beautiful quality of that sound. I felt I could dive into it, be surrounded by its beauty. Before I could fully analyze it, three girls behind her opened their mouths and added their voices to her.

"What is it?" I whispered. "How do the sounds float in the air like that?"

"Those are sopranos," Maalik said. "And yes, their voices ring like a musical instrument. They probably had the talent on earth, but they've perfected it here."

They sang in a language I didn't know, and I couldn't interpret the words. But the message resonated with my soul, so beautiful that I felt as if the Darkness were peeling away from my heart, revealing a fragile, bruised soul, too raw for exposure.

The men in the row behind the women joined in, and the song rushed over me like a wave of heat. My eyes burned, and for a brief moment, I felt fear. Was this the moment my soul would incinerate and I would turn to dust? A feeling like I'd never known before welled up in my chest and burst forward, so overwhelmingly beautiful that my throat ached to sing, my voice wanted to join to theirs. I couldn't keep this to myself, and if I died in this moment, it would be in a moment of pure and exquisite joy.

Joy.

Was that what this was?

My shoulders trembled, and the burning in my eyes spilled forward, racing down my cheeks in rivulets of water. I wanted to hold the song in my fingers, press it into my heart.

Then the song ended, and the angels around me clapped heartily as the lights in the auditorium turned on. I didn't want it to end. I sat very still, hoping I could keep the feeling with me as long as I didn't move.

I sensed Maalik's eyes on me, and I shifted my head enough to meet his gaze. Something like triumph glowed there.

"I knew it," he said.

I tried to speak but couldn't. Blinking and regaining my composure, I tried again. "Knew what?" I whispered.

He reached a hand out toward mine, and I yanked mine back, fearing his touch. He met my eyes, an intensity burning in their golden depths that made my heart do a tumble.

"Knew you would like that," he said.

Somehow I didn't think that's what he'd been thinking.

The atmosphere seemed different at breakfast the next day.

Or was it just me?

Laughter broke out down the table as somebody sent a grape rolling past the trays. The joviality didn't end there, and someone else added a pancake to the food train. I let out a squawk of surprise when a piece of biscuit landed next to my tray.

"It's a game of Skyball!" someone shouted, and napkins and grapes shot across the table.

A napkin slapped Jerahmeel in the side of the face.

"Hey!" Jerahmeel said, his face going red. He jumped to his feet, balling the napkin up in his hand.

"I'm sorry," Daniel said, getting up as well. "We were just messing around."

Jerahmeel's fist tightened, and red and black colors shot off him like sparks. "Mess around with someone else," he growled, and then he stormed away, not even bothering to move his tray.

"What was that about?" I whispered, leaning my head toward Iblis. "I thought he was going to hit him!"

"I know!" Iblis breathed, her blue eyes large and luminous. "And I thought there wouldn't be fighting in heaven!"

Maalik and Grigori, another second year who always seemed to be near him, overheard, and they laughed at that statement.

"First of all, you're not in heaven," Maalik said, his golden brown eyes crinkling at the corners.

Didn't I know that.

"And second of all, while it doesn't happen as often as on earth, we still get into fights and brawls up here. How else do you think the First War happened?"

Daniel shook his head, his black hair bouncing from side to side. "I definitely had different ideas about the afterlife."

"We all did," Maalik said. He stood, shouldering his bag. "Depending on what religious beliefs we were taught."

"And in the end, we all end up here." Lieke stood also, mimicking Maalik. "Seems kind of pointless to have any kind of belief on earth."

"Not at all." Maalik waited as the rest of us gathered our things, then spoke again, as if he wanted to make sure we all heard. "Everything we learned on earth prepared us for life here. Some come better prepared than others. Some people fly through the academy training — quite literally — because they acquired more spiritual knowledge on earth. Others have to start at the beginning."

So maybe he just wanted to make sure I heard.

"Some aren't going to make it through at all," Daniel said, casting a glance after Jerahmeel.

"Yeah," Lieke snorted in agreement.

"You're being too hard on him," Iblis said. Her wings opened and closed gently, a soft breeze whispering over us. "We don't know what experience he's coming from."

We wandered out of the cafeteria, but we stayed as a group, and the conversation continued.

"What I do know is every time I look at him, I see red and black colors swirling off him. And I don't need a class to tell me what that means," Lieke replied.

"Is there a class on that?" I asked, my interest piqued. I certainly saw plenty of colors, but I didn't know what they meant, either.

"Not yet," Abaddon, another second-year, said. "You'll start your classes on Aura Interpretation in your second year."

I paused at the fountain and opened my book to check my schedule. I recognized the building lit up on the map, and I paused to mouth the symbols beneath.

"Du-mah Bu-il-ding. Building." I smiled as I figured out the pronunciation, even if it had been tricky. Then my eyes flickered to the top, where I read, "In-tro to Cel-es-ti-al His-tor-ee." Ha! I'd gotten that also.

"Looks like you're going the same place I am."

I turned toward Kerubiel as he approached, and my body flushed warm for some reason. It was both a pleasant and unnerving sensation. "Hi."

"Hi." He gave me an easy smile and shoved his hands in his pockets as he matched my stride. Today, shades of orange, brown, and green rolled off him.

"What class is everyone else going to?" I nodded toward the rest of my dormmates. I spotted a few of his, as well. They had already gone inside the Dumah Building, but I knew I hadn't seen them in my class last time.

"Most everyone has a history class right now. But we go to different ones. You and I get the history class for dummies."

"For dummies?" I furrowed my brow, unfamiliar with the word.

"No offense intended. It's how they see us. Not how I do."

That did not clear things up. "But why?"

"Well, I guess we didn't learn enough about heaven in our last life. Or what we did learn, they need us to unlearn it."

"Indoctrinate us with falsehoods," I said. But this time my usual fury was tempered with another, trembling emotion: fear. A nagging fear that maybe I was the one believing falsehoods.

"Exactly. Make us see things the way they want us to."

"Mm-hmm." Why was I so threatened by what they had to say?

Kerubiel opened the door for me, and I stepped inside, and then I drew to a halt so suddenly he almost crashed into me.

"Jez! What is it?"

"Look!" I sidestepped to the left, putting a few more inches between us, and pointed. My finger shook, and I hoped he didn't notice.

Kerubiel craned his head and laughed out loud.

Two angels stood in the next hall over, their arms locked around each other, their faces attached at the mouth, the embrace both passionate and lustful.

CHAPTER SEVENTEEN

"What are they doing?" I hissed.

"It's called making out." His tone was mocking. "Never tried it?"

"But here—in Arcadia—" I couldn't get my words out. They tripped over each other, and my eyes darted into the corners of the hallways, waiting to see the wrath of God descend upon them, to see them incinerated to energy particles right before my eyes.

"What's the big deal?" Kerubiel eyed me.

"It's forbidden!" I screeched.

The angels heard me. They turned their faces our direction, but I took off down the hall.

"Jez, wait!" Kerubiel hurried to catch up with me. He reached for my arm, but I slammed away from him, taking deep breaths to calm my heart.

"First the touching," I gasped out. "Now this—this—"

"Kissing?"

"Kissing!" I knew this word. This one physical act had led to the downfall of millions of souls. It was the gateway sin to damnation. "How?"

Kerubiel studied me. "It's a nice thing."

"That's why it's forbidden!"

The classroom door opened, and Master Remiel stepped out. He looked at us both with concern on his face. "Is everything all right?"

Kerubiel turned to me. "I think she—"

"Everything's fine." I flung myself past them, careful not to brush against either of them.

My thoughts whirled in confusion.

Maalik had to have been telling the truth. Touch was not forbidden.

What else was I mistaken about?

"All right, class," Master Remiel said, stepping up to the white board. "We're going to continue where we left off last time." He drew a line across the board. "But first, did anyone go the library and study any of the topics we discussed?"

He swiveled to face us, and I thought how sad it was that he'd retracted his wings. His magnificent white wings should never be hidden.

Most of the students lowered their heads or dropped their eyes, but I didn't. I just shook my head. I couldn't even properly read yet.

"Great, then I know what to go over." He smiled, and the other students lifted their gazes, chuckling in appreciation also. Above the line on the board, he drew a giant circle. "When we were created by the Father, we lived here."

Zophiel raised her hand. "Created how?"

"You'll learn about the creation of souls in your third year biology class. For now, just understand that the Father formed each of us into spiritual beings."

"All of us?" a boy with curly blond hair and wearing the colors of the Emet dormitory asked. "That's billions of people."

"Billions and billions, Camael. And the Father created all of us before any other creation."

Kerubiel gave a derisive snort. "I bet he was tired after all that."

"Indeed. A day of rest has always been a part of the schedule."

"So he created all of us." Zophiel leaned forward. "What did we do?"

"We lived. This was in Shamayim. Time wasn't measured for us the way it is now; we don't have a sense of how long we were there."

"Like, we lived in houses?" A girl with long red hair chewed on the end of her stylus. I couldn't tell what dorm she was from, as she hadn't changed out of her earth clothing yet. She had a screen open on her book, and new words had been written across the top. "Like we did on earth?"

"In a similar way, Lailah. We organized according to friends and relations. Not families at this time, since such a thing didn't exist. All of us were family, but with so many of us, it didn't feel familial. It felt friendly.

"But we were also primitive. We had feelings and no way to channel them. We had no physical bodies, even though we were created in a semblance of the form we are today. We couldn't feel, we couldn't touch."

Couldn't touch. Those words resonated with me. I looked down at my hands and ran them over my arms, covered by the soft sweater of my dorm. I couldn't touch.

I couldn't touch.

Maybe it was just me.

"We could only learn and develop so much in Shamayim, and our father saw this. He knew we needed a place to go where we could develop not only physically, but spiritually and mentally. So he created a world and gave us our first task: come up with an idea involving the new world that would help achieve this goal." Remiel smiled, though the expression seemed tinged with sadness. "This was the last time all of our father's children worked together on a project."

"What happened?" Camael asked.

I knew what happened. My father submitted a plan, a perfect plan. Each one of them would be sent to earth with a body and a clear directive from which they could not stray. Guaranteed redemption. Guaranteed salvation. It was benevolent and loving and unselfish.

But the Favored One had a different plan, and for even considering a contrary way, Hasatan was slammed down to Sheol, a new place created just for him.

Not that he went quietly.

I did not speak, though. I wanted to hear how Remiel would tell this story.

"Several plans were put forth, each of them holding merit. There was some squabbling and disagreement on our parts, but in the end, we knew the final judgment lay with the Father."

"Several plans?" I interrupted. I furrowed my brow. "There were just two."

The other students looked at me, but I kept my eyes steady on Remiel.

"You are misinformed, Jez. Thousands of excited, eager-to-please angels submitted a plan."

"No." I shook my head. "Only two. And for even attempting to subterfuge the plan of the Favored One, the second was cast away into Darkness."

"First of all, the proper term is the Firstborn. Now let's analyze what you think you know. From your perception, there were two angels vying for their plan to be chosen. Am I correct?"

"Yes."

"But one never really had a chance. So by simply submitting his plan in opposition of the chosen plan, he was punished. Correct?"

His eyes were steady on me, unerring, and I nodded, finding my voice to be hidden.

"My statement that thousands of plans were submitted conflicts with this knowledge because it would mean either thousands were also punished like the one you reference, or that the one you reference was not punished the way you have been taught to believe. Also correct?"

He'd gotten to the heart of the matter, and his words struck a nerve. I sank lower in my seat, wishing the other students would look somewhere else. Now my voice whispered out of me. "Yes."

"Let your belief be challenged then, Jez, and this will not be the first time. For I also submitted a plan to the Father. I can even pull it up and show you, for my memory of the first existence is strong and clear."

"First existence?" Lailah interrupted. Her stylus scribbled like crazy across her screen. "I thought our earth life was the first existence."

"It's the first one you can remember right now, but it was your second existence. And this is your third. All of them tie together into one eternal life." He addressed her question before facing me again. "My plan was presented to all of us souls, along with thousands of others. For eons of time we debated the plans. We discussed the pros and cons while our Father readied the interplanetary system for us, preparing us to live on a world with physical bodies.

"Eventually, all but two plans were rejected, including my own. While I felt the sting of not having my plan chosen, I recognized the flaws in my own thinking, for we had spent decades debating them by now. There were two plans left, and they were similar in almost every way."

"What were they?" Zophiel asked, her eyes alight with interest.

"Both involved us coming to earth and procreating as man and woman to receive our bodies. Both allowed us to be born, grow, and die. But one of the plans wanted to make all the decisions for us so we would never know hurt or sin or pain. It guaranteed a way for us to return to Shamayim with the Father, not losing a single soul to Darkness. The other plan called for each of us to fall and stumble along the way, to make our way through mortal life with no memory of heaven, to feel pain and sorrow and sin."

"There!" I blurted out, sitting up straight in my seat. "Isn't it obvious which is the better plan? Why would anyone choose to feel pain? Why would any caring *father* require his children to go through that?" My heart pounded in my chest at the boldness of my outburst, and I heard the murmurs of agreement around me.

"That was what many of us said then, too. Why? Why would we want that? And then the Father pointed out, if we didn't feel pain, we couldn't feel pleasure. If we didn't know sorrow, we couldn't know joy. And if we never fell into sin, we couldn't escape into the Light. Once that was explained to us, we made our decision. We didn't want a half-life on earth. We wanted the chance to experience it all. The good and the bad."

"But not everyone," I said, rattled. The way he described it, the other plan did sound better. Even to me, it was appealing.

Pleasure. Joy. Light. I wanted to feel those things.

"Not everyone," Remiel agreed. "What do you know of this part, Jez?"

I shook my head. I wasn't about to elucidate the situation. My knowledge was not the same as theirs, and I didn't know who was right at the moment.

I did know that Hasatan did not go down without a fight.

"While most of us agreed that the plan the Father chose was the correct one, a good number of angels did not. They wanted the experience the second plan provided: going to earth, getting a body, and a guaranteed return." Remiel let out a sigh. He turned to the white board and drew three stick people on one end. On the other end, he drew six more. "One third of the souls rebelled, pulling away and vowing to see the second plan through to the end. What followed next was the First War."

Remiel put down his stylus and faced us, forcing his lips to curve upward into a smile. "We will start on the First War in our next class. In the meantime, are there any questions?" His gaze scanned the room before landing on me. I shook my head.

"Again, I encourage you to go to the library and look up what you've learned. Many great books have been written on the subject."

I refrained from an eye roll. Yes, many great books written by angels. How unbiased could they be?

Master Remiel watched me as I got up and left the classroom. But I had nothing more to say on the matter.

"You seem to know a lot about this," Kerubiel said, catching up to me as I exited the building.

For once, I didn't want to talk to him. He confused me. I quickened my pace instead. "I know some things."

"How?"

"I just do," I snapped.

He lifted his hands and stopped walking. "Fine. Jeez. Sorry."

I could tell from his posturing that I'd offended him. But I didn't care.

I wanted answers, and I had no way to get them.

"For what it's worth," Kerubiel called after me, "I think the other plan would have been better also."

I stopped and turned to face him. I studied him, a quiver in my lips. "I'm not so sure," I said.

"You seemed pretty sure in there."

"I'm not anymore. And those who chose it paid a price."

His eyes widened. "So some did choose it? They got to go to earth and live out the second plan?"

"No." I turned around and continued marching to my dorm. "It didn't play out that way."

※ ※

They said all of the books ever written were in the library.

I went there after dinner, running my fingers over the spines of words too lengthy for me to sound out.

What was I looking for, anyway? It was like I'd said before. The only thing I'd find here would be angel doctrine.

Demons couldn't read. They certainly couldn't write.

But they had communicated with humans before. Perhaps a human might have written their story.

Even as I considered it, I disregarded the thought. Such a book could exist, but the distorted words and confusion behind them would not shed any light on my troubled soul.

I returned to the dorm, glad that Iblis had gone to Shema. I still couldn't go. I feared what so much Light would do to me.

I took my sweater off and stood in front of the mirror, tracing the chains on my arms. As long as the chains bound me to Sheol, the presence of anything holy could immortally wound me. It was why Barachiel had shielded me when he brought me here, because even the Light from the academy was too much for me at first.

But I had grown accustomed to it enough to tolerate portions of it. I wasn't quite sure what that meant.

I dug my finger into one of the chain loops on my arm, feeling the thickness of the metal as it wrapped around my skin. It was more than just a mark. I swiveled slightly and looked at my bare back in the mirror. Not even tiny humiliating wings like I had let Iblis believe marred my skin.

I sighed and put the sweater back over my arms, a heavy weight in my chest. There was a part of me that wanted to be what everyone else here was. But I carried these constant reminders that I couldn't be. It wasn't up to me. Everyone was free to decide except me.

Iblis had her assignments spread out around her desk. I sat down at her chair and rifled through the books, curious about what she was studying but not curious enough to try to read.

The dorm door opened, and I stood as Iblis came in. I worried she would be upset about me looking at her books, but then I saw her red eyes and the tears on her face.

"You've been crying," I said.

She rolled her eyes and dropped her agenda on the desk. "Yeah. Stupid emotions."

She sank down onto her bed. I hesitated, worried about getting too close. But she needed me. She was my friend, perhaps my only friend. I sat down beside her, keeping very still to prevent myself from bumping her. "What's wrong?" Something had to be wrong for her to be crying. I had been the cause of tears too often not to know that.

My gut twisted within me.

"It's nothing, really. Shema talked about inclusion and acceptance, and it made me think of Jason."

Jason. I racked my brain, trying to put a face to the name. This wasn't someone I knew. "Is he in our dorm?"

She gave a dry laugh and shook her head. "No. He's my boyfriend. Was my boyfriend. I'm dead now, so . . ." She shrugged. "I don't imagine he still thinks of me as his girlfriend."

Ah. I remembered now the conversation we'd had about him several weeks earlier. "But you still feel connected to him," I said, leaning back.

Iblis nodded."Of all the people I miss, he's the one I miss the most. Not because I loved him the most, but because whatever connection we had is gone now and will never happen again."

"That is sad," I said. It had not occurred to me before that such a thing would be sad. I searched my brain for a solution. "Maybe he'll come here too."

Iblis wiped her tears away. "I would never wish that on him. He would have to die as a teenager to come to the academy. I don't want that for him. I want him to live a long and happy life. To live. And that means without me."

"But he will die someday," I said, grasping at straws. "Maybe then you will find each other."

"By then he'll have married. He will have fallen in love again. I will be a distant memory." The pain showed in her eyes.

"What if he doesn't? What if he keeps on loving you until the day he dies?"

There was a flicker of something on her face, and she said, "Well, I will definitely still be here." But then she sighed, and the flicker was gone. "What kind of life would that be? To spend every day pining for the dead? Besides, he is human. Humans can't stay devoted to something they can't see for very long."

Oh, there was so much truth in that.

I retired to my own bed, thinking of Iblis and her Jason. Would they be together if he were here? Would they *kiss*, like the angels I'd seen in the hallway?

Were all of the angels kissing except me?

We reposed in silence, letting our minds reflect over the happenings of the day. I closed my eyes and drifted away into unconsciousness, a semi-dream state where I could imagine a different kind of world. One where I could be who

I wanted to be. One where I got to choose. One where I had wings.

One where I could kiss.

An angel's face popped into my mind, and the desire to touch my lips to his burned so poignantly in my chest that for a moment I worried I'd caught on fire.

Jez.

The whispered call jarred me from my rest, and I sat up, guilt racing through my veins. My traitorous thoughts consumed me.

Jez, came the call again.

I sat up. He wanted to talk to me? Fine. I had questions also.

CHAPTER EIGHTEEN

I made my way out of the dorm and through the quad, to the fountain which chattered quietly into the silent night. The moon glowed overhead, almost as bright as the sun.

I looked into the waters of the fountain and watched as they churned and blackened. There was my way to Sheol, and I didn't want to take it. Sighing, I jumped feet-first into the chilled water.

The chains around my arms tightened, pulling me down. Pulling me home. My feet landed on solid ground, and the dry, heated air warmed me immediately, sucking the moisture from my skin and clothing. I turned, searching in the dark for my father.

"Report, daughter."

The voice came from behind me, and I swiveled again. A shadow faced me, dark and scintillating, the outline barely visible against the flames of hell in the distance. I swallowed as fear leapt up from my belly. The wrong word, and he'd have my hide. "I do not have the dagger."

"And why not?"

"I was interrupted when I was about to take it. They are watching me. They are more suspicious of me."

"Of course. Judging you before they know you. Self-righteous as ever. You will have to be sneaky. You will retrieve a dagger."

Again, the command, and my body flinched. I would have no choice next time but to take it. "Yes, my lord. But when I do, I will likely be expelled from the academy. There are many more things I can learn from them if I'm permitted to stay."

"Such as?"

"There are advanced classes for second years. We're taught how to use our powers. They teach us how to read different languages. I could become quite useful."

"Yes, you could," he said, but there was something else in his tone. Like he wondered at my motivations.

I wasn't sure of them myself.

"You are not the only one, you know."

I stiffened. "The only what?"

"The only one I have my hopes on. There is another besides you who can accomplish your mission."

My heart stuttered slightly. His warning was clear: I was dispensable. He could destroy me as readily as he created me. "Good for you," I said, keeping calm. "You won't need someone else. I will fulfill the mission."

"Good."

He sounded smug and sure of himself. I lifted my chin, thinking of my questions. "They said there were many plans submitted before the First War. Not just yours and his. That you weren't punished for submitting a plan."

"Did they say that?" A dark note entered his tone. "And what did you say?"

"I said what I've always been taught," I snapped back. "That you were treated unjustly."

"And they said?"

"That I was mistaken."

"Are you?"

I took a step closer, trying to make out his features in the darkness. But he remained wrathed in shadow, as always. I did not even know what my own father looked like. "What about the promises you made?"

"I've kept my promises." A hand snatched out of the shadow, long, knobby fingers with misshapen nails. It wrapped around my arm, igniting the metal beneath my skin, and I screamed as the razor sharp pain cut through me. "The New Rule is about to begin. You will usher it in, or you will be eliminated. Your entire purpose, the reason for your creation, is now."

The pain wrapped around my neck, my shoulders, entered my head and inflamed my mind. My cries melted into those of a thousand other anguished souls, and my edges frayed, sparks of energy breaking off and soaring away.

"The fulfilling of all things is at hand. And my kingdom will be a part of it. My kingdom will be the New Rule. I have foreseen the days to come."

He released me, and I gathered the pieces of my being together, sinking to my knees and letting the energies drift back to me. I trembled from the mere memory of the excruciating pain.

His hand fell near my head, and I flinched, but his flesh did not touch mine. "Come, child. You've won many souls for my kingdom. Now it is time to fulfill your destiny and bring me the academy students." He chuckled grimly. "Free will? We will offer them a choice. Either they join me, or their souls will be set free. Permanently."

I shuddered. The daggers could not destroy an immortal soul, only dispatch the energy particles. And the daggers couldn't hurt beings of Light.

But Hasatan knew that. So there must be something else he had planned.

The sharp nails dug into the scalp of my head, and again the pain from his touch seared through me. "You will bring me a dagger. My time is almost at hand." He inhaled sharply. "I can smell it."

He released me, and I collapsed on the hard ground, my fingers grasping for something to hold onto, something to ease their trembling. Fear rocketed through my veins, and I panted, the sour taste of sulfur in the back of my throat.

"Go now and do," he said, his voice haughty. "Retrieve the dagger and await my next command."

"I will do it," I said.

And I would. There was no failing this time.

I did not sleep when I returned to my dorm. I lay on my bed, staring at the light glow of the ceiling, sick and twisted thoughts churning within me.

I rolled over onto my side and faced the wall. Tears pricked my eyes.

For the first time, I understood.

I wasn't bound by free will. Choices didn't trap us. They gave us options.

But I was not created by their Father. I was created by Hasatan, and he had me playing by a different rule book. I had no choice.

The hot, stealthy tears dripped from my eyes and over my nose and down the side of my face. Each trail left a burning path down my skin. Remorse was poison to a demon, having a conscience was toxic to a dark angel. But I did not touch them or try to wipe them away. I deserved them.

As soon as the sun rose, so did I. I pulled my sweater tight around me and left the dorm, heading straight for the library. It was time for breakfast, but Maalik would come here eventually for our study session. I would wait.

I sat in the library and traced circles with my stylus on the table. My agenda dinged with a message, and I opened it, wondering who it would be from. Dreading who it might be from.

Kerubiel's face shown from the little icon. I mouthed the letters as I read them out loud. "Where di-d — did — ya-oo-u — ya-oo — " That one gave me trouble until I realized I was over thinking it. Then I got it from context. "You. Where did you g-o la-s-t na-i — " The rest of the written word was unfamiliar and confusing, but it hardly mattered. I knew what Kerubiel was asking, and a chill ran down my spine. I stared at my screen, unable to respond. Had he seen me? How much had he seen?

The table jostled, pulling me from my thoughts as Maalik settled his bag on top and sat across from me.

"You skipped breakfast," he said, then he peered closer at me. "Are you all right?"

I shook my head. "I mean, yes. Yes, I'm fine."

"What you really mean is, you're not." Maalik leaned toward me across the table. "What's wrong?"

How could I even begin to tell him about the secret rendezvous with the devil last night? Not to mention my mission? And now Kerubiel, who may have seen me cavorting with demons? So I just shook my head again. "I still have trouble fitting in."

"It's not even the middle of your first year. By the end of this year, GAA will feel more like home than anywhere you've ever lived." He gave me a curious look. "If you've even had a home before."

"Sort of." I did not want to talk about my previous existence. Instead, I remembered what Kerubiel and I had seen yesterday. "Maalik, I have to ask you. You said . . ." I took a deep breath, feeling as if just speaking about this bordered on blasphemy. "You said touching is not forbidden."

"Right."

A slight smile quirked the right side of his lips, and the sudden wonder of what his lips would feel like if they touched mine leapt into my mind, and a strange tickle rushed up my belly. I forced my eyes to remain focused on his face. "But yesterday I saw two angels . . . kissing. Surely kissing is forbidden!"

"Ah." He gave a wistful sigh. "Of course it's not. Why would you think that?"

"Because it is expressing a carnal lust. A sinful desire. Even in Arcadia such things cannot be allowed!"

"Jez." Maalik folded his fingers together, his gaze serious. "So there are laws and rules in heaven, but it's not the way you imagine. That's a fourth year class. We do have to learn to tame our carnal desires, and there are acts we are expected to refrain from for our own good. But for now, in Arcadia, we're to let our consciences guide us. The closer we are to the Light, the better decisions we make. On our own, without having someone set down rules for us. By the time we get to be third years, most angels are walking in the Light and living by the rules of heaven without having to think about it."

"So then kissing's not allowed?"

Maalik chuckled. "Kissing's always allowed. It's not just an expression of sinful desire, as you put it. It's also an expression of love and devotion."

Love and devotion. The words sent a shiver down my spine. If he touched his lips to mine, would it mean he was devoted to me? I banished the troubling thought. "But how? How is that permitted? Angels can't possibly be encouraged to nurture such feelings!"

"And why not?" A challenge entered his expression, and he settled back, his jaw tightening. "We went to earth to gain bodies and discover the glories of being a physical entity. Our bodies are different now, but we haven't forgotten. We remember the joy of food, and sleep, and a warm bath, and a mother's kiss, and the caress of a hand. These feelings and understandings make us stronger. They make us better. Why would we want to forget them or pretend they don't exist?"

He brought up excellent points. But I could not wrap my mind around it. "I thought—I thought heaven was the one who decreed such things as forbidden."

"Sounds like we have a lot to clear up from your former education."

"Yes." I nodded, my eyes glazing over as I studied the marbled flooring beneath the table. "Maybe we do."

"So I thought we'd get started."

Something heavy thumped on the table, and I lifted my face to see a thick book resting in front of Maalik. He met my eye and grinned.

"Reading material."

I arched an eyebrow. "You want me to read that?"

"We'll start with this. You're very smart and acquiring knowledge quickly. Why read about Jack and Jill when we can read Genesis?"

My heart gave a little patter of uneasiness. "Genesis?" Something about the word had my skin crawling.

Maalik opened the book and turned it around to face me. "Right here," he said, pointing at a large and gilded letter C.

"Ca-ha—" I began.

"Ch. Those two letters put together make a new sound."

"Right." Not off to a great beginning. "Chuh-ap-ter Oh—"

"This is another weird one. Sometimes, O makes a 'wuh' sound. That happens here. So it's the number one."

"Gotcha." I breathed out slowly. "Chapter one. In—"

"Th also makes a new sound. That's 'the.'"

"In the be-ginn-ing, God—" A shudder ran through me when I said the name. Had I ever dared utter that word aloud? My face grew hot, as did my torso.

"Remember R? It does interesting things to consonants, also."

I listened as Maalik told me the rules, nodding my head and wanting to tell him I wasn't ready, I couldn't read this.

But another part of me tingled with anticipation. I was reading holy writ!

"Keep going."

"God cre-ate-d the he-a-ven—"

"Just heaven."

"And the eh-ar-th." The heat was increasing, creeping up my neck and into my hairline. "And the earth w-as wi-th-oh—"

"Without."

"Without fuh-or-m, and voh-id." I stopped and fanned my face. The warmth on my arms was growing unpleasant.

"Good job with that word. Void. Keep going."

"And dark-ness was up-on the fuh-ac—"

"This is another rule. When you have an e . . ."

His explanation evaporated around me as I plucked at the sleeves of my sweater. Hot. I was getting too hot.

"Jez? Start there at 'face.'"

I started up again, only now it was with eagerness to finish. I needed out of the library. "Face of the dee-p." Fire! Fire on my arms! "And the spi-rit of God—"

The moment the word left my mouth, flames exploded from my body.

I heard Maalik yell, but all I could think was how I needed to get the flames off me. I screamed and tore at my sweater and the button-up shirt I'd put on beneath, but both had burnt into ash.

It was the chains. They glowed red hot, flames wicking off them, daring to burn anything that got close. My body wracked with torment, the burning fire licking my exposed skin.

"Be still, Jez!" Maalik had taken off his jacket and moved to wrap it around me, but I shied back.

"Don't touch me!" I cried.

"I'm trying to help you!" he shouted back.

"And I'm trying to protect you!" I screamed.

That stopped him, but only for a moment. Then he thrust the jacket over my shoulders.

I clutched at it, feeling the satiny cloth inside as it dampened the heat of the chains.

Maalik reached out as if to grab my arm, and I was too beat to stop him. But instead of closing around my arm, an fiery jolt shot through me to him that had him yelping and jerking backward.

I closed my eyes and sank to the ground, letting his jacket billow around me. There must be something good in him, something strong enough to put out the flames, because his jacket soothed my skin like a healing balm.

"Let me see." He crouched in front of me, a healthy distance between us this time.

"It's all right." I shook my head. "They've burned me before."

"This was my fault."

I looked up and saw the torment on his face. Why did he care if he hurt me, a demon of Darkness? Not too long ago, I was certain that if given the choice, he would have gladly sliced me through with an archangel's sword.

"Let me see your arms," he said again.

I removed his jacket and held my arms out, hands fisted. My skin had been burned, but the burns faded as we watched, soaking back into the chain-ridden skin of my body.

The chains did not disappear. They still glowed, though the heat had lessened. Instead of orangish-red, they glowed a faded copper color.

Almost as if testing to see if it would happen again, Maalik snatched at my wrist with his fingers. The same painful shock rippled between us, and he sucked in a breath and pulled back.

"It's forbidden," I said, understanding crashing down around me. "It's forbidden for us. We cannot touch." Not for them. But for us.

"You . . ."

"The Forsaken," I said, clarifying. "We never got bodies. We don't get to experience all the glories of being a physical entity." For the second time in one day, my eyes filled with tears, and the sadness and unfairness caused me to bow my head and shudder.

Maalik sat beside me without saying a word. When I finally lifted my head, his eyes were still on me.

"I am sorry."

"You?" I scoffed. "What do you have to be sorry for?"

"Many things. Let's start with my ignorance. I thought I knew everything about you when I met you, but I know nothing about those from Sheol."

"Aren't you taught about us in your history classes?"

He shook his head. "We learn about the First War and the part the Renegades played in it. Third and Fourth years can take a specialized history class that delves into the underworld, but most of us as Guardians don't need that information. So my knowledge of you was mostly hearsay and preconceived notions I brought with me from earth."

I attempted a smile. "So I'm not as bad as you feared?"

"I didn't know the demons could feel."

"Well, of course they can!" I said.

"I mean, I knew they could. But I thought they only felt evil and malice and Darkness. Not . . . the same things I feel."

I fell silent. He wasn't too far off on that. My feelings had been changing and developing ever since I'd arrived in Arcadia. In Sheol, there was no place for such tender and weak emotions.

"And I apologize for not knowing what would happen if you read the Word. I should have cleared it with Barachiel first."

"He might not have known, either," I said. "Since none from Sheol have ever been able to read."

"Perhaps," he acknowledged with a head bob. "And I'm sorry you can't touch." His voice lowered to a hush, and the fingers of his left hand reached out toward me, tracing the space on the floor between our hands.

The sincerity in his words opened something in my chest, as if it had been a closed box and now Maalik had unlocked it and slowly wedged it open. The pain in my arms dissipated even more. "It's all right. I'm used to that one."

He nodded at me, his eyes moving to include the chains, now a dark gray, that wrapped around my arms. "What's with the chains?"

"They are a reminder." Like I needed one. "That I'm not one of you. The ends of the chains rest in Sheol. That is where my home is. Unlike you, I am not a product of free will. At any moment, if my master calls me home, I must obey." I lifted my gaze and met his as I said the last words. Guilt and displeasure teased my insides, and I hoped fervently he would remember my words in the days to come.

"Come on." Maalik stood and waited for me to join him. "Let's visit Barachiel and make sure you're all right."

"I'm quite fine now," I protested, not anxious to see the archangel who perhaps also knew about my midnight escapades.

Maalik would not hear of my protestations, though. He dragged me along to Barachiel's office in the administration building, casting glances my way with a concerned expression on his face.

CHAPTER NINETEEN

"Barachiel is not in," Master Selaphiel said, greeting us at Barachiel's office. "Can I help with something?"

I saw Maalik's hesitation as he glanced at me again, wearing his jacket now since my own clothes had been burned to ash. I fingered the silken fabric inside, the rougher exterior of the woven cloth, and wondered how I could feel this so easily but not touch Maalik.

Because I was a demon. I thought the judgment against me harsh and unfair, and I resented it.

"We had an issue during our study time. I feel like I should speak with Eldermaster Barachiel."

Maalik met Selaphiel's eyes. I expected her to take offense or try to coax the information out of him, but she merely nodded. "I will summon him. Come inside. He will come when he is done teaching."

We stepped inside and sat in chairs just within the office. I waited for Master Selaphiel to pick up a book similar to mine so she could call Barachiel, but instead she made a motion in the air as if writing with her finger. "Can I get either of you two something to drink while you wait?"

I shook my head, but Maalik said, "Water would be nice."

While Selaphiel stepped away, Maalik leaned toward me and whispered, "It's polite for humans to offer a drink while you're waiting for something, and it's customary to accept, even if you only ask for water."

"But I'm not thirsty," I said, furrowing my brow. "And I'm not human."

"None of us are," Maalik replied. "It's a comfort thing. It makes us feel a little bit more human. And we liked being human."

I nodded, understanding. "And if I want to appear human also, I should try to act this way."

"Well." Maalik lifted one shoulder. Behind him, his wings shifted as if they wanted to unfold before they remembered the cramped space of the chair. "I was thinking more so you could experience a little of what it's like to be human. Since you never — never mind."

Maalik shifted away from me, and awkwardness fell between us. I didn't know how to broach it, so I remained silent.

Selaphiel returned with a glass of water for Maalik, then she sat at Barachiel's desk. She kept her eyes down, her fingers occasionally moving across a flat surface I couldn't see. After only a few moments, Barachiel shimmered into the room.

Maalik stood at once. "Master Barachiel, thank you for coming."

I stood also, though I was still trying to get over his abrupt appearance.

"I'll give you some privacy," Selaphiel said, and she left the office.

"Did you fly here?" I asked, unable to keep the questions at bay.

"Of course." Barachiel smiled at me like a doting grandfather, as if all my questions were reasonable.

"But we didn't see you. And your wings aren't out."

"My wings are always out. You just can't always see them. The same goes for my personage. I can render myself intangible by shifting to a different plane when I wish. It makes it easier to maneuver through solid objects."

"Of course," I murmured, echoing his earlier words. But the rules of this dimension were so different from the one I came from. Assuming they would be the same had been a mistake.

"So what has happened? Are the two of you arguing again?" Barachiel looked back and forth between us, his eyes falling upon Maalik's jacket across my shoulders. He blinked once and then focused his gaze on Maalik. "Or not?"

"No." Maalik shook his head, his posture respectful and proper. "We were doing our study, and I thought it would be, ah, appropriate—" his eyes cast downward for a moment before looking up. "I decided to introduce her to the Word."

I waited to see if Barachiel would react to this confession, but he only nodded.

"Trying to be funny?" he said, and Maalik's cheeks turned a rosy hue.

"Maybe a little," he admitted.

"So what was the problem?"

"She—" Now Maalik was more hesitant, glancing at me and stumbling over his words. "They had an unexpected affect. They . . . she . . ."

Heaven's throne. I'd have to help him out. "My chains began to burn. They caught my uniform on fire and burned it to ash."

Barachiel's eyebrows shot up. "That is unexpected."

"So it's not my fault?" Maalik exhaled. "I thought it was something I did."

"It was something you did. You had her read the Word. But the result was unanticipated and certainly not your fault." Now Barachiel's eyes bored into mine. "I placed a protection around you when you arrived in Arcadia, Jez. A protection to keep you from being injured by the holier Light surrounding you. That protection should last through your entire first year. It should include any additional Light and knowledge you acquire at the academy. Unless the protection has been weakened or violated, you should not be susceptible to heavenly wards and enchantments."

My mind reeled as I tried to take in the full meaning of what he said. "There are heavenly enchantments?"

Barachiel nodded. "For the safety of demon and mankind alike. Some things should not be known, so there are safeguards to keep certain knowledge from falling into the wrong hands at the wrong time."

"So you do intentionally hide knowledge from us," I said, my anger growing.

Barachiel did not answer, but I saw a fire of challenge flicker in his eyes. "Can you think of anything that might have caused your protection to weaken?"

A question with a question. My stomach churned as I remembered my visits to Sheol.

"What sorts of things could cause the protection to weaken?" Maalik asked, his eyes steady on Barachiel.

"Breaking the academy rules. Breaking the celestial laws. Inviting a demon into your life. Allowing devils to influence your choices."

Hanging out with demons in Sheol.

Barachiel did not list that action, but my conscience pricked.

My conscience! The realization that I had one and it was speaking to me made me gasp out loud. Both Barachiel and Maalik looked at me.

"You have something to say? Something that might enlighten us?"

I knew the truth burned in my eyes. I stared back at Barachiel, shame heating my face. I did not want Maalik to know the depth of my wickedness. "I might know what I did," I hedged.

"So you did do something?" Maalik asked. His wings fluttered open.

"It wasn't intentional," I said, and I couldn't meet his eyes.

"I will take care of this, Maalik. Let me see your hands."

He hesitated, and I looked over at him, for the first time wondering about him.

Barachiel was still waiting, and Maalik held his hands out, palms up. Black fissures lined his skin.

"Go to the Healing ward. We'll remove the Darkness from you."

My heart sank, and I turned my eyes away, unable to look at him. My Darkness had polluted his Light.

He turned and marched out of the office, wings opened and arched in obvious displeasure.

Barachiel closed the door behind him. He settled on the edge of the desk and faced me, clasping his hands together. "What happened?"

I lifted my chin. "Am I commanded to tell?"

"No, Jezbathasat," he said, weariness in his voice. "But I cannot help you if I do not know all the details."

He didn't need to know. I didn't need his help. "I do not wish to say."

"You said it wasn't intentional."

I'd said too much. I pressed my lips together, keeping my silence.

"Very well." Barachiel exhaled. "Has your shield of protection been compromised, then?"

"It's possible," I said.

"I can give you a new one. But if you repeat the same behavior, it will also be compromised. Will you be able to stop your destructive actions?"

I knew I would not. I'd been given a command by Hasatan, and choice was not possible. So I said the only thing I could.

"Yes."

Maalik was angry at me.

Again.

I joined my dormmates at lunch and sank into a chair beside Iblis, who went on to share information from her human history class, where they were studying the different forms religion took on earth.

"But it's like they got it all wrong," Dara said, jumping into the discussion. "None of them ever imagined a place like the academy."

"And yet they got so many things right," Iblis said. "How could they have known about heaven and hell and demons and angels?"

"Because of angel interference," Grigori said. "Haven't they taught that to you yet?"

Both girls shook their heads.

"There's a whole class on it as second years," he said. "All the times angels have interacted with humankind and caused serious mayhem. Some of it brings about good consequences, but other things require a second divine intervention just to fix it."

"But isn't that exactly what we're being trained to do?" Iblis said, her brow furrowing. "Intervene in mankind's life?"

"It's totally different," Grigori said. "We won't be changing the outcome of humanity. Just the life of one man. And you have to know your human in and out so that you can whisper promptings and insights into their ears. Usually you're helping them make a safer choice, not making it for them."

"Usually," Jerahmeel said, coming into the conversation with his usual bluster. "But not always."

He had my attention, and I looked at him. "What do you mean?" I asked.

"Well, obvious." He spread his hand. "Sometimes guardian angels actually step in and take a bullet for someone. Quite literally." His lip twisted. "Other times they sit back and do nothing."

"I don't think the angels are supposed to protect someone physically," Iblis began, but Grigori interrupted.

"There's always going to be exceptions. What if your assignment—?"

"Exceptions. Rarities. An unusual situation." Jerahmeel sneered. "More like the Guardians get to decide who is worth saving and who's not. Or maybe some people get stuck with a lousy Guardian."

"And who's to say that person's life wasn't going to change humanity?" I said. "How are we supposed to know?"

"We aren't," Maalik said, with such force and finality that silence descended upon the table. "We are Guardians, not God. We get our instruction from him. We answer to him. We know our assignment's life mission and help them carry it out. That's all."

"Just more pawns in someone else's game," Jerahmeel muttered. "Nothing's really changed."

Maalik chose to ignore him, but I found myself wanting to talk to Jerahmeel more. He wasn't the first angel to show such anger. If he knew what I knew—

He could be a strong ally against the angels.

Maalik was still talking, and a hard lump formed in my throat as I redirected my attention to him. My eyes swept over Iblis and Dara and the other angels I was coming to know from my dorm.

Hasatan had not told me yet, but I knew it was coming. I would have to fight against them.

Chatters of excitement around me jarred me from my negative contemplation. Iblis clapped her hands, her face alight, and then she looked at me, and some of her eagerness faded.

"Oh, Jez. There's nothing you want to see, is there?"

I blinked at her in confusion. I'd missed something.

Iblis shook her head. "Never mind all that. You can watch with me!"

"Come on!" Dara took her arm and pulled her to her feet. "I already know what day I'm requesting. Let's go put it in!"

I stood up slowly, clutching my book to my chest and watching the two of them hurry out, wings brushing as they leaned their heads near each other. My skin tingled, and I rotated to see Maalik watching me as he slung his bag over his shoulder. But he didn't say a word to me. Instead he stepped up to Grigori, and together they strode from the cafeteria.

Jerahmeel also stood, his lips pressed together and his eyes glaring as he headed toward the doors.

On impulse, I called out to him. "Jerahmeel."

He spun around, his eyes flashing. I raised my hand in greeting and stepped closer.

"I'm Jez."

He studied me, eyes roaming from the sweater—courtesy of Barachiel—slung over my shoulders to my face to my visible halter beneath and then to my shoulders again. "I know who you are," he said.

"Do you?" I matched his stride and moved in front of him toward the door. He did also. "You've already heard amazing things about me?"

Humor! It was my first attempt, and I peered at him out of the corner of my eye to see his response.

"Something like that," he said, and a glimmer of a smile pressed against his lips. He matched my stride as we walked out of the dining hall. "You don't join the first years as often as the others. You skip all the devotionals. And you—" he glanced at my shoulders again and fell silent.

I didn't respond to his attention to my lack of wings. "You mean you go to the devotionals?"

"Yes. I like to keep up on the kool-aid."

"Kool-aid?" I didn't get the reference.

"You know. Like everyone thinks this place is happy-happy joy-joy. It's Nirvana. Almost heaven."

"But you don't think so."

He stopped walking and faced me. "Do you?" He stared at me hard. "Something tells me you don't. Which is the only reason I'm talking to you now."

I had trouble catching my breath, and with a sinking heart, I realized I was right. Jerahmeel would be easy to sway to Hasatan's side. "Why are you so angry?"

"Because—" Jerahmeel's hand closed into a fist and pressed against his heart. He shook his head. "No. You first."

This was a game I could play. "I'm angry because of all the lies. I'm angry because I don't know who to trust. Each side points the finger at the other and says they did it. While the angels sit here in Arcadia, all innocent and benevolent, acting like they aren't the cause, violence and hatred has plagued the world since the beginning of time and driven humanity apart."

"Exactly." He stared at me, his body weaving back and forth as he nodded. "Exactly. You get it."

I waited quietly, but he didn't open up about himself.

"So," he said instead, leading the way back toward our dormitory, "who are you going to see?"

The question caught me off guard. "What?"

"You know, for the great 'viewing day.'" He curled his fingers around the words.

I shrugged. "I wasn't listening. What's it about?"

He arched a brow. "Is there no one you care about back on earth?"

I chose not to respond. He gave me a minute, but when I didn't, he kept on talking. "So Maalik said during winter break, or the holy days, we get to pick a day to view someone we care about back on earth. Just a chance to see them and what they're doing."

"Oh!" Now I understood their excitement. But dread bloomed in my chest. Who would I pick to view? A human who had succumbed to my filthy whisperings? "That sounds rather boring," I said. "I think I'll skip it."

He gave me a bewildered look. "You really don't care about anyone."

"I have no one," I said, my fingers curling into my palms. It had never bothered me before, but now I wondered. What would it be like to care? To feel my emotions stir every time a certain spirit came near my own? "Who will you watch?"

"I don't know that I will," he said slowly. "What if I don't like what I see? I'll just be further tormented here."

"But this isn't the place for torment," I said, trying to make sense of his words.

"Could have fooled me."

We stepped into the dormitory together, and Jerahmeel paused at the stairwell leading to the second story.

"Aren't you going to your next class?" he asked.

I shook my head. I hadn't checked to see what it was, but now that I was here, I didn't want to. I wanted to be alone with my thoughts. I wanted to put words to my feelings and write them down, and suddenly I was so, so grateful that the Fallen and demons couldn't read.

"Me neither." He looked me up and down again. "You could come up to my room. If you want. We could see — if everything works the same in this life."

There was innuendo and hidden meaning to his invitation that I didn't quite grasp, and yet the tightening in my chest gave me the vaguest warning that I should decline. "Maybe some other time," I said, giving a small smile to take any sting out of my words. What sting? What had I said that could be problematic?

It didn't matter. I needed him on my side. Jerahmeel would be easy to turn.

CHAPTER TWENTY

I woke up in the morning with a clear objective: befriend Jerahmeel.

I hated that I had a mission now.

Iblis kept up a constant barrage of chatter all the way to breakfast. I followed wordlessly through the line, loading the same foods onto my tray that she did. Then when she went to sit with Dara, I changed directions and put my tray down next to Jerahmeel.

Iblis cast me a look of surprise and then joined us.

It wasn't as if Jerahmeel ate alone. Our entire dorm was at this table or the ones nearby, and nobody was excluded. The angels were good about that. But even those sitting around Jerahmeel didn't seem to see him, speaking over his head or talking to those next to him.

"Hi," I said, sitting down behind my tray.

Iblis looked back and forth between the two of us and cleared her throat. "Mind if we sit here?"

He gave us a lazy smile and gestured to the table. "Be my guest."

Iblis cleared her throat again and shoved her hair out of her face as she squeezed in beside Jerahmeel and another student. "Excuse me," she murmured, forcing the kids to scoot down.

His light blue eyes met mine, and he gave a little smile. "Good to see you again, Jez."

"Jez, you know everyone," Iblis said. "Are you sure you weren't some kind of queen bee in your old life?"

I had no idea what that meant, but Jerahmeel saved me from having to respond.

"She was no queen bee. She was a goth, tried and true."

Iblis looked at me as for confirmation, and Jerahmeel said, "Just look at her. All in black. The academy sweater does little to hide her color preferences."

I looked down at my black halter, feeling insecure in my outfit. I had never had a choice before and hadn't questioned my desire to stay in what was familiar. But now I didn't like the statement I was making. I looked back at Jerahmeel, ready to deny his allegations, when I realized his perception of me worked in my favor. I needed him to think I was that edgy girl, the one who might have something to offer him. I pasted a smile on my face and said, "You've got me figured out. Guess I'll have to change things up again."

"You won't be able to fool me," he said, and I laughed.

But it hurt. Like I'd pulled a mask over my face that didn't fit quite right.

We moved as a unit from breakfast to the Gabriel Building for our therapy class. The wind had picked up outside, prickling my exposed skin. My hair whipped around me, and I increased my speed. My body might not require a jacket, but I didn't enjoy the cold. I stayed close to Jerahmeel, though agitation fluttered in my stomach. I was playing a dangerous game, and I wasn't even sure I wanted to be fighting on this side.

Eleleth already sat in a chair in the center of the circle, and he greeted us with a smile. "I sense a lot of excitement from you all today," he said. "Preparing for your first Viewing, eh?"

I glanced around and saw the eagerness was visible on my dormmates' faces.

"It's a special time," he said. "For many reasons. Winter break occurs during the Holy Days of many different cultures and religions, which means your loved ones might be drawing closer to the Light automatically. That makes it easier to bridge the gap between earth life and this life. But it's also your first time to see them. While this is emotionally fulfilling, it can also be difficult. There's a reason we make you wait until halfway through your first year to look back. If you find yourself struggling to accept what you see or life here in Arcadia after the viewing, please come find me."

Curious. What might one see that would leave them troubled?

"Probably less important to you this year, but important to the upperclassmen, is the upcoming Skyball game."

"What's special about this one?" Dara said.

"I think I remember hearing about it," Leike said. "What happens?"

"It's the last game before the playoffs in the spring," Maalik said. "Whoever wins this game will have an advantage going into the Championship games. They'll be the only team that has to lose twice to be eliminated."

I knew there'd been three games on campus, but I'd only gone to the first one. Not because I hadn't enjoyed the game, but I'd worried about inadvertently bumping a classmate in the excited scuffle of the game. The vicarious rush I'd felt when I watched the teams intrigued me, as if it were me on the pitch playing instead of observing. The championship game would probably be even more intense.

"Great things to look forward to before the break," Eleleth said. "But before we get to them, let's focus a bit more on your transitioning to angel life. There are only a few people we haven't heard from." His eyes swept over us.

I kept my eyes down and settled into my seat. The earlier energy immediately withdrew, and I was certain none of my classmates were eager to spill their losses from their past lives to a room full of strangers.

But as I glanced around at my classmates, I realized we weren't strangers anymore.

"Penemne, could you open for us? Share your story?"

Penemne was petite girl with olive skin and short, black hair. A perpetual grin clung to her features, and this was no exception. She flashed a smile and said, "Well, it was an extraordinary death. I jumped from a flaming helicopter toward the Eiffel Tower and missed. A stunt move gone wrong. But boy, did I look spectacular flying through the air."

Her comment actually brought laughter. I pictured Penemne launching through the air, arms outstretched, ready to make an amazing landing.

Her smile faded. "In all seriousness, it wasn't nearly so cool. I was born in Guatemala, the oldest of seven children. I left my family behind for a better life. I thought I could make something of myself and send money home to them. I didn't even make it across the border." The bright light had left her eyes, but she lifted her chin and met Eleleth's gaze. "If I can become a Guardian for my younger sisters and keep them safe, safer than I was, that's what I want. That's why I'm here. I will still make something of myself and provide a better life for them."

Eleleth nodded, his eyes burning as they held hers. "You will succeed."

Jerahmeel lifted his face. "This is—."

"You can't swear here," Iblis said, and she giggled uncomfortably. "The sound doesn't come out."

His eyelids fluttered. "Why do some people get guardian angels and not others? Do I get to choose? Because my family needs me right now."

I felt Jerahmeel's anguish rolling off of him and piling onto me. I clenched my fingers together, understanding the colors now. Anger and despair. I hurt for him as if the feelings were my own.

You can work with this.

I heard the instruction in my head as if my father were there beside me. He wasn't, and I knew he couldn't see what happened here in Arcadia. Which meant it was simply my inner voice.

I could exploit these feelings and use them against Jerahmeel. Even though what I wanted to do was comfort him.

Iblis reached out and touched his hand, and a flash of jealousy raged through me. She could do what I wanted. I expected him to shove her off, but his fingers closed tightly around hers, his pain deeper than his pride.

"I'm sorry, Jerahmeel," she said. "Life isn't fair."

Jerahmeel turned his face to her, and green tinged his aura.

"It isn't fair, and it's not over," Eleleth said. "We can help you make sure your siblings get the best Guardians possible."

"Right," Jerahmeel muttered.

Eleleth ignored his displeasure and turned to the next angel. "Hashmal?"

Hashmal shrugged. "Nothing exciting here. I got taken down by the flu bug. Can you believe it? Big ole guy like me taken down by a little flu."

"How do you feel about that?" Eleleth asked.

"Sucks, I guess. But here's not so bad. I'm getting kind of used to it."

Eleleth smiled. "Yes. Here's not so bad. And now you have each other."

"And we can't die again," Arella said. "So we don't have to fear."

The angels murmured their agreement and relief, and I waited for Eleleth to contradict them. When he didn't, I turned to look at him. He glanced at me and held my gaze, as if daring me to say something. To tell them about the dangers of a spiritual death.

Not me. I wasn't going to warn them. Especially not if he wasn't.

The last day of classes for the semester carried an air of expectant anticipation and giddiness. The final Skyball game of the season was that evening, and students couldn't stop chattering both about the game and about seeing their friends from GAA at Sinai, the campus we were playing. All of my teachers, including Master Sabriel and Master Remiel, offered indulgent smiles and let us talk excitedly together while they graded assignments or cleaned the area.

Master Ingram polished the weapons, leaving us sitting on the floor to discuss our Holy Day plans.

"Everyone's going to view their families, right?" Daniel asked. "I'm just eager to know how my dad's doing."

"I'm checking on my boyfriend," Iblis said. "Not that I think he's been waiting for me . . . But I want to know what he's up to. I hope he's all right."

And she hoped he was waiting for her. She didn't have to say it; the expectation in her eyes spoke for her.

I glanced toward the weapons wall. Twice since my last visit to Sheol I'd attempted to sneak into the armory and retrieve a dagger, but both times the door had been locked. When we had class, Master Ingram kept me far from the weapons, sometimes allowing me a bo to practice with but not letting me touch a dagger. Somehow I had to find a way to get my hands on one . . .

"What about you, Jez?" Dara said, drawing my attention back to the group. "Who are you going to view?"

This conversation came up in every class, right before the conversation changed to the Skyball game. I picked up the same lie I'd told for the past week. "My mom." If I could view anyone, if I could find a way to see any person, it would be my mother. I just didn't know how to make that a reality.

The bell chimed in the tower, signaling not just the end of class but the end of the semester.

"You're free to go," Master Ingram said over the flutter of wings and murmur of voices as we stood. "You're welcome to use the armory to practice during the break. Just be sure to check with me so I can open it for you."

I seized on her words, relief dispelling my panic. I could sneak one out during the break. I just needed to find a way to use the armory after it had been unlocked for another student. Maybe even enter with someone else and wait until they left.

Satisfied with my course of action, I followed my dormmates from the room, heading to the Skyball pitch.

It was late afternoon, and the wind had died down, taking a bit of the freezing chill with it. Enough moisture lingered in the air that tiny snow flurries fell around our faces. Knowing we'd be outside for the games, I'd grabbed the thicker winter jacket from my closet. No reason to be uncomfortable for several hour.

I lingered behind my classmates, not because I felt left out but because they were huddled so close together, I knew I'd touch one on accident if I caught up to them.

"I thought I'd find you back here."

I shifted slightly to face Maalik. He approached out of the wintry background, tiny snowflakes sticking to his eyelashes and nose. My heart did a little stutter, and I thought I'd never seen anything quite so beautiful. But even as I thought it, I remembered his reproach toward me.

"I did not think you would talk to me again," I said. "Not after I caught on fire during our study of the holy book."

"Eldermaster Barachiel has asked me to get in one more session with you before the break."

"Oh," I said, disappointment filling my chest. So that was why he was talking to me. I shook it off. "We tried, Maalik. You see what I am now. If you don't wish to continue tutoring me, we can work out a new arrangement."

"The thing is, I don't really know what you are at all. And I'll admit that confuses me sometimes. But something about you keeps drawing me back."

"I'm a curiosity." I shrugged. "A mystery to be solved."

"I want to get to know you more."

For some reason, ire shot through me. "Why have you ignored me since our last session, then?"

His cheeks reddened. "I got a little flustered. I thought I'd figured you out, and I was wrong. I'll tell you something, Jez. One of my biggest vices during earth life was anger. I still struggle with it. It takes me a few days sometimes to cool down and see things rationally, so I'm sorry."

"What did I do that made you angry?"

We'd reached the tall bleachers that overlooked the Skyball pitch now, but he stopped, leaning against one of the supports. I stopped as well.

"Sometimes I don't even know," he said. "That's why anger is so irrational. I was angry when I heard you'd compromised your protective shielding."

"Because it reminded you of my evil roots?" I said, lashing out with harsh words. Almost as if I wanted to see him lose control again.

"Not really. Because I could've hurt you when we read from the Word, and it would've been my fault, but also yours for not taking the care you needed."

"And it made you angry that you took the blame," I said, beginning to understand.

He shook his head. "It made me angry that you would take chances with yourself that way."

His words caught me off guard. I took a moment to analyze them, internalize them, and he watched me while I did.

"It's almost as if you care," I said, speaking out loud.

He smiled. "Yeah. It is. Odd, isn't it?"

There seemed to be a hidden meaning in his tone, something confessional, but the way he smiled, the way his eyes twinkled, made me wonder if I was missing a humorous nuance.

"Come on," he said. "We'll miss the start of the game."

I lagged behind, glad the crush of students had already filled the bleachers. "I'd rather sit away from everyone."

"I know. We can sit in the back."

"But don't you want to sit with your friends?" I spotted Grigori and Abaddon near the front, high up in the tall bleachers and with great views of the pitch.

"I sit with them all the time. How often do I get to sit with you?" He started up the long stairs to the seats at the back.

He could sit with me anytime he wanted. But I didn't point that out. He said it as if sitting with me were a privilege, and I rather liked the way that made me feel.

It was just the two of us in the very back. I noticed the other platform had students with different uniforms than ours.

"Are they from the other campus?" I asked.

"Yes. They're Teles. They look like they're not sure if they're about to become ninjas or do gymnastics."

I narrowed my eyes, trying to understand what he meant. They wore tight-fitting, sleeveless clothing.

"They control things with their minds. I guess they like to be ready for movement. Metas, on the other hand, wear white robes. They're from the campus at Zion, and since they shift into other animals, they keep their clothing loose." He pointed across the pitch. "See the guy from Sinai at the end of the first row? That's Jake. Well, that was his earth name. He's my friend, the one I jumped into the water to save."

"He's at the other campus," I said, catching on.

"Yeah. He has Telesight. He can look in someone's mind and see what they see, or show someone else what he's looking at. I'll introduce you to him after the game."

I nodded, but my mind was tripping, trying to catch up with me. What was happening? Why did Maalik want to sit with me, introduce me to his friend?

CHAPTER TWENTY-ONE

The two teams flew out to the pitch, and he leaned in close to me as the cheering erupted. He was careful not to touch me, but I felt his nearness just the same, a sort of electrical charge between us when he spoke to me.

"Do you understand the game?"

I shook my head, the electrical field between us expanding as I did, almost like it cocooned around us. "Iblis explained a little at the first game, but I don't recall."

"The team in the red is us," he said. "Academy at Yishuv."

Master Sabriel threw the ball into the air, and immediately one of the Yishuv angels hurtled forward, wrapping her arms around the ball and speeding toward the basket on the edge of the library tower.

"That's the Flyer," Maalik said. "She's the only one who can score a basket. The only person who can give her the ball is an Interceptor. She has to wait for it to come to her. There's one exception — the Flyer can also catch the ball from the opposing team's Tosser, but not from our team."

I nodded. I liked his closeness, liked the murmur of his voice in my ear. I liked the tingle of his aura as it mingled with mine at my shoulder.

A small angel in a blue robe appeared in front of the Flyer, and he danced around her, preventing her from getting a good shot.

"That's an Interceptor from Sinai," Maalik said. "They're not allowed to throw the ball. He can take it from anyone, but to get it to the Flyer, he has to fly it over and hand it to her. If he gets the ball—"

The Flyer tossed the ball over his head, and another angel from Yishuv in a red uniform caught it. The blue robed-angels closed around him, and he spun his hand in a circle. A portal opened in front of him, and he tossed the ball through it.

"And that was—?" I asked.

"A Tosser. The only one on the team who can create a portal. They have to synergize with the Interceptor to do so, but they can hold onto the energy until the moment they need it."

I nodded, the game starting to make sense as I watched it play out. "Is that all the Tosser does?"

"The Tosser can throw it away from the goal. They can also throw it to the Interceptor so the Interceptor can fly it to a Flyer."

"So there's a Tosser, an Interceptor, and a Flyer? Those are the three positions on each team?"

"Yep. Simple, huh?"

"Not really," I said. I watched the game, leaning forward and trying to understand it. Then I jumped in my seat. "Oh! Our Flyer just caught the ball from the other team's Tosser!"

He grinned, and his hand came down near mine on the bleacher, just near enough that I felt the sizzle of his energy. "You catch on quickly," he said. "It took me a year to understand Skyball."

The game became more interesting when the Sinai angels began using their gifts to interfere with the game, making the ball fly up or down or out of another angel's arms. But they weren't the only ones. I laughed out loud when the Sinai Tosser handed the ball over to our Flyer, knowing he'd fallen under her empathic influence.

I cheered and clapped along with everyone else when it ended.

"Did we win?" I asked.

"Yes," Maalik said, his eyes also crinkling with joy. "Now we have an advantage in the spring when we play both campuses. Did you see the Zion game last month?"

I shook my head. I hadn't cared to, but now I wished I had.

"Just wait until we play them again. They're the most fun to watch."

"Why is that?"

"Because they can shift. And it's awesome."

I heard his words, but all I could think was how my cheek tingled where he hovered. His lips were so near my skin. I couldn't touch him . . . but if I could, all I would need to do was turn my face, and our lips would meet. We would kiss.

My skin shivered at the thought, and I couldn't help myself. I shifted slightly and met his eyes.

He looked right back at me, and something magnetic held us that way for a sudden eternal moment. The noise around us disappeared, but I was aware of my heart thumping, of the ichor rushing through my veins, roaring like a waterfall. I didn't dare move. I didn't breathe. It was like I was seeing him for the first time.

His eyes crinkled in a smile, and he said, "Hi."

"Hi," I whispered.

He drew back, and he put his hand beside mine again, but this time I saw him check when he did so, and I knew it wasn't accidental that he placed his fingers so near to my own.

Close enough to touch. We weren't touching . . . But I felt something sparking in my soul, as if we were.

With the Skyball game over, the semester ended. The other campus went home, and we settled into a casual routine of meeting up for social activities and extra study sessions.

And of course, the Viewings.

I had not scheduled one. There was no point.

I did, however, corner Penemne after lunch the first day of break. The quiet angel would be the least likely to share my plans with anyone.

"Penemne, do you plan to use the armory anytime during the break? Practice sparring?"

She shrugged. "I hadn't thought of it. But maybe."

"Oh, good." I let out an exhale. "I need someone to practice with. Maybe we can do it on Thursday after lunch?"

"Can we do it next week?"

"Sure," I said. "Anytime. Just let me know, and I'll meet you there."

"Great. I just want to do my Viewing first. Seeing my family is all I can think about. What about you?"

"Yes." I smiled hard and gave a slow nod. "That's all I think about."

Iblis scheduled her Viewing for Christmas Eve, an important Holy Day in her family. And Jason's.

"Are you sure you want to see your boyfriend?" Maalik asked her at lunch when she stood up from the table, already eager to meet Eldermaster Barachiel for the Viewing. "You wouldn't rather see your family?"

She shook her head, her eyes alight with anticipation. "I can see my family next time. I might not always want to see Jason."

He looked over at me like he wanted me to say something, but what? "Good luck," I said. "I hope it goes the way you want."

He rolled his eyes, and I knew I hadn't said what he wanted.

"Thanks!" she chirped, and then she hurried away.

"I was thinking, since tomorrow's Christmas," Leike said, "we should all get together and do something special."

"Like what, exchange gifts?" Israfil smirked.

"I've never been a Christian," Daniel said. "What if we don't celebrate Christmas?"

I wasn't comfortable with the idea either. The whole thought of the Holy Days made me nervous. "I'm not sure it's a good idea."

"It's a great idea, for whoever wants," Maalik said. "You'll find several pockets of students getting together to do so. But no one should feel obligated. There'll be a special Shema service in the morning, and then several musical numbers throughout the day. You might find comfort and joy in attending those."

That sounded more like what I would like to do. I opened my mouth to say so, but Maalik looked at me and spoke first.

"Would you mind if we did another study session tomorrow?"

I blinked in surprise. I'd already started to think of different ways I would fill my day, starting with music. I had not gotten those sounds out of my head and looked forward to hearing them again. But then I realized he was offering me an out. A way to escape all the Holy Days celebrations without looking like that was my intent. "Sure."

"Then I'll see you at the library tomorrow. After the morning Shema."

I nodded. I didn't go to the devotional. But maybe after our session, we could sneak over and listen to the choir sing.

He gave me a smile, then shouldered his bag and headed for the exit. I jumped up and ran after him.

"You said they'll be singing all day tomorrow? After Shema?" I caught up to Maalik on the sidewalk and walked with him toward our dorm.

"You liked that, didn't you?"

I nodded, not wanting to voice how much the music touched me.

"You can listen to it on your agenda, you know."

"I can?"

He held out his hand, and I fished through my bag, finding my book and dropping it into his palm.

"It's not quite the same," he said, "but you might like some of this music."

I watched him sift through tabs, selecting lines and moving them into a folder.

"There," he said, handing it back to me. "Merry Christmas, Jez."

I blinked at him, wide-eyed. I didn't dare say the words back. But he didn't seem to expect them. He just turned and continued on his way.

I sat down at my desk in my room before opening the folder he'd created for me. I clicked on the first item, and the sound of cheerful, soprano voices filled my room. I smiled. He was right; the tone wasn't as pure, the music wasn't as angelic as listening to a heavenly choir. But the music itself lifted me. I settled back on my bed and closed my eyes, letting the Light fill my soul.

And then I sat up, troubled. How could I do this? How could I let the Light and goodness enter me, knowing the betrayal I was planning? My heart tore within me, and the conflict filled me with anguish.

The door to the room clicked before it opened, distracting me from my mental conflict. Iblis came in. She smiled at me, but her eyes gleamed with moisture. I reached over and silenced the music on my screen.

"What is it?" I said, rising and moving toward her. "Has something happened?"

She shook her head. "No, not really. I mean, they warned us, right, that things would be different. That's why they made us wait a few months before allowing us to have a Viewing." She tapped her fingers against her palms.

I nodded. "What happened? What changed?"

"It's nothing. And—everything." The tears overflowed and rushed down her cheeks. "Jason has moved on."

"Oh. But you anticipated this outcome, right?" I had never had a boyfriend or even loved anyone. But when I thought of Maalik and pictured the way his golden eyes seemed to see straight into my heart, I felt a stirring of longing. I would not like it if he looked at another angel that way. Maybe it was a tiny glimpse of the emotional connection Iblis had to Jason.

"I knew it was possible." Her eyes reddened as tears flowed down her face. "I didn't really think he'd move on so quickly! I mean, I died!"

Perhaps I was lucky after all, never being born, never experiencing true heartache. "I'm sorry, Iblis. What did you see?"

She picked up a hand towel from the bathroom and wiped her eyes. "It was Christmas Eve, and there was a party at Austin's house. Jason picked up my best friend Amy and took her there. He has a new car, of course. I thought it was sweet, since I'm not there, the two of them are hanging out. I thought maybe it helped them remember me. They stopped by my parents' house first. My mom cried when she hugged Amy, and Jason gave them a Christmas ornament. It was super emotional, and I just loved him all the more for it. I could see the guilt on his face." She shook her head. "I think he worries they blame him. I saw lots of colors, but I couldn't interpret them.

"Then Amy and Jason left for Austin's party. I should've stayed with my family, but I wanted to watch Jason. I wanted to imagine, for a moment, that I was there with him." She sighed, her breathing ragged. "But Amy started crying in the car, and instead of going to Austin's, they went to her house. To her room. There she fell into his arms, and he comforted her." Her lip twisted. "In a very caring, passionate way."

I had watched similar scenes play out often enough to picture it. "Do you want revenge?" I could make it happen.

"What? No." She sighed and sank into the chair at her desk. "I wanted him to move on, Jez. I didn't want Jason to guilt-trip himself and always feel bad for my death, or be stuck on me forever. But maybe for a year . . . it's only been six months! And now I think, maybe it would have been okay for him to pine for me for all eternity."

"It's very selfish of him to need someone else through mortality," I said. "You'll still be here when he dies."

Iblis looked at me, and then she threw back her head and laughed. "But he doesn't know that. Don't you remember what it was like? One day of loneliness feels like an eternity. It seems like there's no end, and you think, 'I can't take this anymore!' I would be selfish to expect anything else from him."

"I don't understand exactly," I said. "I thought you were upset about this. But if you think he did the right thing, then . . ."

She stood up. "Sometimes I wonder about you, Jez. It's like you don't remember feelings. Some things you just can't explain."

Apparently not.

I skipped Shema the next morning, watching from my window as the other students flocked from the dorms toward the Gabriel Building. The snow fell heavily this morning, and it seemed appropriate the way it blanketed the campus in white. Behind me my music played softly, and I pretended it was my own personal Shema. I wondered what it was like in there, the Light pouring down from Shamayim onto the angel souls. Glorious and beautiful. It made me ache with longing.

I turned away from the window and changed my clothes. I didn't wish to wear this black halter any longer. Or the jagged skirt. I pulled on the plaid school uniform with a matching button-up blouse and a thick jacket over the top. Then I sat in quiet contemplation while the songs spilled over me. Who was I, really? Maybe I wasn't who I'd always thought. Maybe I knew less about myself than my classmates did.

I stood up and went downstairs, heading to the library. I set up at our table, finding a thick tome to open and sound out the words while I waited for Maalik.

A rush of cold air filled the library when the door opened. I didn't turn, but kept my finger on the line of words, mouthing them to myself as Maalik dropped into the chair across from me.

"Hey," he said, and then I lifted my eyes.

His lips crinkled in a smile as he unwrapped a navy scarf from around his neck. His wings trembled behind him, sending powdery mists of snow to the library floor.

"Getting started without me?" he said.

"Yes," I said. "Just wanted to see if I could read this book."

"Well, sorry to cut our study short," Maalik said, a sparkle in his eyes as he pulled the book away from me, "but I have something else in mind for today."

"You do?" I watched him put the book back on the shelf and looked at him in surprise. "What are we going to do?"

"It's Christmas," he said. "And today's my Viewing. I'm not missing it. And I want you there."

I didn't move. "Me?" My voice rose in pitch. "Why me?"

"Do you have a Viewing scheduled?"

I shook my head.

"I didn't think so. So come on. Watch mine with me."

It was a kind offer, a thoughtful offer, but it filled me with dread. My mind flashed back to Iblis' viewing, and how she'd felt after what she'd seen. "What if you don't like what's happening?"

"You realize something after awhile." He shouldered his bag and stood. "The only thing that matters on earth life is preparing for this life. This is where existence really happens."

I stood also. "So it doesn't bother you if you see bad things?"

"Of course it does. But I want to see my family. I remember that earth life wasn't always happy, and I accept that. Some angels don't want to see it, and they decide not to participate in Viewings." He paused a moment, his eyes scanning my face. "You haven't done a Viewing with anyone else, have you?"

"No." There was no one on earth I wanted to check on. For a brief moment, my mind flashed on the hundreds — or was it thousands? — of souls I had led astray during my time in Sheol.

I shoved the thoughts away. I couldn't dwell on them now. I certainly didn't want to see them.

"Come with me." Excitement shown on his face. "You can meet my family."

I imagined Maalik's family would be Lightled, stiff and righteous and holier than thou. "Isn't it private?"

"Maybe." Maalik turned around and headed deeper into the library.

I scurried after, interest replacing my misgivings. "Where are we going?"

"My favorite place on campus." He reached one of the ladders in the back of the room. Without hesitating, he clasped the rungs and pulled himself up. "Come on!" he shouted over his shoulder at me.

Well, why not? I'd always wondered what was up here. I grasped the rungs firmly in my hands and hauled myself up the ladder after him.

We were climbing the library tower. I tilted my head back and looked up, but the ladder disappeared into the roof, too far for me to see. The ground beneath me faded from view long before the ladder ended, and still I could not see the end of our journey. Maalik's wings fluttered ahead of me, and I kept my gaze focused on them. I trusted Maalik, even as I felt a twinge of nerves about our ascent.

He stepped off the ladder first, and I followed him into a hallway with a door at the end. He turned around, his eyes shining with mischief.

"Ready for this?"

"For what?" I asked.

He threw the door open behind him and stepped into open space.

CHAPTER TWENTY-TWO

I gasped when I saw the clouds passing near us. The ground remained firm beneath my feet, but entirely transparent, and I tiptoed after him, my jaw dropping. "How far did we climb? Are we still in Arcadia?" Below us, I could see the snow drifting over the campus. We were above the clouds, and the heavy flakes didn't land on us. I lifted my face and could see directly into the heavens. Stars twinkled in the firmaments. Planets glowed in the distance, large and round.

"Yes. There are still somethings I don't understand, and the tower is one of them. It's almost like magic."

"But we know magic isn't real," I scoffed.

"Yet everything we do now at the academy, when I was a mortal, I would have called magic."

"We are still learning," I said, catching on to what he said. I placed my hands on the railing and looked over the edge. From here I could see the tops of the campus buildings. They appeared far away, but when I looked down on them, suddenly they zoomed in, details becoming clearer. "Are all Viewings done from the tower?"

"Viewings can be done from wherever you choose to be. First years don't know how to open windows, so Eldermaster Barachiel opens one for them. I can create my own. I prefer to be here."

His voice became softer, reverent, almost, as he looked up into the starry sky. Something warm crept up my chest and into my neck, all the way to my cheeks. This was his special place, and he'd brought me here.

"How do you do it?" I asked. "How do you view earth?"

"First you have to think about who you want to see. Make sure your why is pure, that your intent is for their benefit. Then you use your energy to open a window, like peeking into a house to see that person."

He held his hands out, and his fingers glowed orange as his life force gathered at the tips. Then he spun them and spread them apart, and a sphere appeared between them, small with turquoise rays shooting out of the edges. He pulled his hands apart, and it widened until the sphere opened like a round doorway. It paused directly in front of us, big enough for one of us to step through. An earth home appeared, a kitchen with wood cabinets and a refrigerator covered with magnets.

"Is it a portal?" I asked. "Can you step through?"

"No. Windows are similar to portals, but you need to synergize to create a portal unless you have an assignment. We can't descend until we become a GIT."

"Is this your house?"

"My dad's house. My parents are divorced. I lived with my mom. But right now, I want to see my dad."

"How does the window know to open here?"

Maalik chuckled. "I control where the window opens."

So many questions whirled through my mind. But before I could ask, a man stepped into the kitchen. He had a small phone pressed to his ear, and he argued with someone on the phone.

My stomach clenched in recognition when I saw him, and a cold feeling of dread washed over me. This could not be Maalik's father. Please, no. Not this man.

"Who is that?" I whispered, not able to raise my voice any louder.

"That's my dad. He's probably talking to my mom." He rolled his eyes, but there was no anger or even annoyance in his tone.

I closed my eyes, clutching the railing as the world spun around me. The heat of shame and regret rushed up my neck, and I took a step back, afraid Maalik would read the emotions in my aura.

That man was Maalik's father.

The human soul I had tormented as a shadow, fed off for years, led into iniquity and destruction. The man I had ensnared with guile, sated with lies, and torn from his family.

He was Maalik's father.

"Oh!" Maalik exclaimed. "They had the baby!"

I didn't want to look. A terrible dread had seized me, and bile burned my throat. I needed to get away. Before Maalik discovered the part I'd played in his life.

But the baby cried, and my eyes opened of their own accord.

A beautiful, dark-haired woman had come into the room, carrying a baby on her hip.

"Elias, get off the phone," the woman said snappishly. "I need help with dinner, and the baby's hungry."

He held up a hand, silencing her, and continued the barrage into the phone.

The woman huffed and put the baby into a swing tucked in the corner. Immediately the infant began to cry, but the woman set a few dials. The swing began to move, and she walked away from the baby.

"Who are they?" I asked, wishing I could run from this scene. Wishing I could undo the past ten years.

"My dad's girlfriend and their new baby. Rosana was pregnant the last time I saw her."

The woman pounded away in the kitchen, rattling cupboards and plates while she searched for utensils to begin the meal. Maalik's father left, only to return without the phone just as she dumped the vegetables into the frying pan.

"This is how they are spending Christmas?" I asked. "Wouldn't you rather watch your mother?" *Please*, I thought. As a shadow, the people around my victim had never been anything more than fuzzy shades, but I remembered the feeling of Light that radiated off his mother had been so strong, just her presence had often been enough to drive me away.

But sometimes the man's Darkness had overridden her Light. And that was when I fed the most.

"I know how my mom is," Maalik said. "It's my father I worry about."

He kept his eyes trained on the scene, and I forced myself to look back. This was my doing, this man's isolation from his family. I should face it.

Rosana started yelling at Elias when he returned, but he ignored her. Instead he opened the fridge and hunted around. I sensed Maalik tense beside me.

"Here." Elias set a can of soda on the counter. "You finish making dinner and I'll do the laundry. Does that help?"

Maalik drew in a breath and exhaled. "A soda. He was looking for a soda." He laughed out loud.

"You thought he was looking for . . ." My voice trailed off. I knew what he'd feared, but if I said it out loud, he might guess I had more knowledge than I should about his father.

"A beer, or whiskey, or something. My dad's an alcoholic," Maalik said, his eyes bright. "He was never sober. For eight years, my mom put up with him and his abuse."

"Then what happened?" I whispered.

"She left him. He's had a bunch of girlfriends since then, but this one I think might last. I check on them every year."

"Only once a year?"

"Yeah. If I check too often, I don't see enough change, and that's discouraging. But just now, they were fighting, and my dad didn't grab a beer. And he didn't yell at her or — or hit her."

My eyes turned back to the open window before us, where Maalik's dad shuffled clothing from the washing machine into the dryer. It had been years since I'd goaded this man to sin. He'd become less accessible, and I'd moved on to easier targets. My shame burned me. "What changed?"

"I think losing me was a big part of it."

I swiveled to face him, my heart feeling twice its normal size. I would have been there, a shadow haunting his family when he died. "How did his behavior affect you?"

"The way it affects most kids. I was angry and rude and obnoxious. And I drank a lot too."

I didn't want to hear this. I didn't want to think I had any cause in Maalik's life being unhappy.

But Maalik couldn't seem to stop talking, now that he'd started. "You heard how I died. A swimming accident?"

I nodded, my eyes glued to his face.

"I didn't go into detail in the group." He looked away from the window and met my gaze. "But the accident was my fault. We'd been drinking. I was drunk. I brought the alcohol. When my friend fell in, I went in after him. Which was stupid. If I'd been sober, maybe I could have saved him. But instead I killed us both."

My throat ached with unshed emotion. But he remained stoic, so I forced myself to be as well. "I thought you would have been like Iblis. Someone who went to church every Sunday and believed in—" My voice caught. I still couldn't say the word.

"Oh, I believed in God. I hated him. I was so angry for what he'd done to my family."

"But he didn't do it." I whispered the words out, almost against my will.

"I know that now."

My mind whirled, trying to digest this new information. "And they let you into the academy?"

"Everyone gets in, Jez. We're still learning. Once we're here, we decide if we're staying or going."

"And you decided to stay," I breathed. It seemed unreal, that someone with that venomous attitude would want to be here.

"I almost didn't. I almost decided I'd rather have my hatred and my anger than trust a God who let such wicked things happen."

I clutched the railing. "You almost became a Fallen?"

"Almost." A small smile graced his lips. "But the masters here, they don't want us to fall. Especially Barachiel. He convinced me to stay. And try again. And again and again and again."

"Try what?"

"To change. To believe." He put his hand next to mine on the railing, like he'd done at the game, close enough that the energy of our souls sizzled between us. "I repeated year one three times before moving onto year two."

"So you've been here for four years!"

"Yep."

And here I'd thought he was class leader because he'd been so perfect on earth . . . because he'd been the perfect example.

"Do you despise me now?" he said, his voice teasing. "Because I'm not the guy you thought I was?"

I shook my head, still trying to understand. "They gave you so many chances."

"As many as I wanted. Jez."

I lifted my face when he said my name, his eyes peering into mine.

"You get these chances also. If my soul could be redeemed, so can yours."

For a moment, I let myself hope. The idea that I could become someone as whole and good as Maalik washed over me like warm sunshine. I inhaled it, held it close to my heart, and believed.

And then I remembered.

He did not know everything I'd done, the souls I'd destroyed. His own family that I'd destroyed. I was not like him. And I could never be.

"I am past redemption," I whispered, looking back into the darkness of space, at the twinkling stars.

"Nobody is, Jez."

"You wouldn't say that," I said, my voice trembling, "if you knew what I've done. What I was."

He bent his head closer to mine, his aura expanding, reaching out as if to envelope me. "I accept you."

I took a step back, away from his energy field. I didn't argue with him. Because I couldn't tell him.

※ ※

I checked the message on my screen for the third time.

Meet at the armoree after lunch, I'd said to Penemne.

Okay, she'd replied.

I allowed myself a small moment of satisfaction that my writing had improved so much. But now I sat on my bed in my dorm, alone because Iblis had decided Jerahmeel needed to be more social, and she'd made him go on a walk with her.

Penemne should be at the armory now. Master Ingram should be unlocking the doors now. It shouldn't be too much longer.

My pulse thumped in my throat. Soon, I'd fulfill my mission.

My screen dinged with an incoming message.

Waiting for you, Penemne said.

Coming, I said. *Warm up with out me.*

Still I sat. I picked up a book and tried to sound out letters, but the words danced around on the page, illusive. I couldn't concentrate and put the book aside.

Fifteen minutes. Twenty.

Penemne texted again. *Still coming?*

I exhaled. *Sorry,* I said. *Something came up and I'm late. Don't wait. I'll practice by myself.*

She didn't respond, and I stood slowly, giving her time to put away her weapons and leave the armory. She'd reserved it for an hour, but only forty minutes had passed. I shouldered my bag and left the dorm, doing mental calculations as I went. Master Ingram would come by and lock the door. I needed to be in and out before that happened. Then I would pretend like I'd never made it there at all, and nobody would be the wiser.

But I had to hurry. I had to time this window just right.

Students milled about the quad and walked along the sidewalks. I didn't look at them and hoped they weren't looking at me as I walked into the Uriel Armory. I strode confidently down the hall to the weapons room, then glanced around, my hand on the door.

Nobody in sight.

Heart thumping in my ears, I pushed open the door and let out an exhale when it wasn't locked. I'd almost hoped — I shook it off. Time to act.

I entered the weapons room and pulled up short when Penemne turned, her short dark hair swishing with her head when she faced me.

"Hi," she said, flashing white teeth in a smile. "Our hour is almost up, but we have a few minutes, if you wanted to spar."

She was still here. I stared at her in disbelief, my plan fading to ruins at my feet. "I can't believe you waited," I said, trying to hide my distress.

She shrugged. "I didn't mind. It's a lot more fun to spar with someone else. Here." She tossed me a bo. "We're not allowed to touch the daggers without a master present, but I'm getting pretty good with a bo staff."

"Thanks," I said, catching it. I cast a look of longing at the daggers. But I couldn't do anything about it now. If I ran over and grabbed one, she'd see me. All of the academy would know.

I would just have to do it some other time.

The second semester started without fanfare. The Holy Days were over, and every first year had assuaged some of their homesick feelings by having a Viewing.

Except me. And I wasn't homesick. But I got sick every time I thought of home. It was only a matter of time, I knew, before my father demanded my attention again. And I got nervous every time I thought of it.

"Why do we use a book instead of the screen when we practice?" I asked Maalik as we sat in the library together during the first week of classes. "Is it easier to learn that way?"

He shrugged. "I don't know. I could probably teach you with the screen also. But there's something about real books, feeling the weight of the book in your hand, turning the pages . . . It's just me. Personal preference."

I looked down at the book open on the table in front of me, and suddenly it had greater value.

"You're doing so well with reading and writing," he said. "Soon you won't need me anymore."

I lifted my face, taking in his features, the Light that seemed to constantly glow around him. "That's not true."

He smiled. "I mean my teaching skills."

I didn't like the thought of not having these sessions. What would I do without his steadying presence, his quiet confidence? He saw something in me, something good. He believed in me.

He believed a lie.

I looked away, turning my attention back to the book.

"You all right, Jez?"

I lifted my eyes without moving my face. "Yes."

He tilted his head. "You seem nervous."

I dropped my gaze. "I'm fine."

He was quiet a moment, and then he said, "There was a time I was really good at putting on a brave face too. It seemed like the more something bothered me, the more I pretended like it didn't. And you seem like there's something really bothering you."

I met his eyes, and my ability to lie to him melted away. "There is something," I said quietly. "But I can't tell you."

"Does it have to do with your past existence?"

I nodded.

"Listen to me, Jez." He shifted in his seat, that earnest expression crossing his face. "You're different now. That girl from Sheol, that girl who arrived in Arcadia four months ago—she's not you. You don't have to hang onto the past."

I yearned to tell him. But as if sensing my desires, the chains around my arms tightened and grew hot, threatening to burn me, to expose me. "I'm still bound," I said softly.

"You can be free. It's a choice, Jez. Once you decide, you'll be set free."

"Choice." I fought to keep the snarl from my voice. "There is no choice."

He sighed. "There is always a choice."

"Maybe for people like you," I said.

He fell silent, and I felt the painful sting of victory. But it didn't make me feel better.

"Leandro," Maalik said quietly.

I furrowed my brow, studying him. "What?"

"Leandro was my earth name," Maalik said. "That's who I was."

I caught my breath. Earth names were special; they were intimate in that they represented an existence the angels had left behind. There was no need to speak of them here. "Leandro," I whispered, and a surge of energy leapt from me to him, a feeling of connection that hadn't been there before.

"I made a lot of mistakes with that name," Maalik said. "But none of that matters. In Arcadia, I was given a new name. My first name, and everything I did wrong as Leandro was put behind me."

"Leandro," I said again, loving the feel of it on my tongue.

He smiled. "It's a nice name. But now I am Maalik. I'm different." He leaned toward me. "Who are you?"

He was asking for my name. My real name, just as he'd shared with me. But I couldn't share mine with him. I wasn't a new creature, and revealing my name would reveal who I really was. I stood up, pushing my chair back.

"You don't want to know," I said, and I fled the library.

CHAPTER TWENTY-THREE

Meet me at the Skyball pitch during lunch.

I reread Kerubiel's message three times as I hurried to Creations class. We hadn't spoken since he'd told me about kissing, and I hadn't responded because I wasn't sure if I wanted to meet him. Something about him drew me toward him like a moth to the flame. Or, in my case, like a Forsaken to the Darkness. He also brought out my predator instincts, awakening in me the desire to feed.

And for some reason, these things made me wary of him.

Today Master Sabriel handed us large pots of beautiful colors and a paintbrush, and she told us to recreate our favorite view of the sky.

"What are we painting on?" Dara asked, dipping her blue-handled brush into the yellow paint.

Sabriel laughed, her face crinkling with delight. "Oh yes, I always forget that first years expect a canvas of some kind. Just paint it directly on the sky, my angelings."

The students looked at each other with wide eyes, but I had never painted anything before, so it didn't matter to me.

"No need to clean your brush between colors, either," Master Sabriel said. "You may begin."

Paint my favorite view of the sky.

A few months ago it would have been blackness, the sky with no moon and no clouds, just a blanket of dark.

But now my thoughts flew to how the sky had looked when I stood on the tower beside Maalik, feeling his spirit beside me, feeling his Light and warmth igniting me with hope and longing.

Such a bittersweet memory.

I dipped my brush into the black paint and then waved it in front of me. Sure enough, the coloring stuck to the sky above me, immediately transforming the light blue into a night sky. I brushed more on, and more, so it blotted out the light, and a feeling of such misery and sorrow filled me that I gasped out loud, forcing back a painful stinging in my eyes. Out. Out with the Light.

No, I thought. *The Light cannot be expelled. It's forever a part of me now.*

"Jez," Master Sabriel said, approaching behind me, "remember where you are. Try to leave the past behind you."

I didn't even turn to her. The angels all said this as if they thought it a simple task. "I'm not done." I pictured again the planets and the space spread out in front of me and Maalik, as far as the eye could see. Inspired by the view, I dipped my brush into the white, so bright it almost glowed. I poked at my night sky, dabbing big dots and little pinpricks, trying to emulate the stars as I had seen them.

Almost, but not quite. The stars held too still. They didn't flicker and burn as they had from the tower. I added a bit of yellow to some of them, but it still didn't give the effect I wanted.

"Very nice, Jez. I'm impressed."

Master Sabriel was back, and she paused behind me. "The stars in the firmament are beautiful, indeed. I'm pleased they've made an impression on you."

"But it's not quite right," I murmured, studying it. "They aren't alive like in the sky."

"Then give them life. Just like I've been teaching you since last semester."

Use my soul energy to create. I closed my eyes and tried to drum it up, but this was different than using it to control the elements. I felt energy sparking in my soul, but it wouldn't pass from me to the painting. The sky remained dull and inanimate.

"Like this." Sabriel summoned the energy into her fingers, where it glowed on her tips.

I could do that. I concentrated and managed a handful of sparkling energy.

"Now give it life."

I shook my head. "I don't know how to make the energy pass from me to it."

"You control the energy. Just send it." She pinched her fingers together and blew on them. The sparks flew from her hand into my night sky, and immediately, the stars flickered to life.

"Oh!" I cried, because the beauty enraptured me just as it had on the tower. It brought back the feelings Maalik had awakened in me. I wanted to fall into their depths. I wanted to be near him again just to feel of his soul.

"Try it," she said.

I pinched my fingers together and blew, but instead of scattering over my night sky, the energy fell from my fingers toward the ground.

"It's all right." Master Sabriel smiled at me. "You're improving. Soon you'll be able to."

She left me, and I exhaled, staring at my scene. The fact that I'd created it at all left me bursting with happiness. Until I remembered what else I'd learned up there on that tower.

And if Maalik knew, he would never speak to me again.

I pulled out my book and opened Kerubiel's message.

OK.

While the rest of my dormmates moved from Creations class toward the cafeteria, I clutched my schedule to my chest and made my way to the Skyball pitch. The towers of the opposing buildings faced each other, though all remained quiet with no practice or game going on, as all sports ceased during the second semester when the upper years went to earth on assignment. I stood on the field and imagined what it would feel like to glide through the air, flapping those magnificent wings and throwing a ball around—for sport.

"There you are."

I turned around as Kerubiel approached. His light hair was shoved out of his face, and the Darkness framed him like a shadow he carried around. I took a step toward him, reaching out as if I could gather his shadow into myself.

His eyes darted to my hands, and he reached out also. I yanked back, catching myself before I gave into the magnetism.

"What's wrong?" he asked, tilting his head.

"I can't touch you," I said.

"You keep saying that. Why don't you try it?"

I shook my head. "I can't."

"There's a lot you're missing out on." He stepped close to me, so close that I took a stumbling step backward.

My heart rattled at his nearness. "Can you harness your energy for creation?"

His eyes glinted. "I can create lots of things."

"Show me how. I can harness the energy, but I can't send it anywhere."

His lip twisted. "Watch this." He cupped his hand and inhaled, closing his eyes. I studied his hand, and a moment later, the crackling energy I expected snapped in his palm.

"Yes." I looked at him and then summoned my own energy to my hand. "Now what?"

"Now you tell it to do what you want. You're in charge. Do I have your permission?"

Permission. The word filled me with trepidation. The Forsaken could not influence mortal souls without their permission, which mortals were keen to give in many ways, through actions, feelings, and even words. I wouldn't give mine away so easily. "Permission to do what?"

"Permission to show you what I can do with my energy."

He kept his clear blue eyes on me, waiting for my answer. The Darkness flickered around him, inviting me. It was comforting, somehow, soothing to the aches in my heart.

"Yes," I said, making up my mind.

A hint of a smile creased his lips. He bent his head near his hand and whispered, "Enter."

The flickers lifted from his hand and flew into my body. I stiffened. A strange thickness filled my chest.

"Be still," Kerubiel said. "If you won't let me touch you, this is the best I can do. Close your eyes."

I stared at him, doubting him.

"Do it," he said. "I won't hurt you."

I felt compelled to do what he said. I closed my eyes.

A sensation like tongues of fire crept up my soul, exploding from my stomach and caressing me with heat and pleasure. I gasped, and my eyes flew open, wide with astonishment. I'd never felt anything like that before.

"How are you doing that?" I cried.

He smirked. "Imagine what I could do if I could touch you."

The pleasant feeling left me reeling. I closed my eyes, not wanting it to end, but recognizing the danger. I'd given my will over to him, and he could control me. Just as a Fallen controlled an Underling on earth. Except I hadn't let him drink from my soul. I didn't belong to him.

"How did you know how to do that?" I whispered. This was knowledge of Darkness. He had not learned it here.

"What's your real name?" he asked.

I peered at him through hooded lids. I wanted to feel his energy again. I wanted to feel that exquisite pleasure. "Do it again."

He grinned. "Tell me your name."

A tiny flicker of energy caressed my neck, teasing me, and I let out a breathy sigh.

"Do you like how this feels?" he asked, curiosity tinging his voice.

"I've never experienced this," I admitted.

"If you only knew, Jez. When two human bodies come together, touching, with nothing between them, it's the most marvelous feeling in the universe. It's paradise."

I believed him. This was desire? No wonder humans fell so easily. I didn't even have the weaknesses of the flesh to tempt me, and I wanted to give into this heady feeling.

"Your name," he said.

"Jez," I breathed. "Jezbathasat."

"Jezbathasat," he whispered, and I felt a sliver of my soul leak away from me, feeding into his energy.

My eyes snapped open, and the hazy fog enveloping my mind vanished. I straightened up, eyes widening. "You tricked me!"

He held out his hands, taking a few steps back. "No, I didn't. I did exactly what you wanted me to."

He'd manipulated me, and I'd fallen for it. Me! "What are you going to do with my name?" I demanded. What would he want with that information? Names were valuable. They had power. That was why Maalik sharing his with me had been special, intimate. And why I hadn't shared mine. A Fallen could not control an Underling without knowing its name.

He studied me coolly. "I'm trying to figure you out."

"And I played right into your trap," I breathed, furious with him. Furious with myself.

"It looked like you were enjoying it."

I trembled at my own weakness, because I had enjoyed it. But now I felt used and tarnished and broken. "How could you?" Tears pricked my eyes.

"Calm down," he said. "It's not like I was trying to hurt you. You asked me to show you, so I did. I didn't do anything you didn't want."

His cold words rang with truth. I had brought this upon myself.

I turned and marched from the field, suddenly glad I'd never had a body. What a terrible idea, giving such strong feelings to a human!

"Jez!" Kerubiel called after me. "Come on."

I did not glance back.

For the next few days, I tiptoed around my classmates on eggshells, expecting Kerubiel to blurt out my name at any moment, or share my secret with the other students.

Worse, I feared he would tell Maalik. My skin prickled with fearful apprehension of what Maalik would say if he knew. It there was any way for me to keep my identity a secret from him forever, I intended to find it.

When Kerubiel did nothing, didn't even approach me or speak to me again, I slowly began to relax.

Just when I thought everything would be fine, Hasatan's voice woke me in the night.

"Come, Jezbathasat."

The voice echoed through my mind and around me in my bed, and I opened my eyes and sat up. Indignation burned through me, and I wanted to refuse him. But even as I was thinking it, my legs were swinging over the side of the bed and I was exiting my room.

I couldn't refuse. There was no choice. I belonged to him, and he commanded, and I obeyed.

I had forgotten my jacket, but my chains burned as they pulled me toward the fountain, dragging me to Sheol. The frigid air vaporized around me, enshrouding me with a cloud of steam. The portal hissed in front of me, melting the ice in the water.

There was no point resisting. Anger and resentment brewed within me, but I stepped through the portal.

As soon as the blazing heat of Sheol blasted my skin, fear replaced my resentment. Shadows and Darkness lurked just out of sight, and I remembered my task and my failure to complete it.

"Daughter." Hasatan's shadowy figured stepped in front of me. "You have the dagger?"

The only correct answer was yes. But I didn't have it. "No, but—"

My explanation was cut off by searing pain as the chains got on fire, charring my skin as I screamed. My hands grabbed at them, desperate actions to remove the pain, and were rewarded with blistering burns across my palms.

Abruptly the burning stopped, and I doubled over, panting and trying to catch my breath.

"Failure is not an option," he growled. "Bring me that dagger."

I wheezed, unable to speak. I realized it wouldn't matter that I'd attempted to take the dagger. All that mattered was I hadn't succeeded.

"How is your learning coming along?"

I still couldn't answer. The pain was receding, but my mind screamed with the memory of it.

"Can you read?"

I forced my head to bob.

"Good. You will be a valuable asset when you leave the academy."

Yay for me. I closed my eyes, wishing I could cease to exist. Maybe if I failed, Hasatan would kill me.

"You will retrieve the dagger before two moons have passed," he said, his voice booming with command.

My body stiffened, and my throat strained with words. "I will retrieve it," I managed to gasp out.

I knew without a doubt that I would do it.

There was no other option.

※ ※

"I can't believe how quickly you've picked this up." Maalik beamed at me, the pride evident in his eyes as he closed the book I'd been reading from. "I suppose I shouldn't be surprised. It's a lot easer to learn in this realm than on earth. But soon you'll be able to pick up material from any language and read it."

I offered a smile, though I felt uneasy inside. That's what Hasatan wanted. Someone who could read.

I wore a thick jacket, even inside the library. The marks from the burns had faded but weren't gone. Not yet. Every time I moved, I received a visceral reminder of my father's command and what I'd promised to do.

I hated this. Somewhere, my feelings had changed. I did not want to fool the angels at Arcadia. I didn't want to betray my dormmates.

I did not want to lie to Maalik.

"You're a good teacher," I said.

"Come on." Maalik put the book back on the shelf and returned to me. "Let's go for a walk."

Something bright and strong filled my heart when I stood next to him, pure and light, like the music when the angels sang. I compared it to the spark of energy Kerubiel had manipulated me with, and my face warmed with shame. How could I have taken pleasure in something so false?

My thoughts must have shown on my face, because Maalik nudged me with his book. "What's on your mind?"

"I can't reveal," I said automatically, and he laughed.

"I've told you just about everything about myself," he said. "And yet, you're still playing mysterious."

"Because you are good," I said in all seriousness. "My thoughts often revolve around who I was. And what I did."

He fell silent as we walked through the quad, stepping past other angels on their way to class or out for a stroll. He sat down on the edge of the fountain, and I joined him. The water remained off for the winter, and I touched the frozen surface. There was no visible sign of the portal I'd taken to Sheol just days before.

"I don't think I knew you before," he said. "I've searched my memory for anytime I might have interacted with you in the first existence, and it comes up blank. Of course, I don't remember everything yet. Maybe it will come to me."

"You didn't know me."

"Are you sure? Do you remember?"

"Nobody knew me," I said.

"Somebody had to know you."

I shook my head. Maalik knew I was a Forsaken, one of the souls damned to live out its existence in Sheol, but he didn't understand everything about me. "I wasn't there in the first existence."

"Everyone was there."

"I wasn't." I lifted my head, my heart pounding nervously in my throat. Was I sure about telling him?

He cocked his head, his aura flashing a deep purple. Could he see mine? What did it say about me?

"You can trust me," he said, patting my finger with his book.

I smiled slightly. That was how he'd taken to touching me. He carried his book under one arm when we were together and used it to nudge me or poke me. Somehow, it warmed my heart as if it were his own hand.

"Well, if it isn't our little vixen, Jez."

The shiver of warning crept down my spine even as I turned my head to see Kerubiel approaching.

Something in Maalik's expression hardened. "What are you doing here, Shade?"

Kerubiel lifted his chin, smugness radiating off of him. He shoved his hands into his pockets. "You say that like it's an insult. Shades have a very powerful influence on other beings. Wouldn't you say so, Jez?"

Chapter Twenty-Four

I glared at him, face warming with embarrassment as I remembered our last encounter.

Kerubiel's eyes looked at my hand, pressed nearly against Maalik's, and then he smirked at Maalik. "But maybe you already know about the influence of shades."

"No one's influencing anyone," I said, incensed by the insinuation.

"Let it go, Jez," Maalik said. "He doesn't know anything."

"A lot," Kerubiel said. "I know a lot. Don't be fooled by her innocent face. You don't know what she did with me on the Skyball pitch."

I could not look at Maalik as the heat rushed to my eyes. I clenched my fists, panic racing through my veins. Behind us, the ice cracked in the fountain, and Maalik glanced at it.

So did Kerubiel. Then he looked at me. "I'm still figuring you out. I don't have all the answers, but I'm close. Somehow I suspect your name is a clue to it all, Jezbathasat."

"What?" Maalik said, his tone of voice changing. "What did you say?"

I closed my eyes, fear flooding me. Kerubiel had just done it for me. Revealed what I was. Who I was.

Kerubiel didn't miss the reaction. "That means something to you. What is it?"

But Maalik was looking at me. "Is that your name? You told him your name?"

"It just kind of slipped out," I said, helpless before him.

"You could say she was caught up in the moment," Kerubiel said, that smirk back on his face.

Oh, how I wished I could smack him. "He manipulated me!"

Maalik stood up, and I watched him anxiously.

"Where are you going?"

"To see if what he's saying is true," Maalik replied, not even glancing at me.

I stood as well. "You could just ask me."

Something darkened in his gaze. "Somehow I doubt you would tell me the truth."

His response stung, and I stumbled backward. Just like that, and now he didn't trust me?

Kerubiel regarded me as Maalik walked away. "What does he know that I don't?"

I spun on him. "This is all your fault."

He lifted an eyebrow. "No, it's not. You're keeping things from all of us, and that makes it your fault."

I glared at him, hating that he was right.

I left Kerubiel at the fountain and ran back to the library, where I assumed Maalik was, searching in the books for information about me.

But I didn't find him, even as I ran among the shelves. So I sat down on the floor and removed my agenda.

Where are you? Can we talk?

I sent the message to him and held my breath, waiting for his response.

When it came it, was harsh and loaded with emotion.

Now you want to talk? I've been trying for weeks to get you to open up. But apparently it wasn't that you didn't want to talk, just that you didn't want to talk to me. Maybe you should stick with those you're comfortable with.

It took me nearly ten minutes to decipher the message, and each word felt like a slap to the face. He hadn't said it, but I could feel the words as if he had: *Stick with your kind.*

He didn't tell me where he was, and I didn't ask again. I comforted myself with what he'd told me before, that he was prone to anger and sometimes needed a moment to cool down. I'd give him time.

Maalik skipped meals, not joining Table D. And as one day turned into two and two turned into three, I wondered how long it would take.

Or maybe, now that he'd discovered the truth about me, we were through talking.

A coldness sank into my soul at the thought, and a sorrow I hadn't thought myself capable of accompanied me to each class and every activity.

"Today we are going to work with the elements to see which one you are most inclined to." Eldermaster Barachiel walked among us where we stood on the grassy lawn, each of us with our feet apart and palms facing the ground.

"Did you go to the library and study the meaning behind the different elements?"

He'd given us the assignment a week ago, but I didn't nod. I had not returned to the library since I'd gone seeking Maalik. I was afraid he'd be there, and I didn't want to intrude on his space.

But it looked like I was in the minority. Most of my classmates nodded. Now I was at a disadvantage because they had studied the elements and I had not.

"Fantastic," Barachiel said. "Make sure you have plenty of space around you. Let's start with drawing up your energy. Go ahead, pull it up from inside you. Let it flow to your fingertips."

I'd had practice with this now, both in this class and Creations class. I closed my eyes and visualized my soul energy burning up into my fingers.

"Now we will cycle through the most common elements. There may be more than one that speaks to you, but there will be one you control the best. Let's start with the earth. This is the power to move mountains, to shake the ground."

To cause cities to be swallowed up. To create valleys and hills where before there were none.

The ground trembled beneath my feet, and I opened my eyes to see the earth shooting upward, creating a mound in front of my face. I gasped and took a step backward.

"Sorry!" Arella said beside me, her face turning pink. "I didn't know that would happen!"

"You did that?"

"I think so." She looked at her open palms. "I felt the energy leave me."

I hadn't felt anything. My fingers still sparked with unspent force. Valleys and hills sprang up around me, and Leike was in the midst of creating a mountain.

"Very good, very good. Those of you who were able to work with the ground, remember that power."

"Earth bender! I'm an earth bender!" someone shouted, and several angels laughed, apparently catching a reference I did not.

"Remember it might not be your only power. Now, put everything back the way it was."

This appeared to be much harder. I watched Arella scrunch up her face in concentration, moving her hands back and forth over the mound. She succeeded in getting it to fall back into the earth, but it looked as if a child had dug it up with a shovel and put it back.

"Looks pretty good," I said, and she gave me a grateful smile.

Barachiel chuckled, and I looked up to see crinkles around his eyes as he walked in front of us. A quick glance showed she wasn't the only one who had struggled to get the earth back down. Leike was shoving the mountain back into the crater he'd pulled it from.

"From your research, what does it mean if an angel is prone to Earth moving?" Barachiel asked.

"It means they are more logically rooted," Iblis said, speaking up from somewhere to my left. "They tend to see things in black-and-white. There is no middle ground."

"That's right. Consider how that applies to you if you found talent in the earth.

"The next element we are going to try is wind. Remember to give this a shot even if you were able to manipulate the earth. You might be able to do both." He held his hands out in front of him so the palms faced each other. "Just like you channeled your energy before, do it again. Only this time, push it between your hands."

I held out my hands the way he did and summoned my energy, hoping this time something would happen. The flickering sparks collected in both of my fingertips, and then they pushed against each other with a magnetic force that shoved me backward. I gasped and crouched to the ground before I rocketed into another angel.

Wind whipped around me and tumbled through my hair like a miniature tornado. I glanced around and saw other students using their hands to manipulate the shape of the wind.

"Good job," Barachiel said, approaching me. "You found a power over an element."

"I — I'm surprised," I admitted, my voice a little shaky.

"Why should you be? Your soul is composed of energy like any other living creature. You've just never learned how to harness it correctly."

Correctly being the operative word, because I had certainly learned how to use the energy of my soul for other purposes.

I got to my feet and took a look around me. The angels who were not manipulating the air looked frustrated or disappointed, including Arella, who's lower lip poked out in a pout.

"You are all doing amazing," Barachiel said. "Who knows what traits are found in the wind manipulators?"

Iblis spoke again. "Loyalty. Unwavering. Someone who is not easily tossed about on the waves."

"Indeed," Barachiel said.

I leaned forward and peered at Iblis, curious. What element had she managed to summon?

"If you do not react to any of the elements today, please do not be alarmed," Barachiel said. "There are other, lesser known elements that we won't go through right now, but I invite you to come and speak with me after class so we can find yours. You also might just need a little more time, and there's no harm in that either."

Anticipation rushed through my veins as I stood with my palms open at my side, anxious to see if I would be able to summon any other.

"The last one we will try is fire. This one might seem unusual because we don't always see fire in the world around us. But it is a natural element created from retrieving and combining multiple elements found in the air, such as during a thunder storm, and in the ground, such as lava melting up from the earth's core. So to manipulate fire, you do have to be capable of either air manipulation or ground manipulation. Unlike the other elements, fire changes the composition of objects in a way that can't be replaced. So take caution when attempting this manipulation.

"Find a focus. Something in nature that you can attempt to catch on fire. The grass at your feet, a nearby tree."

I focused on a tree just in my line of sight.

"Got that? Good. That's the easy part. The hard part will come naturally to you or not at all. Close your eyes and use your energy to connect with the elements that would create a spark."

I did as he said, sucking in a breath and visualizing the electrons of the sky vibrating against each other, generating enough of a charge to create lightning.

I could see them. With my eyes closed, I could see the molecules dancing in the air around me. My fingers twitched, calling them together. With a single force, I could get them to ignite —

A yell rent the air, followed by a shriek and a scream. I opened my eyes, my concentration broken, to see a whirling fireball spinning in Israfil's face. It gathered energy like a vortex, sucking leaves off the branches of nearby trees and adding grass to its escalating appetite.

For moment, I froze, a tremor of fear ripping through me as I saw the fireball as if it were a reflection of a portal to hell. I reacted with one clear thought: put the fire out.

I changed the way I'd been manipulating the molecules and spread my arms, hoping I'd rearranged the oxygen molecules enough to suffocate the fire. And then I lashed out, throwing my vacuum at the fireball.

But instead of sucking the fuel from the fire, a spray of water erupted in front of me, shooting out of the ground and enveloping the fireball. The hosing continued, and my soul's energy grew brighter and stronger as it pulled additional molecules from the air and decimated the fireball.

When only smoky plumes remained, I dropped my hands and took a step back, my heart pounding with weariness coupled with relief. I looked around at my classmates, but none of them were looking at me. Their eyes were on the circle of burnt grass left behind by the fireball and the remains of the water as it seeped back into the earth.

"I'm sorry," Israfil said. "I thought I had it under control, but it got away from me." He spun toward me. "You—you used water."

"Class dismissed," Barachiel said, so loudly and abruptly that it didn't feel natural. The students swung toward him, and then their gazes flickered to me, and I got the uneasy feeling I'd done something wrong.

Iblis picked up her bag and handed mine to me also. "Let's go."

Something felt off, and I couldn't quite tell me what it was. "But why?" I accepted my bag from her but took my time moseying from the field. I glanced back to see several students crowding around Barachiel.

"Keep walking," Iblis said, moving at a quicker pace.

I fell silent and followed her lead, though the nagging feeling in my gut told me this was about me.

Iblis didn't say a word as we moved through the quad, past the fountain. I stared at its icy waters as we passed, as if it could somehow tell me what was going on. Even though she didn't speak, there was a certain urgency to the way Iblis moved.

She bypassed the cafeteria and went straight to our dorm. I followed her in, and only after she close the door did she spin around, arms crossing over her chest as she looked at me.

"You're going to need to come up with some kind of story. If there's something you want to tell me, now would be a good time to do so."

My heart gave a little pitter-patter of alarm. "What do you mean?" I said, suddenly finding it hard to swallow.

"You controlled water," she said slowly, as if that should make it all clear. She stepped toward me almost as if she would put her hands on my shoulders, and I flinched away.

She stopped in front of me and sighed. "Jez, I am your friend. And you can trust me. I'm going to stand by you. But it would be nice if I could trust you also. Now tell me. How did you do that?"

I shook my head, still not sure what I had done. "I don't know what you mean."

She pressed her lips together in a tight line. "I did the studying. I read up on all of the elements."

I still just looked at her, having no idea what she was trying to say.

"Do you really not know?"

"I really don't know," I said, my tone dry.

"Angels have power over many things. The elements, emotions, light and dark. But over one thing they don't have power. Water."

A chill tickled down my spine at her words.

"Who has power over water?" I whispered, afraid to know.

"The demons. It is said to be a power of hell. Water is the devil's domain."

I closed my eyes. And here I had just used water in front of my entire class. It had come so naturally to me, I hadn't even stopped to think about it.

I hadn't thought about it, and that was the problem. I should've questioned why it came so naturally to me.

"Now we'll have to think of something to tell everyone."

I opened my eyes, staring at Iblis' face in disbelief.

"Otherwise the rumor will go around that you're a demon, that you've escaped from hell and are here to infiltrate us."

One eyebrow lifted. "You've put a lot of thought into this rumor."

"It's not that big of a stretch."

"Why do you want to help me cover this up?" I couldn't understand why she wasn't renouncing me and demanding a new roommate.

She tilted her head and looked at me like I was daft. "Because you're my friend. And I don't really care how you manipulated water. It doesn't change anything. But we do have to come up with a good story."

I wanted to laugh. "Then you believe I can manipulate water because I am . . . I am . . ." I couldn't bring myself to say it.

She just stared at me, as if waiting for me to sentence myself.

I tapped my fingers against each other and cleared my throat. "Have there ever been any other accounts of angels being able to manipulate water?"

"I don't know. But I bet we could find out. Wait!" She snapped her fingers, a look of wonder coming over her face. "Yes. The Firstborn could manipulate water."

The Favored One. Of course he could. He could manipulate everything, while Hasatan was given the unwanted element, more of a curse than a compensation prize.

But the bitterness these thoughts usually dragged up remained at bay.

"Iblis, there is something you should know." Holding her gaze with mine, not taking my eyes from hers, I slid out of my sweater. Her eyes shot to my shoulders, probably seeking out my tiny wings. But I didn't stop there. I unbuttoned my shirt and pulled my arms free of it, revealing the chains that wound around and around my arms.

"Take a good look." I lifted my chin and stepped forward, leaving myself open for her scrutiny.

Iblis looked uncertain for a moment, and then she stepped around me, behind me, and back to the front. "You don't have any wings."

"No. I don't."

Her eyes scanned the chains on my arms. "What does it mean? Are you a Fallen?"

"What do you know about the Fallen?"

She scooted past me and sat down at her chair, swiveling to face me. "They came to earth. Upon their deaths, they were judged unworthy to enter heaven and were stripped of their wings. Then they were sent to hell for eternal damnation."

"Some of them choose to go to hell instead of heaven. They want to be there."

"Yes, because living in heaven as an unholy being would be more torturous than living in hell."

"Where did you learn all this?" I asked, curious in spite of myself.

She gestured at the bookcase between our beds. "Books. They're everywhere. And I can read faster than I ever could before. The knowledge just pours into me."

I nodded, having experienced the same thing while learning to read. A spark of anticipation simmered in my belly. Soon I'd be able to read as quickly and easily as Iblis. I hoped.

"So?" she said. "Are you?"

I'd forgotten she'd asked me a question. I regarded her, wondering how much to reveal. The truth would not reassure her. And yet, I found myself reluctant to continue lying to her.

CHAPTER TWENTY-FIVE

"No," I said, deciding to tell her what I could. "I am not a Fallen."

"Then what are you?"

I shook my head. "Something else. And I can't tell you what."

"Are you a Temptare?" she breathed.

I had heard this word before, but it had never been defined for me. "What is a Temptare?"

She cleared her throat. "The Renegades—the ones who chose not to go to earth and get a body—still go to earth, but they have no body, and their purpose is to tempt mankind so that they lose their course and end up a Fallen instead of returning to the Father."

Her definition brought a painful lump to my throat. I had been a Temptare.

"I'm not far from it."

She gestured at my arms. "Hence the chains."

"Yes. They show my lineage."

"Lineage?" She furrowed her brow.

"I can't say anything more," I said.

She smiled, a surprising gesture that dispelled the tension in the room. "But we can safely tell the rest of the first years that you aren't a demon from hell come to infiltrate Arcadia."

A hard knot formed in my chest. I was a demon, and I was from hell, and I had come to infiltrate Arcadia.

Lie. That was all I had. "That is correct."

"So you lied to me when you said you have baby wings you're ashamed of."

"I never said that," I said. "You did. I agreed with you. I never lied."

"Oh." She nodded. "You just let me believe an untruth."

"Yes," I said. That was what demons did. And even after thousands of years, humans fell for it.

It was like they wanted to be beguiled.

She picked up a book on her desk and flipped through it. "We still need to think of a story. We can say maybe on earth you were a mermaid and you brought those powers with you now."

"Mermaids aren't real."

"Yeah, but who's going to argue? Everyone will assume maybe they are and they just haven't learned about it yet."

Perhaps. "Why don't we just tell them I'm not a demon? Maybe it's a new trend. Manipulating water."

"Yeah, maybe," she said slowly. "That might work, since Barachiel was there and he didn't boot you off Arcadia. But we at least need to face it head on. Laugh it off so everyone knows we know what they're thinking."

I wasn't sure how that would help, but Iblis was nodding her head decisively. "Okay. We can just laugh this off." She still seemed awfully calm about this all. "You're still okay with me?"

She gave me a patient look. "Jez, you're quirky. There's been something odd about you since the moment we met. This isn't really a huge surprise."

Her reaction was. But then, I reminded myself, she couldn't remember the first life yet. And she didn't know my role on earth or my contribution to the fallen state of mankind.

I stayed in the dorm the rest of the evening, hoping the interest in my abilities would be forgotten before morning. But I couldn't hide forever. I joined Iblis as we went to Creations class. True to her word, Iblis spent the whole time laughing off my ability to use water.

Master Sabriel had us working with clay, trying to create beautiful pots and vassals for storing water and oil and wine. It wasn't a living creation, though she encouraged us to pour some of our "heavenly souls" into the effort because it would allow us to create more fully and with more beauty.

I knew she didn't want my soul in it, so I didn't try that. Instead I listened to Iblis.

"Can you believe people used to think the only angels who could manipulate water were from hell?" She laughed loudly and shot a glance my direction. "Right, Jez?"

I attempted a smile, though the skin on my face didn't want to bend. "Right?"

"I mean, the very idea of Jez as a demon!" Iblis looked around at our dormmates. "It's ludicrous!"

"Ludicrous," Jerahmeel said, taking up her cry. She cast him a grateful smile.

"But it's unheard of," Dara said, sounding uneasy. "How can she do it?"

"Just because we've never seen it doesn't mean it's unheard of," Iblis said, shaking her head at Dara like this should be obvious. "Clearly she's gifted."

"She did control two different elements out there," Leike said.

Some of the stiffness eased out of my shoulders, and I concentrated on my hands as they molded the clay into an egg-shaped mass. I didn't want to appear too desperate, but they were coming around. Convincing themselves that I could not be the enemy.

"I've never seen an angel do that," Grigori, another second year, said. "But I've only been here two years. I'm sure someone has seen it."

"Exactly," Iblis said, pouncing on that admission. "Just because we haven't seen it before doesn't mean it's impossible."

"It kind of ups her cool factor," Israfil said.

Arella huffed. "Like she needed any help with that."

I lifted my eyes, focusing on her. I knew about humans and their search for coolness. I'd never understood it and never longed for it. I certainly didn't desire it now.

At least, I hadn't until she said that.

Now my cheeks flushed and I looked back to my egg-clay. Why did her words feel like praise? How could I be thinking and acting like them when I'd never been human before?

The conversation moved past me, and I hollowed out my egg, giving up on making a vase and pretending like a bowl was my aspiration the entire time.

I felt the prickle of eyes on my face, and I lifted my head, only to meet Maalik's penetrating gaze where he sat next to Grigori.

He knew. He alone had not said a word while Iblis wove my defense.

He had not spoken to me since the confrontation with Kerubiel four days earlier. I tried to win our staring contest, but when Maalik finally broke my gaze, it didn't feel like a victory.

※ ❦

"Did you see how I actually turned my clay into a tall vase?" Iblis said excitedly as we walked to the cafeteria after Creations class.

"My clay never made it past a hollowed out circle," I grumbled.

What I really wanted was to thank her for sticking her neck out for me. For sticking with me. She'd been glued to my side since the incident in Synergy class, and she made it very clear to any onlookers that I was still her friend and still a part of our dorm. But I couldn't thank her with the other angels around us.

"Well, you can't be good at everything. Since you can manipulate two different elements, including one that no one's supposed to be able to, I don't think you have a leg to stand on."

She was right, and her words made me giggle. "Okay. I'll stop complaining."

We entered the dining hall, but before we took two more steps, Kerubiel stepped over to us.

"Jez. Can you sit with me?"

I turned to look at him in his dark clothing and brooding aura, not diminished by the orange tray of food in his grip. I inhaled, breathing in his Darkness without meaning to. Some part of me flickered, still nourished by the dark.

"I don't think so," I said, withdrawing from him. I took a step backward, putting distance between him and me.

He held up a hand, stopping my retreat. "I just want to talk to you."

His expression seemed nervous, vulnerable, very different from his attitude a few day ago when he'd driven Maalik from me. The memory surged through me, making me angry.

As if reading my mind, Kerubiel said, "No one should make you feel inferior for who you are. If anyone treats you like you are less than them, you should be angry at them. I was a catalyst, not the cause."

His words rang with truth, and my feelings shifted, my hurt at Maalik's abandonment turning into anger that he couldn't even bother to tell me he despised me now.

"Yes," I said. "I'll sit with you."

Iblis cast me a long glance but said nothing.

"I'm outside." He nodded out the doors where I had previously taken a scolding from Maalik.

"Okay."

Iblis stayed quiet until the outer door closed behind him, then she said, "Something going on with you two? I wasn't sure if you wanted to murder him or eat him."

The Darkness called to me, awakening my salacious appetite. "He smells delicious," I admitted.

"TMI!" Laughing, Iblis held a hand up to the side of her face. "I'll catch you later."

TMI. I pondered the letters while I slipped through the line and put a box of fruit on my tray. If I had ever judged Eve for consuming the fruit in the garden, I did not now. If there was one food I could eat all day, every day, it was fruit.

Kerubiel stood with his back to the doors, his magnificent wings open and quivering as he looked out over the blossoming garden. Very appropriate for where my thoughts had just been. He turned at the sound of the door.

"Kerubiel," I said, sitting on the bench and setting my tray beside his.

"Jez." He crossed to me and sat down beside me. "I know what you are."

"What do you mean?" I said, going for ignorance.

"I've wondered before. Because you don't have wings, and because of—certain other things. But when you controlled the water in class yesterday, I knew."

A sick feeling entered the pit of my stomach, and I put down the fruit in my hands. I switched tactics, opting for Iblis' plan now. "You mean the idea that I could be a demon? The idea is—"

Kerubiel bent his face to mine and kissed me.

Or at least, he tried.

The electric shock that jolted through us threw him across the patio and against a tree. I shrieked as the current tore through my body, ripping my skin to shreds and rebuilding it the next moment.

"I can't touch you," he said, but instead of sounding confused, he sounded triumphant. Like he'd just proved something. He looked down at his hands, turning them over, and I could see the lines of blackness cracking across them.

I rose to my feet, shaking my fingers as if that would discharge the raging pain. "You cannot touch me!" I shouted, and the wind roared my fury at him, whipping his hair away from his face and tossing branches at his exposed body. Which I suddenly very much wanted to hurt. I curled my fingers into claws, the image of pouncing on him and flaying his flesh flashing through my mind.

But that would hurt me as well as him, and it wasn't worth it.

The cafeteria door opened again, but this time it was Maalik who came out, and his eyes flashed like lightning in a thunderstorm. "Get away from her!" he shouted at Kerubiel.

I uncurled my fingers, shaking, trying to bring my thoughts back to a logical place.

"Easy," Kerubiel said. "I was just testing something."

"She's not a toy for you to play with!"

I apparently wasn't the only one who could call up wind. An opposing force whipped past us, and Kerubiel's wings trembled in it. As much as I wanted to tear into Kerubiel, I suddenly worried Maalik might do it for me.

And he had no right to defend me when he wasn't even speaking to me.

"Maalik," I said, inserting as much coldness into my voice as I could, "I don't need your help."

"You can go," Kerubiel said. "She and I are capable of taking care of ourselves."

Maalik turned to me, and so many colors flickered through his aura that I couldn't even keep up with them. "Come back inside. He's influencing you, Jez."

"At least he talks to me," I said, quieter now, but keeping the coldness in my voice.

Maalik's eyes lowered, and then he strode back into the cafeteria.

My gaze flashed to Kerubiel, and the anger returned. I balled my fists up.

"I'm sorry. I'm sorry," Kerubiel said, holding his hands up as he approached me, warily, like he suspected my murderous thoughts. "I didn't know it would hurt you. I just wanted to see if it was true."

"We are cursed," I growled, my voice sounding every bit like a demon's. "We are forbidden to know the pleasure and comfort of tactile touch. I thought it was all spiritual beings, but I have learned it is only us. One more gift from heaven." I spat the words out, and fire flickered from my fingers, lancing across them and seeking a hold. I closed my fists, not about to set fire to my clothing again.

Kerubiel's eyes danced to my hands and then back to my face. "You can manipulate fire also. What else can you do?"

"I can burn you!" I screeched, raising my hands and pointing my palms at him.

Never mind that I couldn't hurt him. I had no power over the celestial beings.

Kerubiel didn't know that. He flinched and shielded his face. "Jez, I'm sorry. Chill, okay? I just wanted to see what would happen."

"You touched me!"

"I kissed you." He lowered his hands, something mischievous entering his eyes. "I figured I didn't have anything to lose. If it worked, great, if it didn't, well . . ."

I trembled and shuddered with indignation. "You used me."

He studied me a long moment. "I had a reason." He approached me again. "Are you calm enough to talk?"

"I don't want to talk to you," I hissed.

"Come on, Jez." He settled himself on the bench and gestured for me to return. "I won't touch you. I promise. But at least we got past the pretenses, right?"

That was true. I could not even try to deny what he had witnessed.

Then again, man was easily convinced he hadn't really seen what he thought he had.

"I just want to know more about you," Kerubiel implored, his face innocent and earnest. "Are you a Fallen?"

I regarded him coolly, not returning to the bench. "I'm a demon." That was easier than explaining my true parenthood.

He nodded. "How did you get here? Are you in hiding?"

"Barachiel knows I'm here. He knows what I am."

"But you have a plan, right?" Hunger flashed in his eyes. "Something more than all this stupid Guardian stuff."

Why not lay it all out? I needed more recruits, and this foolish angel did not know the danger he beheld. "I've been sent to gather angels for the Fallen legion. Satan intends to infiltrate Arcadia and wage war on heaven. This time, those who fight on his side will not be punished."

"And those who fight against him?"

I shook my head. My anger was abating, and I regretted my loose tongue. "A New Rule is at hand. All shall recognize his power. His day of greatness is coming."

Kerubiel stared at me, enraptured. "You're beautiful when you speak that way," he breathed.

"Do not come near me," I warned. "I am not subject to the follies of human want and desire."

"Carnal pleasures," he smirked. "Only because you don't know what you're missing."

I hissed at him, ready to lash out again.

"I want to help you," he said. "What can I do?"

Recruit them, by avarice or cunning. Some will look evil in the face and gladly embrace it. Some will turn their face away from the blatant evil but will allow a blind eye to pass over the smaller crimes. Find their weaknesses and exploit them.

Here was one who looked evil in the face and accepted it. He would be useful to the cause.

"You can speak of this to no one," I warned.

"You know I won't betray you. That's why you told me to begin with."

Yes. The Darkness pitched off him in waves, his shadow obscuring the Light even in the garden. I breathed it in, held my breath, felt how it scurried to the ends of my fingers and toes. I opened my eyes and regarded him. Had he been allowed to live into adulthood, Kerubiel would have been a Fallen by choice.

"The generator," I said, remembering I'd asked him about it months ago. "Have you found it?"

He shook his head.

"Find it. And find out how we disable it."

"All right. What else?"

My chest tightened, and I felt nauseous. Why didn't he fight the pull toward the dark? "When the time is right, I will come for you," I said.

With that I turned and entered the cafeteria.

The moment the door closed behind me, Kerubiel's Darkness left me. I blinked against the fresh air in the cafeteria, the sense that a black cloth had just been removed from my eyes. I spotted the angels from my dorm sitting at Table D, their auras of indigo and green indicating their sincerity and friendship.

Icy fingers wrapped around my heart, and I gritted my teeth. I would never be like them. I served a different master.

CHAPTER TWENTY-SIX

"Let's get this over with, shall we?"

Maalik dropped a book on the table in front of me with a bang. This tome was considerably thinner than the one we'd read from last time, but hopefully it wouldn't reduce my clothing to ash.

I looked up at him, at his golden eyes burning with some intense emotion, and I whithered before his gaze. "Fine." He hadn't spoken a word to me since he'd burst out onto the patio where I was talking to Kerubiel the day before. His abandonment hurt me. I thought—somehow I thought we'd connected.

He swiveled the book to me, and I began to read at the top of the page. "'Mar-lee was de-ad.'" I glanced at him for affirmation, but his head was bent, studying his knees or his shoes or something, anywhere but me. I turned back to the book. "'To be-gin with. There is no do-ub-tuh—'" Now I was certain I was wrong because I didn't know this word. But when I looked at Maalik, he still said nothing. So I kept going. "'Whatever a-bo-uht that.'"

I continued in that manner, tripping over words and stumbling with the meanings, but he didn't interject. He let me continue along wordlessly until I turned the page.

"Good." He took the book back and closed it. "You don't need me anymore. You've mastered reading."

His hostility stung. I wanted to ignore it, but I couldn't. "Why are you so angry with me?"

He shrugged. "I'm not." But his every mannerism spoke otherwise.

"Other than interrupting an argument with Kerubiel yesterday, you've not spoken to me since we last met." My voice grew quieter. "Did I do something to offend you, or is it just knowing who I am?"

"Why do you care?" he returned, red and black exploding from his aura.

I could not answer that. I did not want to know why I cared.

"It doesn't matter. You can't change what you are. I can't expect anything more from you."

"So it's back to that," I said, my defenses rising. "The self-righteous, condemning angel."

"And isn't it justified?" he shot back. "What have you done in your spare time to earn my respect?"

My face burned. He didn't know about my visits back to Sheol; he was grasping at straws. But it was an intentional jab toward my admission in Barachiel's office. "What I do is none of your business."

He shrugged. "Then there we are."

"I thought we were supposed to be a family." Something hurt within me, something closed my throat, made it difficult to breathe. Something was choking me.

"Right?" he said. "Aren't we supposed to be transparent with each other?" He narrowed his eyes. "But you don't belong in our family. You never did."

I blinked back the stinging in my eyes. "You don't know anything about me."

"I know everything about you. And I know you'd rather talk to the Shadow Shade than to me."

Green and red and gray spiked off his aura, vying for attention, and I wished I knew what the colors meant. "You mean Kerubiel," I whispered.

"Is there some other Shadow Shade you've confessed your name to? Someone else you're kissing?"

His words lashed out like blades, slashing at me. But in that moment, he reminded me of a wounded human, giving into anger and accusations rather than facing the hurt someone had caused him.

But who? Who would cause Maalik enough pain to make him angry like this?

I could say nothing against his accusations about Kerubiel, because each one of them was true. But I was more interested in his own pain. And not because I wanted to feed upon it, but because I wanted to take it away. "Why are you so upset?"

"I'm not. That's what you are. That's what you're going to do."

His implications and accusations pierced my heart. I'd thought he was the one person who saw me differently. "I guess now that you know who I am, my value has diminished. I'm not worthy of redemption after all."

Something flashed across his eyes, and he took a step back. His mouth worked, but no words came out.

"I told you I wasn't," I said, finding the words for him. "You just didn't believe me." I gathered my bag, clutching it to my chest, and hurried from the library.

※ ※

I escaped to my dorm room, my whole body shaking as if I'd been soaked in ice water. I opened my agenda and searched for the messenger program. A bar opened that read, "To:".

I concentrated as I imagined how to spell his name. "B-A-R-A—"

I got stuck on the "k" sound, but luckily his name appeared in a list of options, and I filed away that the "ch" also made the "k" sound.

Next for the message. This would be harder.

"I hav finished my studees with Maalik."

Something crumpled inside me when I typed his name, and I remembered when he'd showed me how to spell mine, and when he'd corrected my spelling of his. He'd believed me to be better back then. He'd thought I was capable of goodness.

Now he knew better.

"I wil keep practising by myself."

I knew it wasn't perfect, but Barachiel would get the message. And we were done. Maalik and I could not get along, no matter how many angelic interventions we had. He made too many assumptions about me, and too many of them were true.

I didn't go to the cafeteria for lunch. It was better to separate myself from my dormmates.

What did it mean that Kerubiel was a Shadow Shade? I stood up and faced the bookshelf in my room, tilting my head to read the titles. Iblis said she'd learned a lot from reading them. If I was going to acquire knowledge before returning to my eternal position in Sheol, now was the time to do it.

I was looking for information about the shades, but the second book title caught my interest. *A Brief Analysis of the Purpose of the Temptares in the Journey of Man.*

It was that word Iblis had used. I sat down at my desk and opened the book.

Foreword:

When the heavenly hosts accepted the plan to came to earth and learn right from wrong, they knew the choice would not always be easy. But each correct choice would bring them closer to becoming like their heavenly father and eventually returning to their first home, only this time with more knowledge and understanding than could be acquired in the heavenly realms alone.

What no one could know, because it was an unknown variable, was what form those choices would take. With the First War ended and the dust settled, the Renegades could no longer accept the greater Light. A new realm was created for them to live in comfort, but they were not satisfied with this. With Hasatan's promises ringing in their ears, the Renegades developed their own plan to achieve the goal of getting to earth. They took the form of the Temptare and descended to the chosen planet, living among humans as ideas, intelligences, and spirits, ready to lead the Lightled down the jaded path and join them in Sheol.

Why didn't the Father prevent them from this descent? Because what Hasatan didn't know was his plan fit within the great Plan of Happiness. This book will highlight the ways the Temptare separate the wheat from the chafe, and how man is able to more clearly see the differences between good and evil, thanks to the lines drawn by the Temptare.

I didn't like to dwell on the times I'd gone to earth and fed off human weakness, egged it on so I could nourish myself. Those events weren't personal. I needed to eat, and human folly provided the source.

But something had changed since coming here, and now I felt unsettled emotions roiling in my stomach when I remembered the humans I'd ensnared. They weren't mindless creatures to me anymore, and I wasn't sure how to undo that.

My schedule dinged as a new message came through, jarring me from the words I'd stumbled through. Lunch was over, and it was time for my next class. I picked up my screen and read the message from Barachiel.

Thank you for the message. I regret that you and Maalik have decided to end your studies together, for there is still much he can teach you. But I respect your decision. Mind the crossroads, Jezbathasat, for they are in front of you.

He used my full name, like I needed another reminder of who I was.

An image flashed behind his message: the Uriel Armory.

My next class was weaponry. My resolve hardened. It was time to steal the dagger, and nothing prevented me from doing so now. My loyalties to my dormmates had been severed.

🪶

I slipped in a little late to class. My reading had distracted me more than I expected, but I was also pleased at how well I'd been able to piece together the unfamiliar words, using both my knowledge for the language and inference to decode the writing.

Master Ingram glanced at me once when I came in, her eyes dark and mistrusting. But I found a seat near a window in the back and folded my hands in my lap, the epitome of humility and servitude. She returned to speaking to the other students gathered at the wall.

"Now that we are into the second semester and you've learned how to fight with bos and sabers, your next step is to claim your dagger. We've used them before, and you may already know which one is yours based on the previous times we've touched them. The dagger you choose will become a part of your soul. It will understand your needs and fight for you without you having to control it. It will match your personality, whether it is used primarily as a defensive or as an offensive weapon.

"From where you stand, you may already feel a call. Close your eyes and listen."

What the sky? It couldn't hurt. I closed my eyes.

"Take a deep breath. Inhale and let it out, see if there is a tug on your breath. A tug toward a dagger."

A tug? I felt a distinct pull, so strong I lurched to my feet. My eyes shot open to be sure no one had seen, then I put my hands on the windowsill behind me and lowered myself down again.

But something called me. My heart pattered in my neck, and I couldn't have been more shocked if Master Ingram had walked over to me and presented me with a weapon.

There was a dagger on that wall for me.

"Open your eyes. If you felt a pull, move toward it. If you didn't, step forward and try again."

I watched as each student stepped toward the wall. Some broke off and went to the right or left, following the call of their dagger. And my ichor thumped in my ears, possessiveness curling my fingers. What if someone selected my dagger?

"When you think you've found your dagger, hold your hands in front of it, palms out. You don't have to guess. The dagger will leap into your hands."

I held my breath with anticipation as different angels approached the wall and held their palms out. Several of the daggers trembled in place before releasing themselves into the hands of the angels, and their cries of surprise and pleasure echoed through the armory.

I had thought at this moment I would feel rage, watching instruments of destruction in the hands of the self-righteous angels. But instead I felt the same fluttering excitement. One of those daggers was mine. What did that mean?

My eyes fell on a dagger no one had approached, and even from here I could see the flames of purple and green emblazoned on it, burning as if the dagger itself were actually a light.

I could not take my eyes from it.

"What if my dagger is not here?" Daniel asked. "What if it's at one of the other campuses?"

Master Ingram smiled. "Those sorts of mistakes are not made here at the academy. Every student at Yishuv has a dagger in this room. Some have been here for eons, waiting for the right angel. Others were only recently created in the forgery, delivered especially for your arrival."

"Who makes them?" Israfil asked, studying the sapphire-blue blade in his hands.

"There are angels who specialize in this, working with this material. It's not a skill we teach at the academy, but there are more opportunities for learning outside of your education here. Luckily there is a place for every skill set."

The students nodded at this information, and at least I wasn't the only one new to this. An entire angelic culture existed in Arcadia and Shamayim, and I didn't know anything about it. Forsaken existed in a sphere without purpose, seeking out a meaningless existence of longing and desire.

We deserve this also, I told myself. *We deserve to have beautiful things, to experience it all, to have a culture.*

I would get that dagger, and I would help the Forsaken take that first step to reclaiming what should've been theirs.

I sat quietly and gave no indication of the dark thoughts filling my mind.

"Now that you have your daggers, I would like you to become familiar with them. Let them rest in the palm of your hand, get used to their weight. Toss them back and forth. Next class we will practice sparring with the daggers. I'll bring in second-year students to teach you different things they've learned with their daggers. Remember, your assignment will have a mission to fulfill on earth, and your job is to help them finish the mission. Sometimes there will be attacks on your assignment, both spiritual and mortal, and you must be able to fight them off."

Attacks on humans? She gave us too much credit. We could trick and cajole and ensnare a soul, but we could not physically attack a body.

Master Ingram continue to walk among the students, sharing information and demonstrating different holds on the daggers. She didn't look my way again. It was as if I wasn't there. Obviously she did not consider me part of the class.

The bell tolled outside, and Master Ingram said, "Go ahead and put your daggers away. They will be waiting for you for our next class."

"When do we get to keep them on us at all times?" Israfil asked.

"When you graduate from second year to third year and receive an assignment. If you don't have an assignment, there's not much purpose to having a dagger. We don't have anything to fight here in Arcadia."

I knew it was not my imagination that her eyes swept toward me on my place at the windowsill. But I kept my expression neutral.

Of course, if she could discern auras, she could probably read my feelings. Perhaps even my mind.

So I worked hard at keeping my emotions neutral as well. I did not allow myself to formulate a plan. I would have to fly by the seat of my pants for this to work.

I filed out with the rest of my dormmates, neither at the back or the front of the crowd. I did not glance behind me as we left the room. I walked with my peers to the front of the building and then out the doors. We walked together to the quad and then disbursed to different locations, some to the library, some to the gardens, some to the dorms.

Only then did I turn around and head back for the armory.

There were no classes in session at the moment, and I saw no signs of any teachers either. I made my way stealthily to the back of the building.

I put my hand on the closed door and felt the first moment of hesitation. Was that a footstep behind me?

I remained still a moment longer, listening. I risked a glance behind me and exhaled in relief when I saw nothing. The time was now.

CHAPTER TWENTY-SEVEN

I pushed on the door, surprised it wasn't locked. The armory was empty. It seemed everything was working in my favor today. I crossed the room in several quick strides, my chest heaving when I came to a stop in front of the daggers.

The green and purple flamed dagger fairly hummed at me. I took a step closer and watched it vibrate on the wall. It was waiting for me. I wouldn't make it wait any longer. I held my hands out toward it, palms facing forward, and without a moment's hesitation, the dagger leapt into my hands.

"What are you doing?"

I whipped around at the sound of a male voice, my heart skyrocketing.

Jerahmeel stood there, his wings closed and arched over his head. He studied me with a calculated expression on his face.

"It's my dagger," I said by way of explanation.

"You didn't pick one today."

"This one picked me." I didn't bother to explain the politics behind why I wasn't allowed to participate.

"But why are you here now? We had to leave our daggers behind after class."

"I just—I wanted to touch it. I should've been allowed during class."

"That's all?"

A female voice sounded in the hallway, sounding as if it were getting closer. Jerahmeel's eyes shot to my hands, still clutching the dagger, and then to my face.

"You better hide," he said.

Hide? My eyes cast around the armory, riddled with weapons and chairs and a series of hanging bags used for hand-to-hand combat practice, and I remembered she still hadn't taught the Five-Point.

I darted as fast as I could to one of the bags mostly in shadow and then ducked behind it. I slipped the dagger into the band of my skirt and made myself as tiny as possible where I crouched.

"Hello?" Master Ingram entered the room. "Jerahmeel? What are you doing in here?"

"You caught me." His tone had just the right amount of chagrin and teasing in it. "I just wanted to take a look at my dagger again. And I figured, since you didn't lock the door, that must be okay."

"Just because a door is unlocked doesn't mean you have free access to every room on campus, Jerahmeel. We do expect you to be self-governing and understand that you are not invited everywhere."

"Right. Well, I wasn't so great at the self-governing thing on earth, so you might have to cut me some slack."

His tone had become more sarcastic, and I peeked around the bag. Master Ingram did not look pleased. She crossed her arms over her chest.

"Did you touch the daggers?"

"No, ma'am. You did say to leave them there until next time."

She didn't react to his mocking. "These daggers are dangerous. There's a reason why we don't allow them in the possession of a first or second year. So let me make it more clear to you. Unless you have been invited to enter a room, if the door is closed, don't go in."

He leaned toward her, smirking. "Got it. But you might consider locking the doors."

He whispered the last words as if revealing a secret. "You know. For those angels like me who maybe aren't so bright."

He gave a sly smile and then strolled out of the room, hands in his pockets.

I stared after him in total shock. Why had he covered for me? And he was way too good at playing the rebel. When they discovered the missing dagger, the blame would be placed squarely on him.

Master Ingram took a deep breath and smoothed the front of her dark pants. Her wings fluttered, and though I couldn't perceive an aura around her, I imagined she felt agitation. With a quick look around, she turned and marched from the room. She faced the room after she stepped out, scanning the corners again, as if sensing she wasn't alone. I pulled back behind the bag entirely, afraid she'd feel me out somehow. Then she closed the doors, and the lights flickered out, and then there was the unmistakable click of a lock.

She'd locked the doors.

I was locked in.

My heart pounded so loud I worried the sound would draw her back. How would I get out of here?

I waited in the darkness for a breathless amount of time. But even with no lights, the armory wasn't total darkness. The sun dipped down below the horizon, but I still didn't move. Eventually, the moon came out, lighting the interior of the room again

I was certain it was safe now.

I rose and walked to the door, then examined the locking mechanism between the doors. I put my hand on the door, leaning closer, and the mechanism unlocked.

I jumped back, surprised. And then I realized the lock was meant to keep people out — not in.

I could get out.

I stepped into the dark hall and closed the door behind me. Someone might notice the door wasn't locked in the morning, but the blame would not fall on me. My hand brushed against the dagger tucked safely in my waistband. Never again would I be without it. ·

Iblis looked up from her desk where she read from one of the many thick books from the academy the moment I entered the dorm room. "Where have you been?" she asked. "I looked for you at dinner. I even asked Kerubiel, and he didn't know where you were."

"I was studying," I said, taking my cue from her open book. "At the library."

"I messaged you."

"Did you?" I pulled out my agenda, buried in my book bag. I opened it and touched the surface. The screen sprang to life, showing her message.

Where are you? Want to sit together at Shema?

Followed by another message from Kerubiel: *You promised to tell me when it's time.*

And yet a third message, and my heart did a funny tumble when I saw the image of Maalik's face: *Could we talk sometime?*

I ignored the last two. Kerubiel would see me soon enough and know I hadn't taken off yet. As for Maalik, we would just argue.

And I would not be able to hide what I had done from him.

"I can't go to Shema," I said to Iblis.

"Oh. Because of . . ."

"The whole hell stuff. Yeah. And why would Kerubiel know where I was?" I scowled, irritated that she thought we were connected somehow.

"Well, it's obvious there's something between you."

"There's not," I huffed. I took off my sweater and climbed into my bed, glad I didn't have to hide my wingless state from her anymore.

But I still needed to hide the dagger. I faced the wall and pulled it from my waist, admiring it. It warmed in my hand, and a desire to protect and preserve surged through me. With this dagger, I could keep the Darkness at bay. I could stop those who wished ill and harm on heavenly beings and defenseless mortals alike.

But that wasn't what I would do with it.

I slipped the dagger under my pillow and lay my head upon it. I wouldn't keep it on my body. It would be safe in my room.

I hardly slept that night, certain an alarm would sound, ring out among the archangels and masters, warn them a dagger had been taken. But morning came with no such alarm. Breakfast turned my stomach, a mixture of nerves and guilt preventing me from consuming anything imbued with Light. I expected at any moment someone would come to summon me, or a message would appear on my screen requesting my presence in the Eldermaster's office.

None came. Was it possible the missing dagger had been overlooked?

"You have all discovered a propensity for at least one manipulation," Barachiel said during out next Synergy class, walking among us where we stood on the field. "And I know you are eager to learn how to control that element. But today I want you to start small. Sit on the grass. Feel the soft blades beneath your body. Use a small part of your energy to summon forth the tiniest particle of your element. Then play with it. Hold it in your hand. Keep it small. Nothing bigger than a marble. You may begin."

We glanced around at each other before settling into the grass. I wasn't sure of the size of a marble, so I watched those around me. No one had brought up my watering abilities since that day weeks earlier, but I wasn't about to call attention to myself again. So I focused on the air. I held my hand out to it, pulling the energy from within my core and calling the wind forward.

A tiny breeze blew across my palm. I stared at it, unable to hide my wonder. Though I couldn't see the air currents, I felt the sensation flickering over my skin.

A shadow fell over me, and I looked up in time to see Barachiel. He crouched in front of me.

"Why are you playing with air when you could play with water?" he asked softly.

My face warmed. "Apparently I have the ability to play with multiple elements."

"You have a unique ability. A power. You shouldn't hide from it."

I glanced around at my classmates, absorbed in their own attempts to call forth the elements. "I-I can manipulate three of them."

"Fire?"

I nodded.

Barachiel settled back on his heels, appraising me. "Then we are lucky to have you on our side."

"Can all the Forsaken master the elements as I have?" I whispered, barely breathing out the words. I hoped no one could hear me.

"Usually the Renegade angels are only able to manipulate water," Barachiel said, matching my tone. "But clearly you are not the same as them. Don't be afraid to experiment with the other elements."

I nodded, encouraged by his words. I extended the fingers on my left hand toward the dirt, and this time I intentionally called up water from within the ground. Drops of moisture gathered at the surface of the soil, and then they floated up to my palm in tiny droplets. The water was crisp and cool to the touch, and I marveled that I could feel it.

I rolled my palm over and let the water float into the air. A tiny vortex whipped about on my hand. I dipped my fingers into it, running my fingers around it. Then I envisioned it shaping into a ball of water and air. It reformed, coalescing into a ball the size of a grape. It hovered just above my hand, almost touching me but not quite.

I looked over at Iblis and was not surprised to see her manipulating the air, several blades of grass rolling around in the air current she held in the palm of her hands. She looked up and met my eyes, and she smiled. I couldn't help returning it. I felt a surge of satisfaction at my ability to do this task as well as her, perhaps even better than many of our classmates.

"Good job out here."

I looked away from Iblis' eyes as Jerahmeel walked over to her.

"Thanks," she said, her cheeks reddening.

He smiled and gripped her shoulder, then raised his eyes to me.

"You too. Looks like you're doing great."

He gave me a knowing smirk, and I scowled at him. To Iblis he might have sounded friendly and sincere, but I knew he was reminding me of our encounter in the armory. He moved away from her, closer to me.

"Stop watching me," I hissed.

"You definitely intrigue me," he said.

Iblis was looking at us. I kept my voice calm. I didn't know why he'd covered for me when I stole the dagger, but there had to be something in it for him. "What is your gift with the elements?"

"Fire."

"Sounds like you two would make a good match," Iblis said, her voice slightly strained. "Jez can do fire also."

"You can do fire?" He swiveled toward me again.

I didn't answer, just glared at him the best I could. He needed to go away before he let something slip.

"Students, after you've done this exercise with your element, you're free to go," Barachiel said. "If anyone has any questions or needs further practice, don't hesitate to ask."

Jerahmeel turned back to Iblis. "Are you headed to lunch?"

"In a moment." Iblis looked to me. "There's something I want to check in the library first."

I could tell I was expected to follow. I didn't want to go to the library. It reminded me of Maalik and our last exchange of heated words. I hadn't responded to his message, but I couldn't help looking for him anytime we were in the same room. Which wasn't often. I'd been skipping meals and avoiding both him and Kerubiel.

Jerahmeel nodded. "I'll see you when you get to the cafeteria then."

"Come on." Iblis lead the way without asking me if I wanted to go, which meant I didn't have a chance to object. I just trailed along behind.

The empty great room echoed as we walked in. My thick-soled shoes made hollow thumps as we walked across the floor.

"What are you looking for in here?" I asked, disgruntled at having been virtually dragged here.

"I just want to see if there's any precedent for an angel to do what you can do."

"You mean, manipulate water?"

"I mean, manipulate three of the elements."

I tilted my head back and stared up at the bookshelves that stretched so high into the ceiling I couldn't see the tops. "How can you even begin to find something in here?"

Iblis held up her agenda. "On our tablets, of course! They tell us where every book in this library is."

"And what if its way up there?" I said, nodding upward.

"That's what the ladders are for." She stepped over to one of the shelves and rolled a ladder across the floor. I had not noticed it until now.

I stepped forward and put my hands on the rungs, suddenly wanting a reason to climb to the very top. And then keep going, all the way into the atmosphere, and maybe I could disappear before I committed my act of treachery.

"Here we go . . . angels and their powers. There's like, a hundred books on the topic. They're in the west wing of the library. This could take a while to locate." Iblis started off in another direction.

"I have a better idea," I said, not moving.

"Oh?" She turned around, one eyebrow shooting up. "What's your idea?"

I remembered Barachiel and the way he encouraged me in class. "I think I'll just go ask Barachiel." The angel had always been honest and forthright with me. I felt safe in assuming he would continue to be so.

"Well, that takes all the fun out of it, doesn't it?" She placed her hands on her hips and pouted, then shrugged. "Just in case he doesn't know, I'm going to see what I can find here. Let me know when you're done talking to him. If lunch isn't over, we can meet up and talk about what we find out."

"Okay."

I turned around and walked out at the library, eager to accomplish my task now that I had set my mind to it.

Just as I was about to step inside the administration building, my agenda vibrated in my bag. I pulled it out, expecting a message from Iblis. Maybe she'd found something.

Instead, Barachiel's face showed next to the scrolling letters.

Please come to my office.

That was all it said, but the ichor in my veins ran cold.

I'd been discovered. They knew about the dagger.

I turned around and estimated the distance from the MAB to my dorm, my heart pounding. How quickly could I retrieve the dagger? I could open a portal straight to Sheol and be gone before they noticed.

But I didn't know how to open a portal. And they would find me.

I clutched my bag to me and let out a slow exhale. I'd just have to lie. Unless he searched my room, they wouldn't find the dagger on me.

I stepped inside, trembling with each step. I didn't frequently see other angels coming through here, and the times I'd been in the building, there hadn't been a lot of foot traffic. My mind fleetingly went back to Maalik, thinking of our trip to Barachiel's office together.

I banished those thoughts from my mind.

Barachiel's door was open, and I was about to step inside when I heard the hurried, rushed voice of someone speaking in anger.

"There is evil in her soul. I feel it every time she's around me."

CHAPTER TWENTY-EIGHT

The female voice whispered out harsh and angry, and I froze. There was no doubt in my mind that she was speaking about me.

"I know your feelings. We have felt the same as you. But I promise, there is a purpose far greater than you or I can imagine for her presence here."

"There can be nothing that justifies bringing such corruption into our holy realm."

"Mind your temper, Ingram." Barachiel's voice came, soft and gentle. "You do not know of what you speak. Remember the prophecy. 'The illegitimate girl so high, high, not low, the late return will make the grieved ones contended.'"

Silence followed after his words. And then she hissed, "Do you think she's the one?"

"I am watching the signs. Do not let your anger blind you. There was much suffering in the past. But not only was she not the cause, she wasn't even there. You must keep your emotions about you."

"She was in the armory! I know she was! I could smell her!"

"I do not doubt you," Barachiel said.

"And yet you do nothing! What is she about? You should find out!"

"I've been given specific instructions to let her be."

A stunned, hushed silence followed his pronouncement. And then Master Ingram said, her voice sounding strangled, "To just let her be?"

"Yes. Just like we do with the humans. We can aid, we can protect, we can advise, but in the end, what is going to be will be."

"And this comes down from the courts?"

"From the Father himself."

I clasped my hands over my mouth to keep from gasping out loud. I backed down the hallway, not because I didn't want to hear more, but because I was afraid the very beating of my heart would be audible. The words pounded in my head. The Father himself? He was aware of me? It was inconceivable that he was not only aware of my presence here, but that he had some superior plan for my life. Me, a Forsaken, no, worse. I was not even one of his creations.

I exited the administration building, my feet tumbling over one another. I could not ask Barachiel my question right now because it had morphed into a hundred others, and I wasn't sure which was most important.

One nagging thought came back to me. Why had Eldermaster Barachiel summoned me? If not to confront me about the dagger, why? Had he wanted me to overhear? And if so . . . what did that mean?

My agenda dinged again as I approached the library, and I pulled it from my bag, my hands shaking so bad I struggled to open it. Was it Eldermaster Barachiel, asking if I'd heard?

It was Maalik.

I would really like to talk to you. There are things I need to say.

I read his message three times, taking deep breaths to clear my head each time. Did he wish to berate me some more? To tell me off for good this time?

Whatever it was, the time had come to keep my distance from him. I put the agenda back in my bag and pushed open the library doors.

"Iblis?" I called, seeking her out in the mass of books. "Iblis?"

"Jez?"

Her voice came as a small echo from somewhere deeper in the library. I moved that direction, seeking her out. I needed to tell someone what I'd heard, and quickly, before I forgot.

I spotted her partially up a ladder. She climbed down, a book clutched under her arm.

"I found this one," she said as she descended. "It talks about angels and their abilities. It's called *Angelic Abilities through the Ages*. But I'm not sure if it will be as specific, so there's another book listed in my tablet that has case studies, but I haven't had a chance to look for it yet. What did Barachiel say? You're back quickly."

I shook my head. "I didn't really understand. He said something about the fulfillment of a prophecy, something about revelations."

She jumped the rest way to the ground from the third rung of the ladder. "Prophecies? Revelations? Seems like an odd thing to say to you."

"He didn't say it to me. I overheard it."

"Did you talk to him at all?"

"No."

"Tell me what he said."

I narrowed my eyes, trying to remember the exact words. "To leave me alone . . . because this is the way it has to be . . . that the—" I stuttered on the word but managed to eek out, "Father is aware of me. And he quoted a prophecy or something that made no sense to me whatsoever."

Iblis' eyes went large. "Yeah, that's kind of epic! Who was he talking to? Did you see?"

"Master Ingram. And it sounds like she hates me."

"Of course she doesn't hate you. She's just a bit rigid. Why would you think that?"

For starters, she suspected me of having taken the dagger. But Barachiel refused to confront me over it. Of course I couldn't tell that to Iblis, so I said, "Just her tone when they were speaking."

"Do you remember any of the prophecy?"

I shook my head. "No. Something about an illegitimate daughter and contending."

She mouthed the words to herself. "What does it mean?"

"I was hoping you could tell me."

"We'll figure it out." She looked down at the book in her arms, and then hurried over to one of the tables. Her agenda lay there, and she opened it up, scanning the tablet within. "But we'll have to get to it later. Jerahmeel is waiting. Said he wants to talk to me."

I'd completely forgotten about him. "Go. I'll see what I can find."

"Good luck." She tucked her books under her arm and quickly strode out of the library.

Then I was alone, in this place that reminded me so much of Maalik. I spun in a slow circle, taking in the rows of books. The sheer amount of knowledge in here overwhelmed me. I approached a table and slowly sank into a chair, trying to imagine where I would begin. I'd never done any sort of research before, and my reading skills were still elementary.

I remembered the book I'd started back in my dorm. I could continue with that one, but now I had more I wanted to understand. And I wanted someone to help me with it.

I opened my agenda, waking the screen on my tablet and pulled up the messaging program. I had keyed in Maalik's name before I even realized it.

No. I couldn't be around him.

But he would be able to help me.

But he won't help me, I reminded myself. No matter what he was capable of.

Who else was there? Kerubiel. I dismissed the idea almost immediately. He was a little too eager, and I didn't trust him.

Jerahmeel.

He was with Iblis right now, and I didn't want to pull him away from her. He always seemed calmer around her, and he felt like a loose cannon sometimes. But maybe after school . . .

I hesitated as I spelled out his name, and not because I wasn't sure of the letters. I didn't want to reveal what I'd overheard. I needed to get his help without arousing his interest.

His face popped up in the receiving line, and I slowly wrote out, *Can you meet me at the library after school?*

The words came to me easily, the spelling more natural.

It took a few moments, but then he responded, *Yes. I'll come after class.*

I checked my schedule and to see what class I had next. Creations. I should go early, since nothing I'd created thus far had turned out correctly. But that only made me want to skip the class entirely.

I left my agenda on the table and walked along the back wall of the library until I found a shelf with long, colorful books no thicker than my pinkie. I sat down and pulled one off the shelf. The child on the cover sitting next to a large bear indicated this was a book for kids.

I couldn't help the smile as I opened it, imagining a young human listening to this book at the feet of its mother.

Mother. I'd had a mother. I took a deep breath, trying to still my thoughts before they went there. The thought of her dredged up emotions I couldn't control. Fear mixed with . . . what had she made me feel?

The Forsaken didn't love. We weren't capable of it. We had no conscience. That was one of the curses heaven left us with.

But I was certain my mother had loved me. What did that mean? Was she not a Forsaken?

I could almost feel it, almost remember it. That feeling of loving and being loved, that fiery emotion, burning like liquid fire in my veins.

I could not let myself remember it. It would distract me from my mission. And I was so very close to completing it.

I focused my attention on the book, which was much easier to read than the one in my room. It told a story about a little boy who relied on his stuffed animal to help him deal with his feelings because he thought the animal was alive. Eventually he figured out it wasn't, and he was able to talk to people around him about what he felt instead of an inanimate object.

I sat there with the book open across my lap, trying to make sense of it. Was there a deeper meaning? Why was such a book created for children?

I picked up another and read through it, then another, small pictures and understandings of mortality falling into place. The books were easy to read, and each one made me feel a little more human.

"Jez?"

I looked up at Jerahmeel as he stood over me, his hands in the pockets of his pants, wings tucked and folded behind his shoulders. His light, curly hair fell across his face.

"Thanks for coming." I dropped the book onto the ground beside me and jumped to my feet. Jerahmeel's eyes checked my movements, and he tilted his head, reading the titles of the picture books beside me. Then he looked back at me with a curious expression on his face.

"A bit of nostalgic reading?"

"Nostalgic? Why?"

He shrugged. "I thought maybe the books meant something to you. Maybe from your childhood."

Of course. Why else would I be reading children's book? I didn't answer the question and looked back at him instead.

"I need your help. I want to research something, but I don't know how. I've never had to do research or use the library, and I'm not sure how to begin."

He nodded. "Sure. Right. Well, I'm not the best, but I do know the theory behind researching."

That was several steps ahead of me. "I appreciate it."

"What class is it for?"

If I told him it wasn't for a class, he would only be more intrigued by my choice of personal study. So I said, "History."

"That's a hard class. You must have a big essay to write for it."

I just nodded. "I'm supposed to be looking at prophecies and revelations."

"That's pretty broad." Jerahmeel pulled out his agenda and moved the stylus over the screen. "What kind of prophecies?"

"I don't really know."

"Well." Jerahmeel gave a short laugh and shook his head. "No wonder you're not sure how to get started." He swiveled his screen to show me. "These are all the books in this library that mention prophecies."

"Wow," I murmured. The list scrolled off the screen, and I realized there must be hundreds. "Can we just pick one?"

"Go for it."

I touched a title on the screen, and it grew larger. Jerahmeel turned down an aisle, scanning book spines. He had to move a ladder and climb up a few rows, but then he retrieved a book and brought it down to me.

"Here you go."

I thumbed through the book. "Okay."

"Yeah, you look about as thrilled as I do every time I get a homework assignment." He gave a short laugh. "I've never been in the habit of doing them."

I scanned the table of contents. The book was broken into three parts: Prophecies about humanity, angelic prophecies, and prophecies about the end of times. I moved to a table and sat down. "Why?"

"Seemed like a waste of time. When would I need the information?" He rolled his eyes. "Now I have to take Earth Biology because I'm not ready for the heavenly version."

I was itching to peruse this book, but his words also made me curious. "I'll probably have to take that too. Why was learning a waste of time?"

Jerahmeel settled across from me, leaning back in his chair and playing with his stylus. "I had my family to take care of. I needed money, not knowledge."

I knew about the desire for lucre and money, but only from a theoretical point of view. "Money isn't real."

"Not here, it isn't. But on earth, it meant maybe I could keep my brother and sister alive." A muscle twitched in his cheek. "Since my mom was set on getting us killed."

A few silent words slipped out in his sentence, and I knew he'd uttered some colorful explitives. I put my book down, far more interested in his story now. "Your mother wanted you killed?"

"Not so much. But she didn't do anything to keep us alive, either. It was up to me. And a lot of good I did. I'm dead now."

I flashed back to what he'd said in TLG. "You were shot in a house?"

"Yeah." His nostrils flared. "It was supposed to be a quick job, one that would arrange my family's safety for a few months. Instead I died. I was worse than my mom."

The anger and helplessness glistened in his eyes. I felt for him. But it was an opening, an opportunity I should not neglect. I swallowed hard and said, "There might still be a way to help them."

He met my eyes. "How?"

I lowered my voice. "The angels are not the only spiritual beings with the power to visit earth. Other beings are even more powerful and have great sway with humanity." So far, every word I'd uttered was a truth. The Fallen could control a mortal. All they needed was the mortal's name and free will, and the Fallen could feed off the Underling's soul, gaining enough of a semblance of a physical body to interact with humans, to threaten them and manipulate them.

He held my gaze steady. "You have a way to get to earth?"

I nodded. I might not have the power to open a portal to earth, but I knew who did.

"Does this have to do with that dagger you took?"

I sucked in a breath. "You haven't told anyone about that, have you?"

"Of course not." His eyes gleamed, and he leaned forward. "My brother's still alive, right?"

Like I knew. "Have you seen him here?"

"No."

"Then." I shrugged.

Jerahmeel settled back, looking satisfied, and I hated how easily fooled humans were.

"So what's the plan?" he asked.

"I don't have one yet." I closed the book of prophecies and tucked it under my arm. "But I will let you know when I do."

Hope and anticipation gleamed in his eyes. That expression used to mean fulfillment and satisfaction for me. But now, something wholly unpleasant twisted in my gut.

I pushed off from the table and left the library. I couldn't change anything about this situation.

I became more and more frustrated as I perused the book I'd taken from the library. I knew it was a truthful book. I had to shield my eyes from the Light, and my chains grew hot in warning. If I didn't find the answer quickly, I would have to give up.

The book listed prophecy after prophecy, but in such language that it made no sense to me, with talk of beasts with seven eyes and seven horns and crowns on each horn. Certainly none of the prophecies seemed like something that might involve me. There were prophecies about kings and landslides and birds eating the flesh of the kings and falling stars and so many other things.

My shirt began to smoke, the discomfort finally becoming more than I could bear. I closed the book and shoved it aside. There had been so many others. Maybe another book would yield something relevant.

It would have to wait. Though the other students were at Shema, I didn't want to return to the library yet. I'd sneak over after breakfast and get what I needed before class.

I hurried through the line the next morning, grabbing a yogurt. I could eat this while I walked to the library, and I wouldn't have to waste anymore time.

Or sit at Table D with my dormmates and pretend we were all still friends.

The moon had almost finished its cycle, and Hasatan would call me to report any day now. I would give him the dagger. And my betrayal would be known. The more I distanced myself from them, the better.

I made it out the doors and nearly to the fountain when a voice called after me.

My heart stopped at the sound of Maalik's voice. For a moment, joy burst into my chest, sending flutters of happiness through my body.

Then I remembered the way he'd treated me at our last session.

I stopped in my tracks and spun around, anger rushing through my veins. "What?" I said, moving toward him, holding onto my anger and letting it fire through me. "Come to berate me for something else?"

For some reason, he smiled, which only angered me more. "I knew you'd react this way."

CHAPTER TWENTY-NINE

"What does that mean?" I demanded. "You figured my limited emotional maturity would compel me to react this way? That I wouldn't be able to control myself?"

"No. I knew you would be angry with me."

"And I have every right to be! What, we're talking now? Because you decided it's okay?"

"You're right. You have every right to be angry with me."

I hadn't expected him to apologize so readily. But I wasn't ready to let him off the hook so easily, even if a part of me, some weak, wannabe-human part whimpered and whined, anxious to be back on speaking terms with him.

"Well, I'm glad you figured that out. I have to get to class." I whirled around.

"Jez." His hand shot out, and he nearly clasped my arm before remembering me and withdrawing. "Do you know why it bothered me so much?"

I swallowed against a sudden closing in my throat. "I don't even know *what* bothered you so much," I hissed. "I'm not sure which of my crimes offended you enough to consider me beneath your approach. Or maybe it's instinctive for you angels to hate the Forsaken. You found out who I am, and now I'm worthless in your eyes."

He blinked at me, and something that seemed awfully like pain and regret flashed through his eyes. "You're wrong."

"Wrong? In what way?"

Maalik moved past me to the fountain and sat down on the wall. "Come sit and I'll explain."

I followed, a burning need to know urging my feet forward even when my mind told me to walk away. The more distance between us, the better.

I sat beside Maalik, close enough that I could see flickers of his aura brushing the fabric of my pants. I inhaled, imagining that we were touching. It almost seemed we were.

Maalik hadn't spoken, and I lifted my gaze to find his golden eyes studying my face.

"Well?" I demanded, unable to take my eyes from his. "What did I do that made you so angry with me?"

"I was jealous."

One eyebrow shot up in surprise. Jealousy. One of the most petty human emotions and the cause of so many crimes and sins of passion. "You can feel jealousy? Why would you be jealous of me?"

"I should not feel jealousy. I'm almost in my sixth year at the academy, and I should've mastered this feeling. I thought I had. I haven't conquered anger yet, but the jealousy caught me by surprise."

"But why would you be jealous of me? Because of my ability with the elements?"

"I wasn't jealous of you, Jez. I was jealous of Kerubiel."

"Kerubiel?" I spoke his name too loudly and glanced around quickly to make sure I hadn't summoned him to us. Then I focused on Maalik. "What could Kerubiel have that could possibly make you jealous?"

"You."

Maalik stated it simply and without apology, no aggression or anger in his tone.

I did not understand his meaning. "Kerubiel doesn't have me."

A ghost of a smile flashed across Maalik's face. "I think part of the problem is that something about you has drawn me to you since we met. But I fought it. It seemed wrong, because of who you are. It took me a while, but I realized I was wrong to judge you for that. Men don't like to be blamed for the fall of Adam, and yet here I was, blaming you for the fall of Hasatan."

His words rang true, striking a chord in me, and I trembled as I tried to discern the different layers of interpretation.

"And I was frustrated. That's not really something I can explain, except, when I saw Kerubiel kiss you, I was furious. I wondered why that was possible for him and not me. The only thing I could think of was because he's a Shadow Shade, and you—and then I was just angry, and I made a fool of myself coming between you. Then you sent me away, and I thought I'd misinterpreted every interaction between us, and —the jealousy took over."

"He had no right to kiss me," I said, remembering that moment with revulsion.

"But he did kiss you. And I can't even touch you without hurting you."

"You're the one I want to touch," I said without thinking. I recoiled at my words, realizing perhaps I should not say such things out loud. My eyes tracked along to the black wings behind his shoulders. "I've wanted to touch you since the day I saw you."

He let out a breath. "So there is a connection between us."

I met his gaze, not sure how to answer that.

"But you weren't sure," Maalik said. "So you sent me away. You wanted to explore a relationship with Kerubiel. Is that it?"

I just blinked at him. I didn't know what he was talking about.

"And that's your right, and I acted like an —." His last word vanished with no sound, and I arched a brow, curious what he'd said. "I should have given you your space to decide who you want to be with."

Finally, something that made sense. "Who I want to be with? I would never choose to be with Kerubiel."

"Then why did you kiss him? How did he do it?"

I shook my head, feeling some of the residual panic from the memory of the pain his touch had caused. "It was agony to my soul." I clenched my hands into fists and stared at Maalik. "I wanted to destroy him for hurting me so much."

Maalik sucked in a breath. "So he can't touch you either."

"Of course not. No one can."

Maalik looked down at the bench where our thighs were nearly touching. "You aura is touching my leg."

"And yours is touching mine."

He looked at me and gave a twisted half smile. "At least our auras can touch."

Was it humor I detected in his voice? I couldn't help returning his smile.

"You are more like us than you realize," he said.

"So," I said, my tone soft, an unfamiliar nuance in my voice, "are we friends again?"

Maalik scooted over a bit and put his hand on the bench. "Put your hand next to mine."

I did, careful not to touch him.

Maalik spread his fingers, so close it seemed like electric sparks danced between our hands. "Do you feel that?"

I caught my breath. "You mean you do too?"

"That's our auras touching." He looked at me. "I believe in you. I see goodness in you. You have to believe it too."

I could not tear my gaze from his, and a whirlwind of conflicting emotions fluttered up in my heart. "There is no goodness in me," I whispered. "My soul is black and dark." I turned my head, pulling my hand from his. Instantly I felt the loss of his aura, so close to mine that I'd felt his soul. "I will never be what you are."

I stood up, cradling my bag to my chest, and hurried toward the Dumah Building, feeling a deeper pain than I'd felt when Maalik wasn't speaking to me. For a moment, I had indulged in a weak yet delicious fantasy: that I was not a Forsaken, that I had followed the Favored One and could be on the same level as Maalik.

But I hadn't, and I couldn't, and realizing what I couldn't have only made it worse.

I hardened my heart. All of this would be over soon.

"The First War in heaven," Master Remiel said, writing the words on the white screen.

Kerubiel sat beside me, and I felt his gaze slide over me, but I didn't turn. I despised that he was the one I would have to work with here. He was who I was allied with.

I wanted to be allied with Maalik. But it would be a different kind of alliance, one of goodness and faith and protection. Two beings wanting to right the injustices and hurts of the world.

A poignant longing filled my chest. Maalik thought I was capable of being that person.

He would soon know how wrong he was.

Master Remiel turned to face us. "What were the sides? If you read the assignment, you'll know the answer."

I knew the answer without doing the reading. The Forsaken and the Favored. But I waited to see what someone else would say.

Zophiel raised her hand. "There were many parties that broke away, but two main ones were the Lightled and the Renegades."

Even their term for the Forsaken was degrading.

I was starting to think it was correct.

"That's right." Remiel nodded. "Several smaller dissidents agreed with neither the Lightled nor the Renegades, but when it came to choosing sides, they paired with the Lightled. For that, they were also rewarded."

"Sent to earth and given bodies," I said, hoping the sadness I felt didn't reflect in my voice.

Camael furrowed his brow. "Why would the Renegades fight against coming to earth? Wasn't that what they wanted also?"

"Yes." Remiel sat down on the edge of his desk. "But they wanted to do it their way, and when Hasatan realized his plan hadn't been chosen, he and the Renegades decided to make it happen by force. When they attacked the heavenly hosts, it was with the full intent to usurp the Father and bring Hasatan's plan to fruition. He promised his angels that not only would they get to earth and receive bodies, but they would also inherit the same heavenly glory the Father had promised the Lightled."

This wasn't the same story I'd been told. I cleared my throat, disliking my uncertainty. "That's not how I've heard it."

Remiel looked at me, and I hated the kindness in his eyes. The pity. "Would you like to discuss the differences? We can meet after class if you prefer."

I shook my head. I was no longer sure that my version of events was the truth. "I thought Hasatan was promised bodies for his angels if they would remove themselves from heaven. Your—the Father created a new realm just for him. But Hasatan didn't trust it. He wanted a guarantee that he and his angels would be treated fairly. When he demanded to be the first sent to earth as proof that he and his angels would receive the same treatment, heaven attacked. The archangels massacred his followers until Hasatan and the Forsaken retreated to Sheol. Once they did, the gates to heaven were forever shut against them."

"Where did you read that?" Lailah asked, flipping through a book on her desk. "That's not in here."

"You can find other books containing similar stories in the library," Remiel said. "But let's discuss what Jez put forward here." He returned to the board and wrote, *Hasatan was promised bodies for his followers if they would leave heaven.* He turned and faced us again. "What do you think about this statement?"

Silence reigned for a moment, then Daniel raised his hand. "Well, I don't think the Renegades would have followed Hasatan unless they thought they would also get bodies."

"Good point. All of the souls in heaven wanted a body. We all wanted to experience the height of emotions and experiences that come with a physical body. So why would they follow Hasatan?"

"Because he offered them a guarantee back to heaven," Lailah said. "Being a Lightled didn't guarantee that. When the Renegades followed Hasatan, they didn't know they were losing the opportunity to go to earth."

"That's not so fair, then, is it?" I said, speaking up again. "They should have been told what they would lose."

"Absolutely." Remiel nodded. "Let's look at the other half of the statement. It implies that the Father wanted them to leave Shamayim. Why would he want that?"

No one answered. I shifted in my seat. I wanted to say it was out of anger or spite, but I'd learned too much in the past few months. I didn't believe that was true.

"He wouldn't want them to go," Camael said. "These were also his children. But he respected their desires. If they wanted to leave, he would let them."

"Exactly." Remiel returned to the board. He drew a line through my statement and wrote, *Hasatan wanted to remove himself and the Renegades from heaven, and the Father told them they could go. He warned them they would lose the opportunity to go to Earth and receive a body.* He looked at us again. "Now, the thing is, the Father told them they would not get bodies. But

Hasatan told them he had a backup plan. He assured them he could get them bodies. The Renegades believed him."

Hasatan lied to them. He lied so they would follow him.

The thought hit me like a punch to the gut. He did have a way for his angels to get bodies, but the way was vile and disgusting. He didn't reveal how it could be done. The fact that it could be done allowed him to create a deception that would sound sincere.

My heart rate quickened, pounding out in the base of my neck.

He lied to me.

"This is truth," Remiel went on. "But even truth can be twisted based on what we think and feel. So don't take my word for it. Study this out. When your memories return, you can evaluate your understanding of events with what you've learned. Now, back to Jez's thoughts." His eyes crinkled as he met mine. He swiveled and wrote on the board, *The Father created a new realm just for Hasatan and the Renegades.*

"Let's discuss," he said. "What happened?"

"Well, we know hell exists," Kerubiel said. "Why did God make it?"

"It wouldn't have always existed," Lailah said slowly. "There was no reason for it when we all lived together."

"It must have been a punishment for disagreeing," Israfil said.

"Hasatan's pride was injured when his plan was rejected," Remiel said. "And not just his. Several of the angels wanted to leave heaven and create their own communities. The Father allowed them to. He created Arcadia and Sheol and several other locations for the angels to spread out while they waited for the chance to go to earth. So this one is true."

Remiel wrote beside the sentence, *The Father loved them enough to create a new realm for them.*

"So hell wasn't a place of eternal punishment," Zophiel said slowly.

"Sheol was a beautiful location," Remiel said. "Much like Arcadia. A land of mountains and rivers and forests and abundance. But it is not that way anymore. Let's examine Jez's next allegation." He wrote across the board, *Hasatan didn't trust the Father and demanded proof they would receive bodies by sending him to earth.*

"Well, we already know the bodies thing isn't true," Lailah said. "Hasatan created that lie to fool his followers. They weren't getting bodies."

"That's right." Remiel sighed. "This entire statement, unfortunately, is a falsehood. It's a lie put forth by Hasatan to enrage the Renegades — who call themselves the Forsaken — and make them feel they were treated unfairly. It was a thorn to motivate them to attack heaven and claim what they thought was theirs."

I sucked in a breath and pulled at the hem of my blouse. My face felt hot.

Everything he said made sense. Prickles erupted over my skin, and a tremble pushed up from my feet, vibrating all the way to my shoulders.

Remiel crossed out the sentence and wrote, *Hasatan told his followers they had been misled and mistreated.*

"Now for Jez's next allegation." He wrote the damning words across the white screen. *Heaven attacked.*

He didn't have to say anything. I knew that wasn't what happened. It was so clear to me now.

Lailah cleared her throat, and my anger flashed at her, at her ability to spout history as if it meant nothing. As if her world weren't dissolving.

"Hasatan was the one who armed his soldiers with weapons forged in Sheol and attacked heaven."

"But it was a rather futile measure," Remiel said, his eyes sympathetic as they glanced my direction. "While painful, his weapons could not destroy an angel. Instead, they forced the heavenly hosts to retaliate. Hasatan's followers became demons and snuck through the heavenly concourses, using their angelic powers for evil. They wounded the souls and hearts of many who had previously been their brothers. They even captured a number of angels and dragged them to Sheol, where they were imprisoned.

"The archangels were called upon to create armies and rescue the imprisoned. We created Light-infused daggers to keep the Renegades back, but as soon as they had been dispatched to Sheol, the Renegades would claw their way back to heaven and begin the battle again.

"So the Father shut the gates. He renounced the heavenly state of the Renegades and took from them their Light. Sheol became a place of Darkness. The last of the Renegades were dispatched from heaven and banished to hell, where they have become servants of Hasatan, used in his plan to deceive mankind and prevent them from returning to heaven. We know them now as Temptare." Remiel walked to the board, crossed through the two words *Heaven attacked*, and wrote, *Hasatan attacked and was defeated.*

"What of—" My voice cracked, and I cleared my throat. "What about the flaming swords?"

CHAPTER THIRTY

"Ah, the great Swords of Truth." Remiel settled back on the desk. "What have you heard about the swords, Jez?"

"That they destroy an demon's soul. Dispel even his intelligence into particles of energy, and he is no more."

Remiel looked out over the class. "Was there ever an angel that you think most deserved to be struck down by a Sword of Truth?"

"Hasatan, obviously," Zophiel said. "He was the one who lied and started the whole thing."

"That's right." Remiel gave a patient smile. "He was not the only one to dissent, nor the only angel throughout the eons to create havoc. But he was the master manipulator that cost the Father a third of his children and continues to con man to his side even today. But if he most deserves to be struck down, why hasn't he been?"

"Because God doesn't dare descend to hell," Kerubiel said.

"Is that it?" Remiel asked, looking out over all of us. He stood and wiped his hands on his white pants. "Your assignment today is to write a two-page essay on why you think Hasatan is still in existence and what the purpose of the Swords of Truth is. Use whatever sources you have at your disposal. Class dismissed."

I stood slowly with the others, but instead of leaving the classroom, I approached Remiel's desk. He returned to the board and wiped it down, then faced me as if he'd known I was coming.

"Yes, Jez?"

I couldn't wait to research and get some answers. I had to know now. "He could cut Hasatan down at any moment. He can be anywhere in this universe that he wants to be, at any time."

Remiel didn't blink. "Are you asking me?"

"No." I shook my head. "Why doesn't he do it?"

"Why do you think?"

I pondered the question. The Lightled on earth would have a much easier life without Hasatan and the Forsaken— or Renegades, or Temptare—whispering in their ears, taunting them and hurting them. They would be much happier.

Wouldn't they? Would they recognize peace without experiencing disharmony?

"It's all part of the plan," I whispered, and my heart twisted within me as Barachiel's words echoed in my mind. *She's part of the plan. Father said to let her be.*

I turned away, my eyes stinging. I was a part of this, too.

I faced Remiel again, one last question on the tip of my tongue. "The Swords of Truth. Do they exist?"

"Yes," Remiel said, a hint of a smile on his lips.

"Have they ever been used?"

He shook his head, a slow backward and forward motion.

"Then why? Why do they exist?"

"That, Jez," he said softly, "is a lesson for another day."

I moved as though in a daze from the Durham Building toward my dorm. That was where I meant to go, anyway, but somehow I ended up in front of the library. Changing my mind, I opened the door and pulled it open.

As soon as I was inside, facing the rows and rows of books, I knew what I wanted to research.

The Swords of Truth.

I opened my tablet and found the function to search the library. My fingers trembled as I wrote out, *sord of truth*. It quickly corrected itself, and I committed to memory the proper spelling of the word.

To my surprise, only a handful of books were dedicated to the subject, and one was written by Master Remiel. Of course.

Did I trust him?

I did.

I moved through the rows until I found the appropriate book, and then I sat down on the cold floor and opened it, searching for answers. I wasn't a quick enough reader to start at the beginning, so I flipped through the pages, scanning.

Near the end, a title caught my eye: "Justice Vanquishes Mercy."

I stopped flipping and read the first paragraph.

For the entirety of creation's history, we have witnessed the great forgiveness and mercy the Father has exhibited. Time and time again, the swords have hung over the heads of the Renegades and Fallen as a tangible but unlikely threat. No demon or dark angel has ever been destroyed or cast out of existence.

Yet.

Mercy has had the reins, and multiple chances have been extended to Hasatan and his followers, giving them every opportunity to turn from evil before it is too late.

Because in the Great War, it will be too late.

The Great War? Was this their term for the New Rule Hasatan planned to initiate? Was the Great War a result of Hasatan's planned takeover?

But then—a cold shiver ran down my spine. The New Rule was supposed to be of the utmost secrecy.

This book had to be thousands of years old.

I continued reading, because I couldn't stop, because my thoughts were harrowed up now in the inevitability of my fate.

During the Great War, after the voice of reason is struck down and lies dead in the street for days, when the Renegades and the Fallen reign freely on the earth, the archangels will descend in their glory and greatness, wielding flaming Swords of Truth in their hands, and will destroy the minions of Darkness and their master for a millennia of time.

I put the book, still open, down on the flooring beside me. A deep ache filled my chest, and hot tears slid down my cheeks.

I would be destroyed in this Great War. Because I was a minion of Darkness. I served one master.

Footsteps sounded on the tile floor, echoing up through my palms. I wiped my hands across my cheeks, trying to eliminate any evidence of crying. I lifted my head as Maalik came around the corner.

I wasn't surprised to see him, just as I knew he wasn't surprised to see me. He crouched in front of me, his golden eyes studying me.

"I was watching for you in the cafeteria. When you didn't show, I thought you might be here." His finger came out, and I flinched when it neared my face. But he came away with a tear on his thumb, and I had felt nothing except for a slight tingle when he neared me.

We both stared at his finger.

"That came from you. And I can touch it." His expression sobered, and he looked back at me. "What's wrong? I can feel your distress as if it's my own."

"How did you find me here?"

"It was a guess."

"But this row? Right here?"

He shrugged. "I don't know. I guess I just kind of followed the feelings."

I wanted to clasp his hands in my own. I wanted to feel his fingers beneath my own.

I sat on my hands to stifle the urge.

"I was reading."

Maalik's eyes landed on the book beside me, and he picked it up. It was still open to the chapter I'd been reading, and his eyes trailed over it wordlessly. Then he put the book down and looked at me.

"Jez, this isn't about you. You're not one of them."

"Maalik." I pulled my knees to my chest and wrapped my arms around them. "You don't even know what I am. I am Darkness. I am evil. This is my fate. There is no redemption for me."

"You're wrong," he said, his voice firm and confident. "Redemption is available for everyone. I've watched it happen. Over and over and over again, we get the opportunity. You're no different."

I shook my head. "I'm completely different. You need to realize that." He would know soon enough, and then he would hate me as I hated myself.

I stood up and tucked the book under my arm, then headed for the exit.

"Jez?" he called after me.

I didn't answer, and I didn't look back.

I went to my dorm room and put the book on my desk, beside the book of prophecies I'd brought back a few days ago. I fingered the spines of both of them. They held answers, but I wasn't sure if there was a point in me finding out the truth. It would change nothing. I still had to follow through on my orders.

Something whispered along the edges of my thoughts, and I sensed the dagger nearby, under my pillow. I sat on my bed and retrieved it, then ran my finger along the sharp blade. I was careful not to prick myself. While the daggers might injure an angel of Light, they couldn't dispatch the angel. They were created to dispatch the angels who turned to Darkness, to scatter their essence so the angel couldn't immediately come back and cause more harm.

I wasn't an angel of Light. And there was enough Darkness in me that I feared what a cut from the dagger would do.

Weapons class was next. I considered staying in my dorm. If we sparred with daggers, I wouldn't be allowed to participate. I couldn't fight in the hand to hand combat either, and first years won't allowed to use the sabers. Only if we used the bo staffs would I be included in the lesson.

Then there was the issue of Master Ingram . . . She clearly suspected me. She hated me. Could I look her in the eye and feign innocence?

My days here were numbered. I need to glean all I could from my classes.

I slipped the dagger back under my pillow and headed to class.

I was the last to arrive. Master Ingram had brought in a class of second and third years, the brilliant white wings of the third years indicating they had already received an assignment and were official GITs. I noticed Maalik right away, and he held my gaze as if he'd been watching for me. My stomach churned. Why did he have to be here, reminding me of my guilt and evil behavior?

Master Ingram's eyes landed on me as I closed the door behind me, and her lips puckered in distaste.

"You can stay at the back of the room. Somewhere by the window and out of the way is fine."

My ire rose at her obvious dislike for me. But I didn't react. It wouldn't make a difference anyway. So I simply nodded and sat down on the windowsill.

"As I was saying, I have a few upper year students here to pair up and show you some sparring techniques. We're not going to use the daggers today, just our hands. First I'll show you a few stances and basic defensive arm motions. Renegades can't touch you, but Fallen can."

I wondered if she would teach the Five-Point now. While it required multiple angels, it was one way to dispatch a Fallen if the angels had no weapons.

And vice versa.

I stood in my spot by the window and mimicked her stance and posture.

"Good, I can see some of you bring experience from your earth life. Any kind of martial arts or kickboxing or hand combat will be useful here. Now, first years stay where you are. Second and third years, please find a student to spar with. Basic steps only please."

I should not have been surprised when Maalik broke away from the cluster of students and approached me, but a ripple of delight flooded through me. Especially after the way I left him at the library. I regarded him wordlessly as he approached.

"Partners?" he asked.

"I'm not allowed," I said.

"Why?"

"Because of who I am. Because Master Ingram doesn't trust me. And because no one can touch me."

"You need to learn these things as much as the rest of us."

Perhaps not. I would never be a Guardian. Or perhaps I needed to know them more. I would be in the middle of a war soon.

Maalik moved his feet hip-length apart and brought both arms up. He bent them at the elbow and turned his hands into fists. "This is a ready position, and it is the basic defensive position during hand-to-hand combat."

I mimicked his stance. "When is hand-to-hand combat necessary?"

"Sometimes Guardians have to physically defend their assignment. The Fallen have bodies like ours, and the Temptare—" He glanced at me and didn't finish his sentence.

So I did for him. "The Forsaken—or Temptare, as you call them—can take possession of human bodies." My guilt burned me, and I swallowed. "But only if they are invited," I added. "A Forsaken doesn't just go around taking over mortals."

"Sure. But a human body can feel an angelic blow. If we have to defend our assignment, we might need to protect them from a Temptare-possessed mortal. For ourselves, it's the Fallen we must watch out for because they're on the same spiritual plane as we are." He cocked his arm at a right angle and swung it across his torso. "This is a right hook, and it's as useful for us as angels as it was on earth."

His grin was infectious, his presence filling me with a lightness I didn't deserve. I followed his moves.

"What about the daggers? Do we strike a Forsaken anywhere and they are dispatched?"

"To be effective, to send the demons back to hell, the blow must be to the forehead. Anywhere else will wound a Temptare for sure, take away their ability to use their powers of persuasion and Darkness, but only temporarily. They can skulk and hide until they are healed. Same with the Fallen."

"How can you stab a shadow in the head?"

"Temptare become more substantial as they feed. It becomes easier to get rid of them."

I imagined holding the dagger in my hand, lifted high over the head of an angel. "What if a dagger is used on an angel of Light? What happens to them?"

"They're wounded, just like when the dagger delivers a blow to a demon anywhere except on the head. But the daggers are designed to banish a soul to hell. That only works on demons. I can't imagine an angel of Light could survive there very well."

I imagined Maalik in Sheol, and I could picture how the Darkness would bleed out his Light. It would drink from his soul and tarnish his goodness. Nothing beautiful and pure could survive in Sheol.

"Your thoughts are heavy lately. What is it?"

I lifted my eyes and met his gaze, met those brown eyes that seemed to radiate Light itself within their golden depths. "I am not good, Maalik. There is evil in me that you can't understand. There's evil around me. Everything I touch becomes tainted. You must stay away."

He didn't tear his gaze from my face. Instead, he took a step closer, tilting his head to look down at my face. "I hear your words. But I don't believe them. And I'm determined to show you otherwise."

A strangled cry rang out in the room, and we both whipped our heads toward the clustered group of students just as Master Ingram spread her wings and took off into the air. In another moment she'd flown over the heads of the class and dropped down beside us.

"Maalik, step away from her." Ingram threw her arm out, physically shoving him behind her. Her eyes glittered, and her chest heaved as she faced me.

"What have you done?" she said.

I shook my head, not even sure to what she referred.

"I know what you are." Her eyes narrowed. "You've brought your sickness and your tentacles here to Arcadia, and if you think you can drag him down to hell with you, you are sorely mistaken."

My face went cold and then hot.

"Master Ingram," Maalik said, attempting to come out from behind her, but she only shoved him back harder.

"I have done nothing," I breathed, trying to control the rising fury in my gut. "I have no ill intentions toward Maalik."

"You are a Temptare," she hissed. "A demon. He was standing close enough to mingle his breath with yours, and you're poisoning his mind with your Darkness. You might have fooled him, but I know what you are, and I will not have it in this classroom."

Maalik tried again to speak, but my temper was getting the best of me, and I raised my voice right over him. "You mean you will not have me in this classroom."

"Interpret it as you will, but when the gates of Arcadia close against the Spawn of Hasatan, you will be locked out, and you will be unable to infiltrate the ranks of Light again!"

She had drawn a crowd. The entire class, including the upper level students, had gathered around, and murmurs whispered through them. I sucked in a breath, my hands hot, and I glanced down to see fire flickering around my fingers.

"You don't know what you're talking about," I breathed.

"I know one thing for sure," she said, her eyes darting to the flames at my fingers. "When Hasatan calls you forward, you will answer him, because you are his slave and you do his bidding. There is no hiding the blackness of your soul, Jezbathasat!"

Maalik shouted something, but I didn't hear it. The power of my full name rushed over me, and I closed my eyes as heat enveloped me, saturating my soul with pain and fire. The fiery lakes of Sheol ambled up my feet and wound around my soul, climbing upward and consuming my hair.

I opened my eyes and realized the fire was real. I was drenched in it. In front of me, all around me, students cried out.

"She is a demon from hell!" A third-year student yanked his dagger from his belt, his white wings whipping about anxiously. "Send her back from where she came!"

As quickly as it appeared, the fire vanished. But it took with it my protection: my jacket, my blouse, leaving nothing behind but the black halter and ragged skirt I'd brought with me from Sheol. The chains on my arms glowed red-hot, my lack of wings apparent to all.

The students rushed at me, daggers raised, and I cried out, dropping to my knees and shielding my head.

CHAPTER THIRTY-ONE

"Stop this!"

Maalik's voice thundered across the room, and I lifted my head to see him standing in front of me. A white light radiated outward from him, preventing anyone from getting closer. The Light created a perimeter around us, a shield, and it infused me with hope and determination. I sucked in a breath. Maalik was a shade?

Not only that, but Maalik had drawn his dagger, and he held it out and away from his body as if — *as if he would use it on his fellow angels.*

For me? In my defense?

I craned my neck and searched for Master Ingram. She stood at the edge of the Light around Maalik, its radiance reflected in her eyes.

The other students hesitated.

"Don't," Maalik warned, and his voice crackled with energy. "Think about what you're doing. Think about it. Take a step back and set aside the irrational human emotions."

"She's — she's a Fallen."

I didn't recognize the third year who had spoken, but he was large and formidable, and I didn't want to fight him.

"No, she's not," Maalik said.

"But that word Master Ingram said," another blurted out. "It spoke of the devil, and then she caught fire."

"Put your daggers away and I'll explain," Maalik said, not backing down.

They focused on him at those words, and then, finally, Grigori put away his dagger.

"I trust Maalik," he said. "If he's got an explanation, I want to hear it."

Abaddon followed suit, and a few others put away their weapons. But a student from a different dorm turned to Master Ingram.

"Master?" she said.

Master Ingram shook her head and took several steps backward. "Listen to your classmate. I lost control. I repent of my error."

Her words were the final straw, and the remaining daggers were sheathed. Still, the students stared at Maalik, waiting for understanding.

Maalik exhaled, and the white light sucked back into him, leaving me feeling vulnerable and exposed. He turned around, his eyes running over the chains that wrapped around my bare arms. "Jez? Are you okay?"

"I'm okay," I murmured, hugging myself.

"What is she?" a third-year girl asked.

"She's an angel," Iblis said, speaking up. She stepped forward from the group of first years, eyes defiant and challenging. She stepped past Maalik and came to my side. "She's our classmate. She's an apprentice. She's learning, just like we are. She's just like us."

I met my roommate's eyes, saw the genuine affection there.

Not just affection, either. I saw trust.

Something cracked open in my chest, broke into a million pieces, and left me raw and aching. I could not betray her. I could not turn against her.

"But she has no wings," Dara said, her voice timid, like she feared retaliation.

"She must be a Fallen," someone else said.

Maalik caught my eye. "Do you want to explain? Or should I?"

I shook my head. I couldn't lie to them and pretend I was nothing more than a fellow student. I couldn't deny that their fears of infiltration and betrayal were very real. But I didn't want Maalik to speak for me. I cleared my throat and stepped forward, vowing to only reveal what I could truthfully.

"My name is Jezbathasat," I said. Silence greeted me, and I spelled it out for them in case they hadn't caught the reference. "Jez, daughter of Hasatan."

The expected gasps and murmurs rose up, and flickers of surprise formed on their faces. A few hands dashed back to their daggers, and Maalik's wings fluttered beside me. At his warning look, their hands stilled.

"I am not your sister," I continued. "We do not have the same father. I am also not a Fallen. I never went to earth. I never chose to follow the—Firstborn. But your father sent Master Barachiel to offer me the chance to come to the academy and learn with the other angels. With all of you."

"Why?" another third-year asked.

"I don't know why," I admitted.

"It doesn't really matter why," Maalik said, interrupting. "I was suspicious when she arrived also. I thought it must be a trick. But she did not ask to come here. She did not put forth an agenda to be here. Our Father wanted her here. He made it happen. And if he calls something clean, we have no right to call it unclean."

"I am not clean," I said, my voice trembling against my will. "But I was given a chance, and I took it."

"How can we trust her?" Abaddon asked, directing his question at Master Ingram. "How do we know she won't use our knowledge against us?"

"We don't," Ingram answered, not looking at me. She spoke carefully. "But we do not put our trust in fallible beings. We put our trust in the Father."

"And he wanted her here," Maalik said, his voice sure and confident. "So take a good look at her. She has no wings. She's covered in chains. And she's an Empatya, one of our own."

"Class is over," Ingram said. "Please go directly to your dorms. If you have any questions or concerns about what happened here today, I will inform Master Barachiel, and you can speak with him."

One by one, the students fluttered out, casting furtive glances my direction. Iblis remained by my side, and Maalik stood like a sentry nearby, ready to launch into his defensive stance if he was needed.

"Go as well," Ingram said, facing us. She didn't meet my eyes, though she spoke to me. "This was my fault, and I accept responsibility. Go now."

Maalik glowered at her, but she didn't look at him either. He led the way out of the armory, and Master Ingram closed the door behind him.

He spun to me, his eyes blazing. "She didn't even apologize to you."

"I am less than nothing to her." I blinked against hot tears, slowing as we walked down the corridor. "I am an abomination. I should not exist."

Maalik and Iblis exchanged a look.

"I'll take her back to the dorm," Iblis said.

"Thank you," Maalik said, touching her shoulder.

Touch. He could touch her. I shivered and wrapped my arms around my torso.

"A moment," Maalik said. "Just give us a moment."

"I'll be waiting by the fountain." Iblis gave me an encouraging smile and slipped down the hall.

"She is fiercely loyal to you," Maalik said.

"That's who she is." And I would not betray her. Which meant I would be destroyed.

The thought filled me with peace, and for the first time, I was certain I'd made the correct choice.

Maalik stopped moving and turned to face me. He held his hand out, palm up, in front of me.

I looked at it and then at him. "I can't touch you."

"You don't have to."

I mimicked him, holding my hand out, but palm down. I moved it toward his, close, closer, until I felt the sizzle between us when our auras connected. A tingling warmth started up in my belly and radiated into my chest, leaving me giddy and euphoric. A Light erupted in the space between our hands, enveloping our fingers.

"You're a Light Shade," I said softly.

"You're not the only one with secrets."

I lifted my eyes and met his. Was it possible? Could his Light eliminate my Darkness?

I wanted to find out with all my heart.

※ ※

"There you are."

Iblis met me at the door when I entered our room.

"Come sit down," she said, ushering me to her bed. She sat down beside me, her eyes brimming with concern. But her lips turned up in a smile. "So. Maalik?"

I clasped my hands together, remembering the pulsing energy between us, even though we couldn't touch. "Maalik."

"Good choice. I wish I could hug you, but, you know, you're kind of weird about that."

"I'm weird about a lot of things."

"How are you feeling? It's out in the open now, at least. You don't have to pretend."

"No." Acceptance washed over me, and my shoulders wilted. I couldn't have kept who I was hidden forever. "It's out now. At least there's no more wondering when the news will leak."

"What happens now?"

Iblis probably referred to my classes. Maybe to Master Ingram. Or perhaps my position in the academy. But I could only think of one thing.

My mission.

"Now I stand up for who I want to become."

※ ※

I knew he would summon me. The two months had reached their end. I was ready. I lay in bed with my eyes open, and as soon as Iblis fell into a restful state, I got up and left the room.

I left the dagger under my pillow.

The call came as I crossed the quad. "*Jezbathasat.*"

"I'm coming," I said. I braced myself for what was about to go down.

The early spring morning held a crispness to the air, but the water gurgled from the fountain as I reached it. The portal opened in the shimmering depths, and I gathered my courage about me like a shield. I would need every ounce of it to stand up to him. I climbed on top of the wall, sucked in a breath, and jumped.

The chains tightened painfully around my arms and shoulders, jerking me hard to Sheol. The water vanished in a mist of heated steam, leaving me outside the crumbling palace that Hasatan called home.

"Daughter."

His voice vibrated around me, shivering up my neck and pulsing in my head. I bowed my head in submission.

"Did you retrieve the dagger?"

"I did." I kept my face down, my eyes on the ground. Humble, meek. Confronting him would get me nowhere.

"Where are the two followers you promised me?"

"I was unable to bring them," I said.

Silence followed this proclamation, and his shadowy figure emerged from the flaming background. He walked around me, a blurry darkness that sucked at the courage in my soul.

"You were unable to, or you chose not to?"

Resolution, Jez, I told myself. I straightened my spine and spoke with as much clarity as I could manage. "I have made my choice."

"Choice?" Something like amusement riddled his voice. "What choice do you think you have?"

Fear raced down my spine, but I swallowed hard and stood my course. "The choice I should have been given in the beginning. I—I choose to follow—" I couldn't bring myself to speak his holy name. Instead, I said, "I choose to be Lightled."

Hasatan said nothing for a long moment, but I sensed him circling me, his fingers of Darkness whispering around my neck.

"So be it," he said at last, his tone neutral. "Give me the dagger, and I will set you free."

I sucked in a breath, my shoulders relaxing. I had expected a fight. I had expected to die. But for him to accept my decision so easily? "You will?"

"Of course. I will use the dagger to cut the chains that bind you to Sheol, and you can return to Arcadia. Be one of *his* angels of Light."

He said it derisively, but I didn't care. My heart swelled with joy, and I felt as if I'd burst. I even felt a surge of something similar to affection for my father. Was it possible he cared for me after all? "Thank you, Ba'al," I breathed out, using the respectful title.

"The dagger, Jezbathasat."

I cringed slightly at the sound of my name. I would never escape my lineage. "I didn't bring it," I admitted. "It's in my dorm."

"Then return and get it. You are bound to me until I hold it in my hands."

I didn't want to come back. I wanted to enter into Arcadia as a liberated soul, throw off the chains of Darkness, and begin a new life in truth.

He saw my hesitation. He stepped closer to me and whispered in my ear, "You will never be free if you don't bring me the dagger. I own your soul. I will relinquish it only in exchange for what you promised me. We had a deal."

I nodded. I had to honor my end of the bargain. "I will return."

A shimmering blue portal opened in front of me. No Light entered this realm, but I could imagine it, just on the other side of of the portal. My soul hungered for it, pulled me toward it. I stepped through, closing my eyes and letting the radiance envelope me.

When I opened my eyes again, I stood in the fountain on the quad. The moon shown down upon the academy, lighting up the dark corners and reflecting off the roofs.

I was almost free.

I would never have wings and I would never go to earth. I would never feel the touch of another being. But I would not be bound to Hasatan and Sheol. I would not be forced to serve a dark master.

My feet flew beneath me as I hurried to my dorm. All was silent as the angels took their nightly rest. I slipped into my room, leaving the door open as I knelt beside my bed. My fingers crept beneath the pillow and closed around the dagger blade.

For a moment, I hesitated. What would Hasatan do with this blade? What evil might happen because I delivered it to him?

Nothing, I reassured myself. He couldn't enter Arcadia or any of the heavenly realms. No angels would be descending to Sheol. He would free me from my bonds, and then the dagger would be useless to him.

I straightened up, sliding the dagger into the waistband of my skirt.

A noise, like a shoe scuffing the tile or a finger brushing the wall, had me jerking my head back toward the open doorway. My heart rate ratcheted, and I hurried to the opening. Had someone followed me from Sheol?

It wasn't possible.

I peered down the hallway. It was empty.

Time to go. I closed the door behind me and lowered my head, crossing the few yards between my dorm and the exit to the building.

The fountain beckoned me forward, already shimmering with the open portal. I slowed as I approached, dread icing up my fingers.

"One last time," I told myself, staring down into the fountain. Never again would I have to return to Sheol.

The back of my neck prickled as if someone were near, breathing on me, brushing their fingers parallel to my skin. I whipped around, searching the quad, but it was empty. No one was here. The chains reddened and burned, calling me down. Brushing aside my trepidation, I stepped into the fountain and let the portal suck me down.

I steadied my feet as soon as I arrived. "Hasatan?" I called, looking at the silhouette of the black palace.

A noise thumped behind me, and a bright light sliced across the open field. I pressed my hands to my eyes, momentarily blinded. In the next instant, the light diminished.

"Well, well, well."

Hasatan appeared to my right, but he wasn't alone. Three Forsaken surrounded him, the blackness around them like a vacuum, sucking up any joy or relief I might have felt.

"Why did you bring them?" I asked cautiously, suspicion lancing through my heart. I told myself to keep calm.

"You brought me someone after all."

"Brought—what?" Suddenly I remembered the thump, the bright light, and I whipped around, fear beating at my throat.

Someone had followed me through the portal.

An angel lay in a crumbled heap behind me, dark wings open and covering the body, concealing the identity. The angel's Light was fading fast, dissipating into the vacuum of Sheol.

One pink shoe poked out beneath a wing, and my heart lurched.

Iblis.

I darted forward, calling her name. "Iblis. Iblis, wake up."

"She is merely stunned from the journey. She will wake and be in terrible pain when she does," Hasatan said. "The Darkness will rip her to pieces as it tears out her Light. I could save her and turn her into a Fallen, but I'm afraid she has too much Light. She wouldn't make a good recruit. But I give you points for effort."

The Forsaken stepped closer, and I could just make out the hunger gleaming in their eyes. Hasatan looked at them as well.

"An angel to feed upon," he mused. "The agony and terror would fuel them with delicious nutrients for years. Especially if they can keep her alive. Feed on her until her soul slowly fades away."

Iblis' body trembled, and she groaned, and then a terrible scream escaped her lips.

The Forsaken lurched forward.

CHAPTER THIRTY-TWO

"Stay back!" I shouted at them. I stood in front of her, spreading my hands out, trying to protect her. Then I remembered the dagger, and I jerked it from my waistline. "I'll send you back to the depths," I growled. Not a life sentence, but they wouldn't be able to return so easily, and they would not be able to satisfy their hunger.

Iblis screamed again, and it awoke something in me. I felt her pain, her terror, her despair. I closed my eyes and breathed it in.

No. This was not my nourishment anymore. I opened my eyes and fought off the desire to feed from her soul.

"Jez!" Iblis cried.

I focused on her. She had sat up and her wings enveloped her, cradling her. She pressed her hands to her head and screamed again as tendrils of Darkness snaked around her torso, danced around her face.

"Help her," I said to Hasatan, my voice trembling.

"Give me the dagger," he said.

Yes, the dagger. I had promised him. I looked at the green and purple weapon, gripped in my hand and becoming a part of me as natural as taking a breath. I did not want to let it go.

"We had a deal," he growled, and Iblis shrieked in pain as fire erupted from the ground, licking at our bodies.

Her body was not like mine. She wouldn't be able to withstand this.

I looked back at her face. Tears streaked her cheeks, but her eyes were focused on mine.

"You stole the dagger for him?" she said, her voice thick with pain and betrayal.

My heart twisted. I couldn't deny her words. "Yes."

"You are everything they said you were!" she shouted. "This whole time . . . I believed in you. And you were working for him!"

"You cannot take evil out of a creature of Darkness," Hasatan cooed, stepping beside me. "It's a hopeless endeavor to redeem a devil." He looked at me and smiled, almost tenderly. "You must realize that, my child. You might try, but you cannot change what you are."

No. No, his words couldn't be true. I was changing. I wasn't the same anymore.

Flames leapt up around us, catching Iblis' hair on fire, burning her clothing. She shrieked and writhed in agony.

"The fire will destroy her," Hasatan said. "It will take the person she is and twist her into a demon, an unrecognizable creature of Darkness. The pain will consume her. Give me the dagger."

I faced him, angry and desperate. "Then you'll help her?"

"Yes."

Then this was my choice. I took a step forward and flipped the dagger around, holding the hilt out to him.

Hasatan took it. I glimpsed the veiny, bumpy flesh of his hand before it morphed into clear skin like my own. He held the dagger carefully in his hands as if it were delicate, as if it were glass and he didn't want to drop it.

"At last," he whispered. "I have a blueprint."

"Your turn," I said, my body quaking with each of Iblis' screams.

He raised his head, a movement of shadow against shadow, but I saw the red gleam of his eyes. "My turn to what?" he purred.

I trembled at the sound of his voice. "To set me free. To help Iblis."

He laughed, a low, rumbling sound. "There is no freedom for you."

Cold filled my soul, stretching outward from my heart to my fingers and toes. "What?"

"I created you. You are bound to me, bound to Sheol."

"But what about—?"

"What about what?" he sneered. "Our *promise*? Our *bargain*?" He laughed, an evil, pernicious sound. "Never make a deal with the devil, Jezbathasat!"

I shook my head, refusing to give in. "I won't stay here any longer!"

"You have no choice!" he shouted. "Free will does not exist here! You must do as I say!"

The chains tightened around me, choking me. I strained against them, but they held me tight.

Iblis' cries had grown quieter, mournful wails that pierced my soul.

"Consume her," Hasatan said, jerking a head at his Forsaken.

No. His Renegades. We turned our backs on heaven, and not the other way around.

Smiles wreathed their demonic faces, once-celestial features now more goat- and pig-like than human. They approached Iblis, fingers elongating, damnation issuing forth from their mouths in cloudy wisps.

Somehow, I found the strength to move. I stepped in front of them, barring them from Iblis. "I won't let you do this."

They glanced back at my father.

"Daughter." Hasatan returned to me. "You are my greatest creation. Perhaps you will also be my greatest disappointment. I understand it's a common problem for fathers. But I did not pin all my hopes on you. Your failure means the chance for another to rise to greatness."

My chest heaved as I glared at him. "You could have been great if you hadn't rebelled."

"Do not speak," he said.

I expected to feel the weight of his command, for my mouth to stop up at the order I could not refuse. It didn't happen. "I don't choose you," I whispered. "I choose the Favored One."

A lightness flooded my soul at these words, burned behind my eyes. A strange peace filled my limbs. I could face evil and not feel despair.

Hasatan turned around and strode away. "Imprison her," he called over his shoulder before disappearing into the flames.

They switched directions, coming at me.

The chains around me loosened, going slack against my body. Startled, I looked down.

The metal lay black and smooth on my skin.

Something about it was different. I lifted a hand and brushed at the chains.

My fingers closed around solid metal.

Astonished, I pulled at the chain, then gasped when it slithered off my skin like a giant snake. It uncoiled and fell at my feet with a rustling clang.

The Renegades stopped and stared as well.

I yanked on the chain, trying to discern the end, and it snapped in my hand. I looked up at the Renegades, and they eyed me. Then one of them gave a war cry and charged me.

I whipped the chain at him when he approached, and it wrapped around him, binding him with a searing red glow. He uttered a howl of pain, and then the chain sucked him into the ground, vanishing with both of them.

The other two stopped, hesitant, but I had more chains. I peeled another from my shoulder and wielded it like a weapon, ready. I took two steps backward and crouched by Iblis.

"Stay back."

I felt their uncertainty. They feared my chain, but they feared Hasatan more. I readied myself.

They came at once, both of them. I lashed out with the chain, spinning in a circle as it wound itself tightly around the first, and then spiraling to include the second. The same red glow enveloped them. Their screams echoed around me as they were swallowed by Sheol.

More would come, and I only had two chains left. I needed to get Iblis back to Arcadia. My hands trembled as I held my palms over her body. I didn't know how to open a portal to Arcadia. And even if I did, I didn't know how to get her through it.

I would have to touch her, and the pain would be terrible. But it was my fault she was here, and I wouldn't let her be destroyed by the blackness.

Somewhere, her Father was out there. Surely he would see her and aid her in this moment.

"Help me," I whispered, squeezing my eyes shut and hoping he would hear someone as unworthy as I. Bracing myself, I scooped her into my arms.

It was like holding a blazing sun against my body. I did not register the sensation of her wings, or the raw, burnt edges of her clothing. I registered only the feeling of my skin melting, peeling from my body in layers, exposing muscles and sinews, ichor bubbling up around the wounds.

Silver ichor. Not black, like a demon's, but silver, like an angel's.

A blue portal spiraled open at my feet. I stepped through it, holding Iblis in my arms. We came out in the fountain in Arcadia, and I doubled over, Iblis tumbling from my arms onto the hard ground below, her clothing stained with my ichor.

It was still night. Had time even passed here in Arcadia? We'd made it back, but Iblis didn't move, didn't stir. Her aura was dim and muted. And I collapsed in the water of the fountain, to weak even to step out. I managed to roll myself onto the edge and then flop onto the ground beside Iblis.

We needed help, but I didn't know how to get it. I lay there, staring at the black sky with the brilliant moon, agony in every part of my being. My body trembled, my spiritual matter reacting to a pain as real as to a physical body.

Without my agenda, I didn't know how to reach anyone. My fingers spread on the ground, pressing into the paved concrete.

I would surely be imprisoned for what I had done. I had stolen a dagger and giving it to Hasatan. But I would rather be imprisoned in the celestial jail than sent to the one in Sheol. My regrets bubbled up from my throat, choking me. "I'm sorry," I whispered to the universe. "Maalik. I'm sorry."

Through my slitted eyes, I thought I saw a light approaching. Coming swiftly. It hovered over us before descending beside me, and the light transformed into Barachiel. The archangel knelt beside Iblis and brushed the hair from her face.

"What is it? What has happened?"

I hadn't noticed Master Selaphiel until she spoke.

"They are both badly wounded. Fly her to the healers, quick," Barachiel said.

Selaphiel gathered Iblis into her arms. Her wings, usually kept hidden, spread out from her body in a ray of golden shine. In an instant she and Iblis turned into a pillar of light and vanished.

Barachiel's face appeared above mine, worry lines creasing his forehead. "Now what to do about you, little one? How do I get you to the healers without hurting your further?"

His voice held neither chastisement nor judgment, only concern. I closed my eyes as a few more tears leaked out.

"Eldermaster Barachiel?"

I sensed another being crouch beside us, and I knew him. I knew his spirit enough that I could feel his presence beside me without opening my eyes.

"Maalik. Why are you here?"

"I felt Jez."

"Curious. Stay with her. I cannot take her to Shamayim, but she needs healing. I will return."

I cracked my eyes open and watch the majestic glory of Barachiel's wings as they spread out behind him, and then he was gone also.

"I'm here, Jez." Maalik lay on the ground beside me, his wings folding over me. Not close enough to touch, but close enough that I could feel the strength of his aura. His Light enveloped me, burning and stinging my raw and exposed flesh, and I uttered a moan.

"I wish I could help you," he whispered.

He wouldn't stay, not after he knew what I'd done. I did not have the strength to tell him, nor did I want him to leave. So I closed my eyes again and let his strength infiltrate me.

I had the sensation of time slipping around me, pulling me in and out, but my soul required rest. I did not object.

And then a moment came when I no longer needed it. I opened my eyes and found myself in a white room surrounded by tall windows. I sucked in a deep breath, the fresh, cool air filtering into my lungs. I felt different. My hands clenched soft sheets beneath me. I was on a bed. Where?

"Welcome back, Jezbathasat."

I turned my head as Master Barachiel came into the room.

Memories flitted through my mind, of sneaking off to Sheol with the dagger, turning it into Hasatan, fighting off the

Renegades, and bringing a diminishing Iblis back to Arcadia. "Iblis," I said.

Barachiel sat at a chair beside me. "She was nursed back to Light under the care of the best healers in Shamayim. She resumed classes a few weeks ago. You, on the other hand, underwent an entirely more difficult procedure." He pulled out a tablet and typed something out.

Weeks. How long had I been here? "How did I get here?"

"The Father sent angels with special gear to help us move you without injuring you further. I could not shield you sufficiently to the keep the Light from harming you if we touched you, and you had already been significantly damaged."

I put my hands out in front of me, searching for the burn marks. The skin had regrown, the charred edges and exposed sinew again concealed. I was startled to see only one chain wrapping around each forearm. "Where are the others?"

"Others?"

I traced my fingers over the tattooed image on my skin. "The other chains."

"Come." Barachiel stood. "There is much to discuss."

He left no room for debate, and I slid off the bed. My bare feet padded after him, and I noted with surprise that I no longer wore the black halter and skirt I'd kept on my body like a second skin. Instead, a long white gown reached from my shoulders to my ankles.

"Where are my clothes?" I asked, a bit timidly.

He spoke to me over his shoulder as we walked. "An interesting side effect of your choices. They dissolved into ash shortly after you were healed."

More questions swirled in my head. We stepped out of the building into the familiar light of the GAA campus. It washed over me, and I blinked, welcoming the warm kiss of the sun. I'd never noticed how delicious it was until this moment.

We entered the X-shaped administration building. I expected to go to Barachiel's office, but we went past it. I noticed he continued to type on the open screen in his hand as we walked, and a moment later he opened a door to a larger room.

"Please, sit," he said, gesturing to the spot at the head of a long, wooden table.

I did, feeling a little unnerved that there were spots for about twenty people, but he and I were the only ones in the room. "What is it?"

"Patience. The others will be here soon."

Sure enough, the door opened again, and Master Selaphiel came in, followed by Master Cassiel. While I watched, several more entered. All of the instructors found a spot at the table, including several I didn't know. Barachiel checked his screen.

"Thank you for coming. We will shortly begin the deposition of Jezbathasat. We are waiting on the witness."

Deposition. My heart lurched. Judgment. I'd known it was coming but . . . somehow I'd hoped to avoid it.

The door opened one last time, and Iblis stepped in. Her skin glowed with health, her eyes sparkling. The dark wings fluttered behind her. Her gaze flew to mine, and I couldn't help my smile of relief. She, at least, was unharmed.

She nodded at me, though her lips did not turn upward, and she settled into a chair beside Master Ingram.

Master Ingram. Uh-oh. She wouldn't have anything good to say about me.

"Be at peace, Jez," Barachiel said. "We have gathered your teachers here to give testimony of your progress during the school year. We also wish to hear in your own words an accounting of the incident that took place in Sheol four weeks ago, by earth's reckoning."

Four weeks. It had taken me that long to heal?

"Before we begin with the recommendations," Master Selaphiel said, "we need to know what happened in Sheol. Please start from where you think is a relevant starting place, Jez, and leave out no important details. What brought you to Sheol, and what has become of the dagger?"

Coldness raced across my shoulders. Of course they knew about the dagger. I bowed my head, my shame heavy on my soul as I spoke.

CHAPTER THIRTY-THREE

"Hasatan allowed me to come to the academy because he wanted me to acquire the knowledge given to the angels. But he had plans, also. His intent was to use me to influence other students and bring them over to his side in Sheol."

"Much as the Temptare do on earth," Eleleth said.

I nodded. "I met with my fellow students and evaluated their weaknesses in the same way I evaluated mortal weaknesses in humanity during my time as a Temptare." I hated using that word. But it was the correct word. That was what I'd been. "I learned which ones were most likely to be deceived by half-truths." I could not look at Iblis as I spoke. Now she knew what kind of a person I truly was. "Hasatan commanded me to bring him two of my classmates and one of the daggers used against the For—Renegades and the Fallen."

"Where did you get the dagger?" Master Ingram asked.

"I stole it." Why mince words? "One of the daggers called out to me. I crept into the armory after class and took it."

"Because Hasatan told you to," Ingram said, her tone deriding.

"And you did exactly what he asked you?" Master Sabriel said, her voice incensed.

My face burned. "Yes."

"She obeyed him like a mindless slave," Ingram said, sounding triumphant.

"I ask you to recall," Barachiel said, "that there is no free will in Sheol. Jezbathasat was not given the choice to disobey. It was not an option. And yet," he faced me now, "you returned to Sheol and Hasatan without any of your classmates."

"Except Iblis," Master Ingram said.

"I followed her," Iblis said. "She didn't convince me to come."

I dared a quick glance at her, but her face remained neutral.

"Continue, Jez," Barachiel said. "Why did you return to Sheol alone?"

"I went back to tell Hasatan I wouldn't do it," I said, my face down.

"You fought off his commands?" Master Selaphiel said, her voice unreadable. "Even without the ability to make your own choice?"

"I tried."

"And you gave him the dagger then?" Barachiel asked.

"No. I did not take the dagger with me. I was not going to give it to him."

"So how did he get it?" Cassiel asked, leaning forward on the table.

"He lied to me, and I believed him. He told me he needed the dagger to cut my chains so I would no longer be bound to Sheol, no longer be his slave. So I returned to my dorm and retrieved the dagger. When I returned to Sheol, Iblis came with me. Her spirit was dying. Hasatan promised to save her and free me in exchange for the dagger. And I gave it to him." My head slumped forward, the hair falling across my face.

Master Selaphiel spoke. "At that point, Hasatan had you both in his clasp. He could have sent you to the angel prison. How did you escape?"

I lifted my face again and met her furrowed brow. "Hasatan left us to the Renegades. But when they tried to take Iblis' spirit, I—" Here I hesitated. How could I explain this? "The chains that bound me fell to my feet. I was able to use them to bind the Renegades and keep them away from us long enough to bring Iblis back to Arcadia. Then Master Barachiel found us." I shrugged. "I don't clearly remember the rest."

Ingram shook her head. "This doesn't make sense. There are too many unanswered questions. How could the chains come off? How did she create a portal to Arcadia? How was she able to touch Iblis? How did Barachiel know to get to them? The whole things reeks of a plot. Hasatan is still pulling the strings. She's an infiltrator, trained in the art of deception."

"Jez?" Barachiel said, his tone mild. "Can you explain?"

I took a deep breath. "I don't know about the chains. And I don't know how Barachiel found us. But I—I knew I had to get Iblis back before her spirit was destroyed. So I . . ." I broke off, not sure how to say it. "I asked her Father. The Father."

"You prayed," Remiel said, his voice still.

Was that what it was? The very idea of a being like me, uttering a prayer, was sacrilege.

"However she did it, the portal was opened," Barachiel said. "The Father woke me from rest, and I followed his instructions to get to the quad immediately. There I found them both severely injured. Although Jez succeeded in carrying Iblis to Arcadia, her soul wasn't prepared for the Light, and it damaged her even more than the Darkness of Sheol damaged Iblis. At great personal cost, she saved her friend."

"Iblis." Master Selaphiel turned to my roommate. "What do you remember? Is there anything you can add to this? Why did you follow Jez?"

"I heard her get up and leave the dorm," she said, focusing her gaze on me. "A few minutes passed before she returned. But she left the door open to our room, so I knew she was leaving again. And I decided to follow her." She blinked, eyes casting downward for a minute. "I hid behind the door in the hallway, then crept out to the quad. As soon as Jez leapt through the portal, I did too."

"Did you know where you were going?" Selaphiel asked.

"No. I don't remember arriving, either. I remember feeling horrible pain in my body, in my soul, like cracks of Darkness shooting through my skin and ripping me apart. When I opened my eyes, we were surrounded by flames. The agony was almost unbearable, splitting me into pieces. But I saw Jez talking to four men."

"Four men?" Remiel asked, jerking forward.

"Well, I don't really know. Four creatures. I couldn't see anything except dark shadows. She pulled out the dagger, and she admitted she'd lied to us. Then she gave it to one of the creatures. That's . . . all I remember."

"You don't remember her bringing you back?" Selaphiel asked.

Iblis shook her head. "If she brought me back, great. I'm glad. But I don't remember."

And she wasn't sure she believed it. Believed me. I blinked back the burning of tears. I'd lost the trust of my closet friend at the academy. My only friend, really.

"She gave Hasatan the dagger," Sabriel said.

"She was tricked," Eleleth said.

"Allowing yourself to be deceived is not an excuse for sin," Ingram said.

"We are not here to render judgment," Barachiel said. "We leave that to the Father. We are here to gather the facts and decide Jezbathasat's future at the academy."

Ingram sucked in a breath. "What difference does it make what we decide if the Father hasn't made a decision yet?"

"We make our decision separately. Now, please consider everything you heard in the testimonies of these two angels while you ponder on what you've personally observed in the classroom setting with Jez." Barachiel turned to Sabriel. "Master Sabriel, what have you observed of Jezbathasat?"

Sabriel lifted her head as she addressed him. "I'm master of the Creations class. I've watched Jez struggle in this class, as creating beauty and life is clearly foreign to her. But she comes and puts forth a good effort. I believe with continued practice and with the correct mind shift, she will prove capable of creation."

"What is your recommendation?"

"I recommend Jezbathasat for continued education."

I inhaled quietly. I thought I was on trial here, but no! They were deciding my future—at the academy. It wasn't possible they would let me stay. Could I actually stay?

Then my hope sank like a rock to the bottom of the sea. After what they'd just heard, they would not let me. I was too dangerous.

"Master Remiel?"

"I have Jez in my Remedial History class. In the beginning, I could clearly see her warring with her former education and the facts I taught her. But she did not show a rebellious or belligerent spirit, and I've seen significant changes in her tone and attitude in class. She brings thoughtful questions and has proved to be teachable. I recommend her for continued education."

Remiel and Barachiel nodded at each other, and then Barachiel said, "Master Eleleth?"

"Jez participated in my group therapy class this year. While she was not very forthright about her past and history, under the circumstances, I considered it an acceptable action on her part. She has shown a surprising amount of empathy and compassion for her classmates, especially considering she never experienced the full range of human emotions and experiences. I believe her capable of growing a conscience and exercising judgment, as well as demonstrating understanding and sympathy for human folly. I recommend her for continued education."

Beside him, Master Ingram took slow, deep breaths. She focused on the table in front of her, her chest heaving with each movement. My eyes fell on her, as did Master Barachiel's.

"Master Ingram, speak your piece."

She slowly lifted her eyes, and they burned into mine. "I doubted her from the beginning. She's an evil being, created from Darkness, and has shown all the traits of her creator: insincerity, deception, disloyalty, dishonesty. Her classmates do not accept her. She is not an angel of Light, and she has clearly demonstrated her willingness to betray those who have shown her kindness and offered her a chance to change. She will not change. She cannot change. I know we preach that all can change when they accept the Light, but she is not one of the Father's children. The rules do not apply to her. I do not recommend her for continued education."

Her words seared into my heart, and I swallowed hard. I deserved that. Everything Master Ingram had feared about me had proved to be true.

Barachiel nodded, then he faced me. "I was chosen to escort Jezbathasat to Arcadia from Gehenna. I've seen many changes happen to the angeling in the time since she was brought here. She has come to recognize truth from deception and gained wisdom. She has the ability to manipulate three elements, which is a unique talent, since Lightled are not gifted with the ability to manipulate water. She gives us an advantage, should she prove herself trustworthy and reliable." His gaze seared into mine. "I recommend Jez for continued education."

"The recommendation has been made," Master Selaphiel said. "By the majority ruling, Jezbathasat has been accepted as a second year student."

My shoulders wilted, and I slumped my head forward. I could not even believe it.

Master Ingram stood up. "We'll see what the Father says. I wouldn't celebrate yet." She glared at me before leaving the room.

Iblis stood as well, and I moved toward her, but Selaphiel intercepted. She put a hand on Iblis' shoulder.

"We teach forgiveness and acceptance at the academy," she said, her words soft. "But if you feel unwilling to be Jez's roommate, or unsafe in her presence, you may request an alternate."

Iblis' eyes met mine over her shoulder, and then she looked again at Selaphiel. "I'll let you know before the start of the next term."

"Very good."

Master Selaphiel moved away, leaving nothing between me and Iblis. Still, I hesitated.

She broke the silence first. "Quite an adventure, huh?" Her smile didn't quite reach her eyes.

"I'm sorry," I said. "I never wanted to see you in Sheol. I couldn't bear the thought of something happening to you."

She tilted her head. "Why?"

"I don't know," I said. "But I knew I would rather experience eternal torment than let your Light diminish in Sheol."

"Why did you betray us?"

She would never understand that it wasn't a choice. That the hardest thing I ever did was not follow through on my father's commands. So I simply said, "I was mistaken." And that was the truth.

"Well." Iblis shrugged a shoulder. "I was also recommended for second year."

"What happens until then? What do we do?"

"We have the summer off. We can brush up on skills. I think we get a few more privileges as second years, also. You missed the Championship game."

I thought of Maalik, and the game we'd watched together, and how I'd hoped to watch the spring final with him also. "Did we win?"

"No."

I barely heard her. I was wondering who Maalik had sat with instead of me.

"Jez?"

Barachiel's voice pulled me from my thoughts. I faced the archangel.

"We are not finished. There is someone else who wishes to speak with you."

I followed him out of the room, thinking of Master Ingram and her allegations. Was there something more they intended to do with me?

I followed Barachiel down the hallway to his office. He pulled the door shut, then turned to face me, his gold wings opening and stretching nearly from wall-to-wall.

"I will need to shelter you for this journey."

"Why?" I asked, trepidation creeping along my neck. "Where are we going?"

"Because you have not yet received the greater Light. Come closer."

I did, almost close enough to touch but not quite. Barachiel enfolded his wings around me, and then the room faded away in a whirlwind of rushing sound, like a great wind roaring past.

I shut my eyes against the brilliance pouring in around me; even Barachiel's shield could not eliminate the radiance.

"It's safe to open your eyes now," Barachiel said. "You're protected."

I squinted one eye open, but all I saw was white. Not white like the snow I'd experienced in Arcadia, but white like I'd stepped into a light bulb. I couldn't even see Barachiel, though I knew he stood somewhere just to the side of me.

"Jezbathasat."

I gasped as the voice seared into my soul, vibrating through my mind and body at the same time. The power behind that one word had me falling to my knees.

It was *him*. The Father.

"Rise, child," he said, his voice kind and gentle, and maybe a touch amused.

I could not get my feet under me. I trembled from shoulder to toe. "How can I be here? Your glory should destroy me."

"You are not made of Darkness as you were only months ago. With Barachiel's help, you are able to tolerate being in my presence."

"Why have you brought me here?" I couldn't see him. I couldn't even tell in which direction he was. The brightness surrounded me from all corners, immense and eternal.

"I would like to know the thoughts that went through your head when you defied Hasatan."

"I wasn't trying to be defiant," I said. "I realized I was fighting for the wrong side. I did not want to betray my friends. I wanted to—I wanted to experience more Light."

"So you chose to follow the Light."

"Yes."

"Do you know why the chains fell off you?"

"No." I recalled how they had piled up around my feet, but I did not understand how that happened.

"The chains that bound you to Sheol were made by Hasatan to control you. He did not create your soul with the ability to choose right from wrong. He created you to be an empty shell, capable of doing and being only what he put into you to do and be.

"However, what Hasatan failed to remember was that I created him . . . and thus I created the power that created you. However small it was, a portion of my Light existed within you from your father's side, and even more from your mother's. And you, Jezbathasat, chose to feed that Light. You let it grow until it broke the chains that bound you to Sheol."

His words painted the picture of a brave soul, someone strong enough to fight against everything they were created to be. That wasn't me. "I stole a dagger just as he asked. I gave it to him. I almost delivered my classmates into his hands. And I still wear chains." I glanced down at my exposed arms, where two chains wound up and around my forearms and over my shoulders.

"That chain no longer binds you. It is a defense you can use to keep the shadows of Darkness at bay. Remove the chain."

Remove it? Could I? I scratched at the metal engraved on my skin, and to my surprise, my fingernail caught on it. My heart rate quickening, I pried it up, and then gave the chain a great snap. It whipped in front of me, whistling through the air. I inhaled.

"Can I get it back after I use it?" I thought of the other two chains I'd used to bind the Renegades.

"Only if you retrieve it. Once it returns to Sheol, it will remain there. So use it wisely."

"So . . . you're not going to punish me?" Did I dare hope?

"Jezbathasat, one thing you will realize is that you have an infinite amount of opportunity. One mistake, or two, or a hundred, does not set your path in stone. As often as you wish to try again, you will be granted that chance. Only when you decide you're done improving are you stuck in your path."

His Light rushed into my soul, sprouting out from my heart with such a beautiful heat that I wanted to cry. "I can stay in Arcadia? Continue training to be a Guardian?"

"My dear Jezbathasat, you have chosen to be Lightled. The choice that was denied you was put in front of you, and you took it. Each moment that passes brings you closer to being a spirit of Light. I give you the same blessing I gave all of my children who chose to be Lightled."

I kept very still, breathless, eager to hear what my blessing would be. But before another word could be spoken, something exploded against my shoulder blades. I whirled around, wondering if something had been thrown at me.

A glimpse of black feathers whipped just out of sight, startling me. I could not see anyone else in this place, and I didn't know another angel had accompanied us. I whirled around, trying to make out another person, and something fluttered above me, pulling on the skin of my back.

Like it was connected to me.

Was it—could it be?

I pulled my shoulder forward and craned my head toward my back.

There, fluttering as if with a mind of their own, opening and closing sporadically, rested a pair of beautiful black wings.

I gave a cry, my hands flying to my mouth, stunned at this unexpected development.

"Go back to the academy and learn all you can, Jezbathasat. Many great things are yet expected of you."

I did not want to leave this moment, this place. I'd never felt such joy and happiness. I sobbed, my hands dropping from my face. "Thank you. Thank you so much."

Barachiel's wings enfolded me once again, blocking out a portion of the Light. But what I felt in my soul could not be lessened.

CHAPTER THIRTY-FOUR

Barachiel returned me to the quad. I stared at my own shadow, with the dark wings spread out wide behind me. I couldn't control them, and I laughed at the way they moved, as if wanting to take flight.

"Congratulations, Jez," Barachiel said, his tone riddled with — pride? "You've done well."

"What happens now?" I asked.

"The school year ended while you were in recovery. Tonight is the Ceremony of Progression. Some students will move onto the next level. Others will repeat the year. Come to the ceremony. Celebrate with your classmates. Wear your ceremonial gown."

"What does that look like?"

"You'll find it in your closet."

I hadn't noticed a gown in there before. I started toward my dorm room, but suddenly I felt an intense longing to see a certain angel.

One whose name had not been mentioned once during my inquisition. Had he been to see me while I was recovering?

Or had he changed his mind about me when he realized the full depth of my wickedness?

He doesn't know the full depth, I reminded myself. *He doesn't know everything you did as a Temptare.*

I hoped he would never find out. That was a different life now. A different me.

Without my agenda, I couldn't contact Maalik, nor did I wish him to see me in this flowing healing gown. I would go back to the room, change my clothes, and message him to see if he wanted to meet.

I prayed he would.

I picked up my pace as I neared the dorm, because now I remembered there was a mirror inside.

And I wanted to see my wings.

Normally students milled about the campus, but I only saw a few angels outside. Third and fourth years walked by, their white wings reflecting the sun overhead. I smiled at them, no longer envious.

I had wings. Beautiful black wings.

I pressed the palm of my hand to the door and burst into my room.

Iblis sat at the desk, and she looked up when I entered.

I halted. "I didn't expect you to be here," I said slowly.

"They told me I had time to decide if I wanted a new roommate. I thought I would see how things are with you first."

She regarded me, her clear eyes flicking over my face and then going to the wings behind my shoulders. A small smile graced her lips. "There's no hiding those."

I could not stop the grin that spread across my face. "He gave me wings," I whispered, still in awe. "I'm Lightled now.

I'm not a Renegade anymore." My throat closed, and I choked on my words, too emotional to continue.

Iblis closed the book she'd been reading. "Well. I think it's safe to say you've changed. And I don't know if I trust you completely, but I'm willing to give it another try."

I beamed at her, wrapping my arms around my torso and wanting to hug her. "I promise not to let you down."

"Jez," she said, hesitantly, "I didn't tell them everything. In the deposition."

I looked at how she fidgeted, a blush creeping over her cheeks as she looked down at her hands.

"What else is there?" I asked, mystified. "What did you conceal?"

"I got a message," she said. "It woke me right before you arrived. It told me you were in danger and I needed to follow you."

I gaped at her, reeling at this new information. "You didn't decide to follow me of your own accord?"

"Of course not. I didn't suspect you of anything. If you want to sneak around, that's your business."

I couldn't even think of what this meant. "Who was it from?"

"I don't know. It came secretly."

I didn't know messages could be sent that way. But someone knew where I was going and wanted Iblis in Sheol.

Whoever it was was no friend of ours.

"Why didn't you tell Barachiel?" I demanded.

"The message disappeared," she said. "And I didn't want to get the sender in trouble. Do you think it's bad?"

Her blue eyes were wide now, troubled. I closed my eyes and considered it. Then I looked at her.

"I'm sure it was nothing. But if you get any other messages like that, let me know."

She nodded. "I will."

My eyes darted to the small room attached to ours, and I pushed past her desk, suddenly anxious to see myself. My wings brushed the edges of the door frame to the washroom, a new, tactile sensation that was completely foreign to me. I stopped in front of the mirror and admired them. Long, sweeping feathers sprouted up from behind me. The ones up top were softer, kind of downy. Then they grew thicker, sturdier. I tried to flap them, but the wings did not respond to me, and I realized I would have to learn how to control them.

I stepped out of the bathroom and went to the closet, searching for the ceremonial gown Barachiel had mentioned. "Have you seen Maalik?" I asked, trying to sound only mildly curious.

"Of course. He's our dorm leader."

I paused in my search. The next question would sound less mild. "Has he said anything about me?"

"Not to me. But then, I'm sure he knew I didn't know anything."

I nodded, feeling a prick of disappointment. "What do the gowns for tonight look like?"

Iblis stood and went to her own wardrobe, opening it up. "Like this." She removed a shimmering white gown with cap sleeves, long and waist-less, though it looked more fitted through the bodice. The academy seal rested over the left breast, while ribbons colored for our dorm dangled from the right shoulder. She held it up to herself and smiled. "We'll look stunning up there in these."

I pictured my new black wings with the white dress. "Yes, we will." I turned away from the closet and picked up my agenda, resting quietly on my desk.

Did I dare?

Yes.

I pulled up the messaging screen and typed Maalik's name. Then I wrote, *Can you meet?*

To my surprise and relief, his response came back almost immediately.

When and where?

The library, I replied. And then I had an idea. *On the tower.*

I'll be there.

My heart fluttered so tightly within my chest that I put my hand to my flesh, almost expecting to feel it pounding its way out. And then I turned and rushed for the door.

"Where are you going?" Iblis asked.

I turned to face her. "To the library."

She lifted an eyebrow. "Last minute studying?"

I opened my mouth to reveal the truth to her, but I saw a glimpse of mischief in her eyes. She was teasing me. She knew what I was doing.

"Yes," I said, lifting my chin. "A very important subject matter."

She laughed. "Good luck, then."

If I knew how to make my wings work, I would've flown to the library. But flying on campus was against the rules, so it was a good thing I couldn't. I simply rushed as quickly as I could. They were more students out and about now, a carefree and jovial attitude about them. I didn't make eye contact with any of them, not wanting to be delayed by curious questions or inquisitive friends.

I hurried into the library and went straight to the back. The ladder was there, the one that stretched up to the tower. I put my hands on the rungs and tilted my face, trying to see the top. I could not.

I started upward, hand after hand gripping the metal rungs beneath me, one foot at a time. Up and up and up. The floor beneath me disappeared, and the books blurred into a kaleidoscope of colors.

Finally I reached the catwalk at the top. I stepped onto it, still holding the railing, and made my way to the door at the end. It opened up at my touch, and I stepped into the fresh air, the wind whipping my hair around me as I approached the overlook.

It took my breath away, just as it had the first time. The sun had begun to set, and stars shimmered around me as if I were in outerspace. Wonder filled my soul. In the distance I could see planets, the solar systems the Father had created. How did this place exist? The elements were strong here, earth and wind and fire and water. I could feel them pulsing around me, ready to be gathered in by experienced fingers and create new worlds, new universes.

"Jez?"

I whipped around at the sound of Maalik's voice. I had almost forgotten we were meeting here.

He approached me slowly, his hands in his pants pockets, his expression inquisitive as he looked me over. "You have wings."

I nodded, suddenly shy. How could I explain what had happened? Would he accept me this way?

"Does that mean you're staying?"

"The Father pardoned me," I said. "I've been accepted as a Lightled."

"I told you." Maalik's face broke out into a wide smile. "I told you redemption was available to all."

He held his hand out toward me, palm out, but I remained where I was.

"I did terrible things, Maalik," I said. He couldn't possibly still accept me. He must not know. "I gave Hasatan a dagger. And I nearly betrayed my friends." Pain over my choices clenched my heart, and hot tears swam in my eyes.

"I know," he said softly, his eyes growing somber. "I know what you did."

"Then how can you stand there and look at me, offer your hand to me as if I were as pure as any other angel?"

"Because I know who you are. I know you're heart. And I knew you would hate yourself even though you didn't have a choice. You are not his daughter, Jez. You are his creation. But not his daughter."

His words of acceptance seared my soul and warmed my heart at the same time. "I don't deserve your friendship," I whispered. "I don't deserve forgiveness."

"Put your hand out."

I did so this time, putting my hand out palm out, as close to Maalik's as a I dared without touching. Our auras mingled, energy crackling between us. Maalik inhaled and closed his eyes, and something in my stomach tightened.

He opened his eyes, the gold swirling in their brown depths. "None of us deserve forgiveness. And yet, I was forgiven. You are forgiven. It's a miracle."

"But you and me—our sins were very different."

"Doesn't matter. I couldn't be here without help, and neither can you. When it comes down to it, we are the same."

We were not the same. I would never believe that. But if he was willing to forgive me, I could accept that. I met his eyes and nodded.

He nodded back, looking satisfied. "I wish I could touch you without hurting you."

"I don't care," I said, longing for his fingers to close over mine. To know what his arms around me felt like. "I'll take the pain."

He dropped his hand and stepped closer. He pushed his cheek against mine, almost, *almost* touching, but not quite. He drew his head back, and my wings gave a great flutter, sweeping forward and brushing his face.

"I'm sorry," I gasped out. "I can't control them."

"I remember what it was like," he said, reaching a hand out to capture the excited wing. And then he paused, his fingers stroking the slanted feathers. "Can you feel that?" he asked.

I uttered a small cry as I realized I could. I could *feel* his fingers caressing the edges of my wings. I felt the texture of his skin, and a warm shiver of delight traveled from the edges of my wings down my shoulder blades, coursing through my body.

"I can feel you," I breathed.

"And it doesn't hurt?" His golden brown eyes were alight with excitement, studying me.

I shook my head. "How? How can this be?"

"I don't know." A slow smile spread across his face. "I can touch you."

"You're touching my wings," I corrected.

"I'm touching you," he said, and his other hand came up and stroked along the stiff bony ridge of my wing, following the trail back to my shoulder blades.

I couldn't argue with him. His touch ignited something fiery and electric within my soul, and there was no doubt he was caressing me. I uttered a soft groan, filled with the desire to pull him close to me and enmesh my wings with his. But I'd have to settle myself with the trail of his fingers along my feathers.

"I'm glad you're staying," he said, grinning broadly. "We have an eternity to learn everything about each other."

I smiled, but my heart trembled slightly, taking the edge off the excitement.

Not everything, I hoped.

Don't miss Guardian Angel Academy, Year 2: Redemption! Available now!

I betrayed them all. I delivered the dagger to the underworld.

And yet, the masters of the academy did not expel me. Instead, they gave me my wings and told me there is a plan for me.

A plan for me? Sometimes it seems they've forgotten who I am. What I am.

I can't forget. Nor can I forgive myself. But there might be a way to redeem myself. When the archangels offer me a chance to go to earth, I snatch it up. It means I'll learn more about mortality. How to relate to humans.

And it means I'll get to spend more time with Maalik, the angel who taught me how to feel joy.

Except earth is dangerous.

Earth has temptations.

Earth is confusing.

And there are too many choices. I don't know what's right or wrong anymore.

And I may have just ushered in the Great War.

Preview:

In the beginning, there was Light, and it cast out the Darkness. But one dark angel did not accept defeat and devised a plan to usher in the New Rule . . .

My first year at the Angel Academy was over.

It seemed like a miracle I made it through. It was a miracle.

I sat in a chair in the back of the auditorium with my wings folded behind me, still getting used to how it felt to have these new objects attached to my skin. And since they were different than the rest of my body, created in a holy, spiritual dimension, they were the one part of me that the other angels could touch.

The fourth years, graduating from the Academy, sat in the front rows of seats. They filed onto the stage, resplendent in their white wings, and received their new orders, along with a golden halo to rest upon their heads.

They would move onto Shamayim to begin their eternal missions, a realm I still found mystical and unfamiliar. I had only been there once, and I have been so dazzled by the Light that I hadn't been able to see anything.

The fourth years sat down and the third years filed up. The third years had received a human assignment and proved themselves worthy to be Guardians. They were still GITs, or Guardians in Training, but as they entered their fourth and final year at the academy, they would require less supervision. They would fine-tune their Guardian skills so that after they graduated, they could continue on as full-time guardian angels or pursue further education for a different path.

I sat up straighter in my chair as the second years stood up and moved to the front to receive their promotion to year three, and I wasn't the only one. The transition from second to third year was the most exciting. First and second years were only GAs, or Guardian Apprentices. But every second year who leveled up became a GIT.

Along with the title change, third year angels were given a set of white wings to signify advancement. They would be given a temporary assignment, a human they could protect while being supervised by Guardian Mentors.

This was my first Progression Ceremony, and I was breathless with expectation of seeing the new white wings.

I knew most of the faces of the second years, though only a few names. First and second years didn't rub shoulders often enough.

Master Cassiel waited as Eldermaster Barachiel called the first student's name.

"Hesediel," Barachiel said. "Recommendation: Third year."

She stepped forward, into a ring of Light illuminated on the stage.

"Hesediel," Cassiel said, "can you recite the words of promise?"

"I can," she said, staring straight ahead, her black wings trembling.

"Please proceed."

She gave a little hum deep in her throat, then she said, "I promise before the Eternal King that I will bless and minister to the soul that will be entrusted to me with compassion. The Father is merciful beyond measure, and I will be an emissary of his mercy."

With those words, a sparkling, pulsing beam of Light descended upon the angel and transformed the black wings and two wings of white.

I uttered a soft gasp, my own wings fluttering behind me. I wasn't sure I'd ever seen something so beautiful. Days ago, I'd never dreamed I could have wings. Now, I already hoped to have white ones one day.

Cassiel handed her a scroll, and she took it before scurrying off the stage. The ceremony continued with the second years from the dorms of Emet and Hesed.

And then Eldermaster Barachiel started in on the second years from dorm Alef, and I paid more attention. As dormmates, we spent more time together. We took our meals together and shared a building. I knew these angels, even though we weren't from the same year.

"Abaddon. Recommendation: Third year."

The angel stepped forward and recited his words of promise to Master Cassiel, and then he received his wings.

"Grigori."

I watched the change occur for each angel, fidgeting with anticipation.

"Maalik."

Just hearing his name sent a shiver of anticipation from me, a feeling that both excited and worried me. There he was. Maalik stepped forward, and I squeezed my hands together, my eyes soaking in his features, the high cheek bones, the light brown hair, the serious expression. I was so anxious for him. Did the angels change when their wings changed?

Would he be a different person? Would all of his time and energy go into caring for his assignment? Would he forget me?

I knew my questions and doubts were selfish, but I didn't know how to rid myself of them. My emotions often ran away from me, and I hardly knew how to find them. They were new to me. In Sheol, the only emotions I'd felt were negative. Pain, suffering, hunger, anger, despair. I'd fed off the emotions of humans, seeking sustenance, desperate to ease the agony of my own existence.

The very memory caused my body to flush with shame, and I willed the memory away. The Father had offered me forgiveness, a chance at redemption, and I was grasping it with both hands. I was not the same soul I had been.

"Maalik," Master Cassiel said, his smile fond as he looked at Maalik. "Can you recite the promise?"

"I can," he said, and he didn't wait to be prompted but launched right into it. No sooner had he finished speaking than the same beam of Light appeared above his head. The Light diffused over his wings, changing the smoky black color I had come adore so much to a pearlescent white. I lifted my eyes to his face and saw the excitement that radiated there.

He was ready for this.

I couldn't help but smile wistfully. If only he knew how great he was. How much he inspired me. I owed a good portion of who I was to him.

The second years filed off, and now it was our turn, the first years. I stood with my peers, smoothing the white gown and double-checking the black wings that sprouted from my shoulder blades. Then I followed my roommate, Iblis, across the row and up the steps to the stage.

Not every student leveled up each year. It wasn't uncommon to repeat a year, and some were even booted from the academy. I had met with my teachers just a few days prior and been recommended to move up to second year. I could only hope that judgment still stood.

"Iblis," Barachiel said, and my roommate stepped forward, her brown hair glossy over her shoulder next to the colored ribbons representing our dorm. "Recommendation: Second year."

She smiled and nodded, and Cassiel handed her an agenda. It was fancier than the ones we'd had as first years with the simple black cover. This one was brassy, and the school coat of arms was emblazoned across the front.

"This will be your agenda for the remainder of your time at the academy," he said. "Keep it safe."

She clutched it to her chest and hurried down.

"Jerahmeel," he said, and my eyes followed the angel who had covered for me when I stole the dagger. As far as I knew, he hadn't gotten in trouble, and I was grateful for that. I didn't want to drag anyone else down. "Recommendation: Second year."

I exhaled, relieved for him.

Barachiel continued down the line, calling forth my dormmates and other first years.

"Kerubiel," he said, and I narrowed my eyes as the shade stepped forward.

More like, sauntered. The smugness radiated off him, his aura an alluring blue and green. The shadows built in his wake, but I wasn't drawn to him as I had been before. My angelic ichor pulsed within me, warning me. Mayhem was coming, and my soul whispered that Kerubiel had a part to play in it.

Barachiel studied him, a slight tilt to his head. "Recommendation: First year."

A few whispers scattered through the angels around me, but Kerubiel was not the first to be recommended to repeat the year. I watched him for his reaction. He gave a smirk and strutted off the stage.

I'd seen that one coming.

"Jezbathasat."

Barachiel did not even bother shortening my name now. I supposed there was no reason; all my fellow angels knew my lineage. But I still winced when I heard it, the constant reminder of where I came from. If only I could get out from under it and get a new name. But the angels had been named for their parentage, many of them carrying a portion of the Father's name in their names.

I was also named for mine.

I stepped forward, trying to stifle the fearful unease that crept down my spine. My wings quivered behind me, opening and closing nervously.

I didn't know what was coming, and I could only hold my breath.

"Recommendation: Second year."

My eyelids fluttered, and a smile broke across my face. I stepped to Cassiel and accepted the agenda, then hurried from the stage before he could change his mind.

"Jez."

I should not have been surprised to hear Maalik's voice in the darkness, but I hadn't expected him. I spun from my walk to the back row and stepped into the shadows, where he waited near the stage. He held his hand out, and I hovered mine over it, allowing our auras to mingle. Delightful tingles ran up and down my arm, and I moved my hand up his arm so more of our auras connected.

"Congratulations," he said, his voice deep and rich. "You moved up."

"And you have white wings." I stepped closer to him, my body nearly pressed against his, and longed to feel his arms go around me. But he couldn't touch me without causing me excruciating pain. Our spirits were not of the same caliber.

Maalik glanced at the scroll in his hand. "I'm to spend the summer with a GM, shadowing humans and practicing my gifts so I'm ready to accept an assignment when the school year starts."

I studied the white wings, the tufts of down on the arches and splaying feathers. "They are beautiful."

"Next year you'll earn them too." He reached a finger out and stroked one of my black feathers.

I held very still, treasuring the touch of his hand. The only part of me he could touch without causing pain was my wings, and I took great pleasure in it every time he chose to do so.

"Do you think—?" I whispered, but Maalik shook his head, cutting off my question.

"We should be grateful for what we have."

I knew he was right; not so long ago, I didn't have wings, and no part of us could touch.

But while Maalik seemed patient and long-suffering, I wanted more. I wanted to hold his hand, to know what it felt like to have his arms around me, to kiss him.

He wouldn't try it. The touch of angels burned my soul. I didn't care, but Maalik wouldn't do it. A sigh escaped my lips, but he didn't notice.

"Come on," he said, pulling on a feather. "There will be a feast after. You won't want to miss this."

Food had a way of brightening any occasion, and I'd grown fond of it. Besides, I was a second year now. I had wings and no reason to be dissatisfied.

At least, that's what I told myself as I trailed after him and tried not to wish for more.

Enjoy this book? You can make a huge difference!

If you enjoyed this book, I'd be honored if you'd leave an honest review on whatever book haunt you frequent. Reviews are indie authors' bread and butter, and we couldn't do it without readers like you!

About the Author

I live in beautiful northwest Arkansas in a big blue castle with two princesses and a two princes, a handsome king, and several loyal cats (and one dog). I fill my days with slaying dragons at traffic lights, earning stars at Starbucks, and sparring with the dishes. I also enter the amazing magical kingdom of my mind to pull out stories of wizards, goddesses, high school, angels, and first kisses. Sigh.

I'm the author of several young adult stories, kids books, romance novels, and even one nonfiction.

You can find me outside enjoying a cup of iced tea or in my closet snuggling with my cat. But if you can't make the trip to Arkansas, I'm also hanging out on Facebook and Instagram. You can also visit me on my website, tamarahartheiner.com. I look forward to connecting with you!

Find me on social media! Join my Cassandra Jones fan club on Facebook. Here we can theorize together on what's going to happen, talk about past events, dive into character feelings, and even give me ideas for upcoming books! Find it on Facebook at "All About Cassandra Jones." And follow me on Instagram @tamaraheiner, where I post all kinds of sneak peeks, do fun giveaways, and enjoy interacting with you! Say hello and I'll say hi back!

Connect with Tamara online!
Facebook: https://www.facebook.com/author.tamara.heiner
blog: http://www.tamarahartheiner/blogspot.com
website: http://www.tamarahartheiner.com
Thank you for reading!

Made in the USA
Las Vegas, NV
29 November 2022